HISTORICAL ATLAS OF COLORADO

HISTORICAL ATLAS OF COLORADO

By Thomas J. Noel,
Paul F. Mahoney,
and Richard E. Stevens

University of Oklahoma Press : Norman and London

BY THOMAS J. NOEL

Richthofen's Montclair (Denver, 1976; Boulder, 1978)
Denver: Rocky Mountain Gold (Tulsa, 1980)
Denver's Larimer Street: Main Street, Skid Row, and Urban Renaissance (Denver, 1981)
The City and the Saloon: Denver, 1858–1916 (Lincoln, Nebr., 1982)
The Denver Athletic Club, 1884–1984 (Denver, 1983)
(with Fay Metcalf and Duane A. Smith) *Colorado: Heritage of the Highest State* (Boulder, 1984)
(with Barbara Norgren) *Denver: The City Beautiful* (Denver, 1987)
Colorado Catholicism (Boulder, 1989)
(with Stephen Leonard) *Denver: From Mining Camp to Metropolis* (Boulder, 1990)
Historical Atlas of Colorado (Norman, 1993)

BY RICHARD E. STEVENS

Landforms (Denver, 1970)
Weather and Climate (Denver, 1975)
Historical Atlas of Colorado (Norman, 1993)

BY PAUL F. MAHONEY

Historical Atlas of Colorado (Norman, 1993)

Library of Congress Cataloging-in-Publication Data

Noel, Thomas J. (Thomas Jacob)
    Historical atlas of Colorado / by Thomas J. Noel, Paul F. Mahoney, and Richard E. Stevens.
        p. cm.
    Includes bibliographical references and index.
    Contents: Setting—Boundaries—Agriculture—Transportation—Mining—Settlement—Recreational and historic areas.
    ISBN 0-8061-2555-1
    1. Colorado—Historical geography—Maps.
I. Mahoney, Paul F., 1938– . II. Stevens, Richard E., 1931– .
G1501.S1N6   1993 <G&M>
911'.788—dc20   93-21919
                                                        CIP
                                                        MAP

The paper in this book meets the guidelines for permanence and durability of the Committee on Production Guidelines for Book Longevity of the Council on Library Resources, Inc. ∞

CONTENTS

PREFACE

Colorado. Rare Colorado. Yonder she rests;
Her head of gold pillowed on the Rocky Mountains,
Her breast a shield of silver, her feet in the brown grass,
The boundless plains for a playground.
She is set on a hill before the world.
The air is very clear, that you may see her well.
She is naked as a new born babe; naked but not ashamed.

—JOAQUIN MILLER

We hope that this atlas will help you better see and understand Colorado. The state's history has been played out on a spectacular landscape. The highest mountains of the continental divide cut the state in half with a two-mile-high barrier, forming a rocky obstacle that long served as a tribal and international boundary and as an impediment to exploration and settlement. Yet the Rockies also contained the mineral riches that excited one of America's greatest mass migrations—the Colorado gold rush.

While mountains dominate Colorado's image and even its license plate, three-fourths of Colorado's 3.5 million residents live on the eastern high plains, not in the mountains. Many other Coloradans reside in the western river valleys. In one of these, the Mancos River valley, prehistoric people built fantastic cliff cities and one of the greatest early urban cultures in what is now the United States. The Anasazi (in Navajo, "the ancient ones") did this three centuries before Spaniards followed the Rio Grande into New Mexico, before French trappers followed the South Platte and Cache la Poudre into the Rockies, and before Englishmen settled New England and Virginia.

This atlas relates the evolving human story of how various peoples responded to the stark and demanding geography of America's highest state.

ACKNOWLEDGMENTS

This book is dedicated to our wives, Vi, Sue, and Betty. Thanks also to our colleagues in various academic fields at several institutions, including Dick Allen, Jay Fell, Ellen Fisher, Mark Foster, Emily Hartman, and Jim Whiteside at the University of Colorado at Denver, where June Callahan and Lee Rozinski of the History Department were essential to this project. John Albright and Liston Leyendecker of Colorado State University helped in various ways, as did Duane A. Smith, of Fort Lewis College; the late Mel Griffiths, of the University of Denver; Tom Corona and Steven J. Leonard, of Metropolitan State College of Denver; and Dennis Gallagher, of Regis University; Jack Murphy and Marie Wormington, of the Denver Museum of Natural History; and Dick Conn, of the Denver Art Museum.

Louisa Ward Arps, Bill Bessesen, Robert L. Brown, Nels Carman, Warwick Downing, Perry Eberhart, Abbott Fay, Ed and Gloria Helmuth, Larry and Joyce Herold, Margaret Jacob, Mary Largsagard, Jim Noel, Jack Smith, and Jackson Thode read and improved all or a part of the manuscript. Many history students at the University of Colorado, Denver, helped refine the atlas, especially Julie Corona, Rosemary Fetter, Marcia Goldstein, Barbara Goldhammer, Jim Kroll, Cathleen Norman, Vicki Rubin, Jim and Cathy Lavender-Teliha, and Nancy Widmann.

The staff at the Colorado Historical Society helped not only in researching but in improving this work. Hats off to Dave Halaas, Jim Hartmann, and Andy Masich. We appreciate the patient guidance of John Drayton of the University of Oklahoma Press. Lastly, dear reader, we thank you for your interest in this historical atlas, the first ever done for Colorado, and welcome your suggestions on how to improve subsequent editions.

THOMAS J. NOEL
PAUL F. MAHONEY
RICHARD E. STEVENS

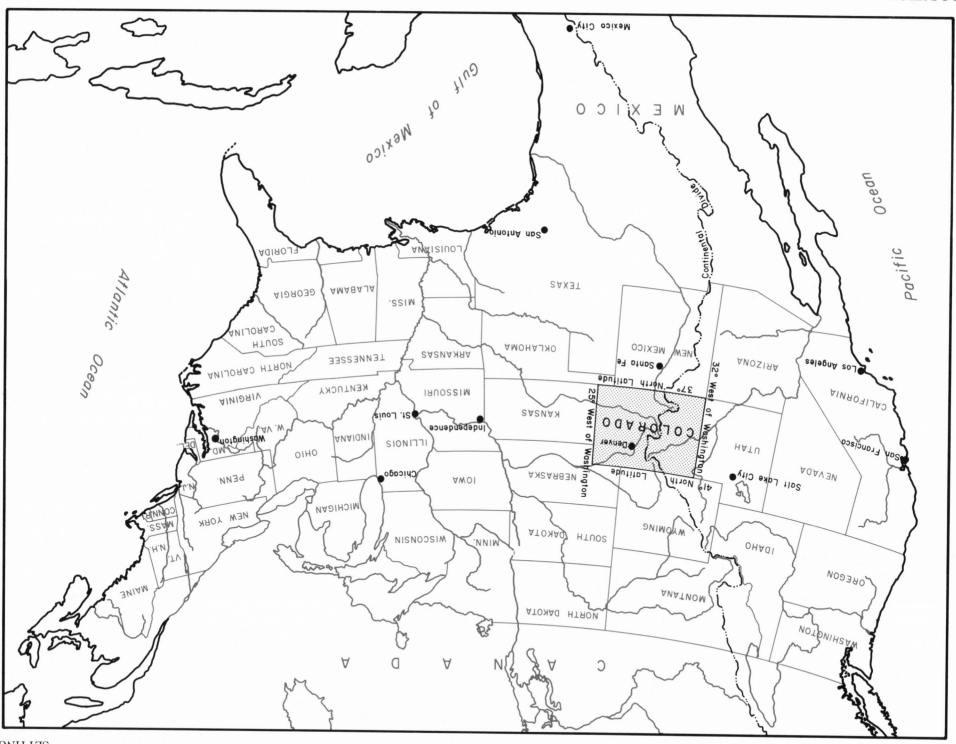

1. LOCATION

Colorado lies about 1,000 miles east of the Pacific Coast and 1,600 miles west of the Atlantic. It is approximately 1,500 miles from both Washington, D.C., and Mexico City, the capitals of the two countries most concerned with its exploration and colonization. Both of those governments, as well as Europeans, were slow to settle Colorado because of its remote location far from any seaport or navigable river.

For centuries Colorado was terra incognita, an obstacle for people trying to get somewhere else. Its forbidding semiarid deserts and treacherous mountains were skirted by Spaniards looking for El Dorado, by Yankee traders headed for Santa Fe, by Mormons flocking to Utah, and by gold seekers rushing to California. The few Spanish, French, or American fur traders and trappers who penetrated the Colorado Rockies faced the Utes. That Shoshonean tribe fought not only Europeans but also Plains Indians who threatened the Ute homeland.

The first U.S. explorers, Zebulon Pike and Stephen Long, either got lost or decided not to cross the Colorado Rockies—the highest mountains in North America. Only after the U.S. government began exploring routes to California did John C. Frémont, John W. Gunnison, and others chart passages through the steep canyons and high passes. If gold had not been discovered in Colorado, it might have been one of the last places to be settled in the contiguous forty-eight states.

Colorado, a Spanish adjective meaning red, ruddy, or embarrassed, is what the Spanish called the river from which Colorado Territory took its name in 1861. Colorado became the thirty-eighth state on August 1, 1876, and was nicknamed the Centennial State. Other monikers are the Silver State (also used by Nevada) and the Highest State (a name shunned since the 1960s by officials concerned about drug use).

Colorado's boundaries have never been changed since they were established by Congress when it created the territory in 1861. The southern boundary with New Mexico and Oklahoma is the thirty-seventh parallel north of the equator; the northern boundary with Wyoming and Nebraska is the forty-first parallel. Other countries sharing the same latitude include Spain, Italy, Greece, Turkey, Afghanistan, and Korea.

Colorado lies in the Mountain Time Zone, which is centered on the 105th meridian from Greenwich, which runs through the city of Denver. The eastern boundary of the state, shared with Nebraska and Kansas, is the twenty-fifth meridian west of Washington, D.C. The western boundary, shared with Utah, is the thirty-second meridian west of Washington. After an international agreement in 1884 to measure longitude from the Greenwich meridian in England, meridians were renumbered. This put the eastern boundary on approximately the 102d meridian west, and the western boundary near the 109th meridian

west. The southwest corner of Colorado touches New Mexico, Arizona, and Utah at the only point in the United States where four states meet.

The state straddles the highest North American section of the continental divide. Elevations range from 14,433 foot Mount Elbert to the state's 3,350 foot low point where the Arkansas River flows over the Kansas border. The average elevation is about 6,800 feet, making Colorado the highest of the fifty states.

Colorado is the eighth largest state in area, measuring about 276 miles north to south and about 387 miles east to west. Colorado's 104,247 square miles form an imperfect rectangle because of surveying errors and the curvature of the earth (the northern state line is about twenty miles shorter than the southern one). Colorado is twice the size of Great Britain and twice the size of all the New England states combined. Coloradans boast that the highest state would also be the largest state—if it could be flattened out.

Although approximately 3.5 million people make Colorado their home, the landscape remains more striking than the built environment. The land, not the people, predominates. Even the sprawling Front Range metropolitan strip between Fort Collins and Pueblo, where 80 percent of all Coloradans live, is dwarfed by the vast prairies and the lofty peaks.

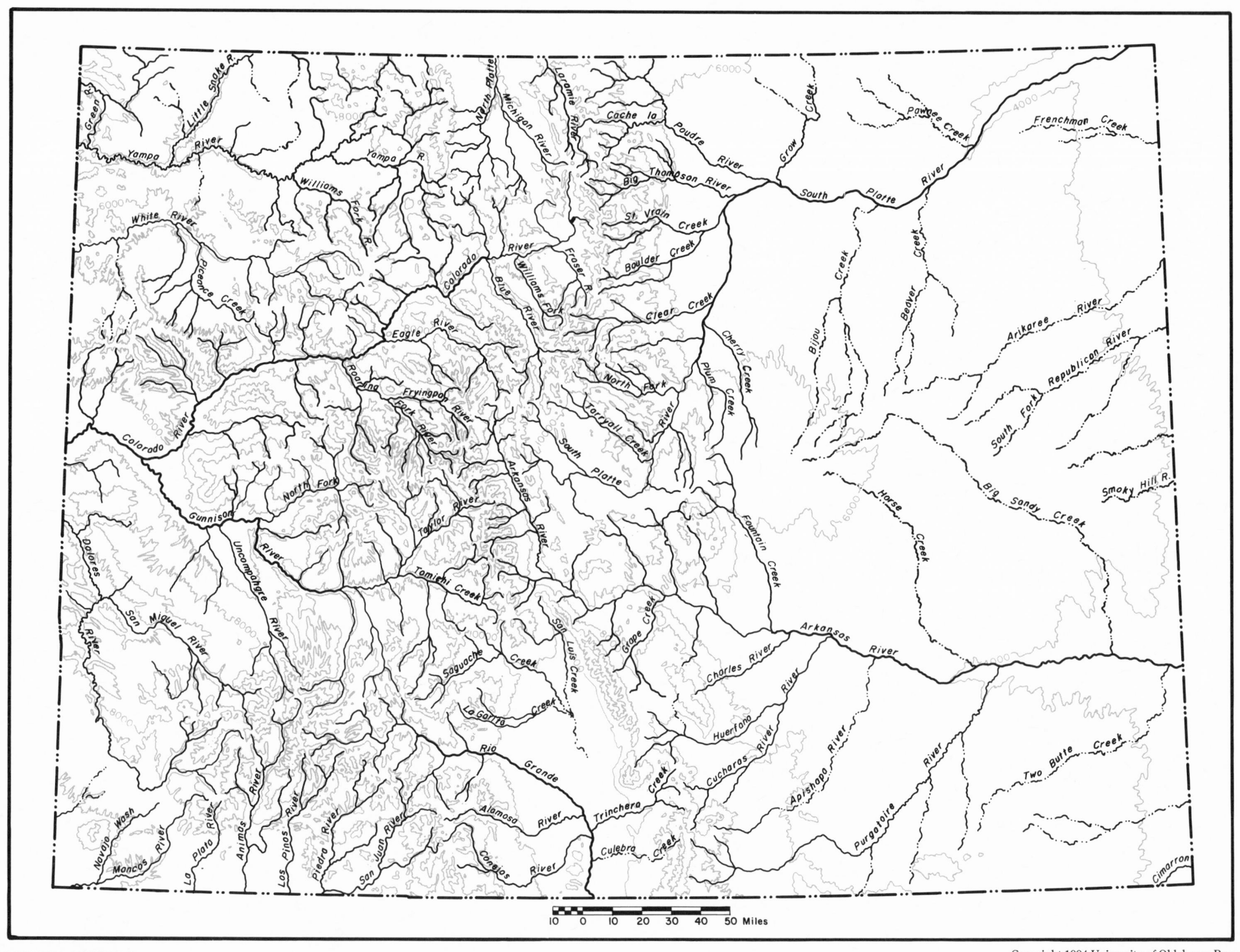

MAJOR RIVERS

2. MAJOR RIVERS

The "Mother of Rivers," Colorado gives birth to four of the major rivers of the American West. All four begin on the continental divide, where rivulets only a few yards apart ultimately lead to the world's two great oceans. The Platte, the Arkansas, and the Rio Grande flow through eastern Colorado into the Gulf of Mexico and the Atlantic. The Colorado River drains the western half of the state on its way to the Gulf of California and the Pacific Ocean.

None of the rivers in Colorado are navigable, but their banks became the main roads and settlement centers. Both the North and the South Platte originate in Colorado, cradled respectively in mountain-rimmed North Park and South Park. Two French explorers, the brothers Jean and Pierre Mallet, called the Platte *la riviére plat* (*plat* is French for "flat" or "shallow"), which Anglo-Americans spelled as Platte. The North and the South Platte merge in North Platte, Nebraska, before joining the Missouri River near Omaha.

The South Platte was a principal route for immigrant wagons and stagecoaches, then for rail and automobile roads. Over two-thirds of all Coloradans live in the valley of the South Platte and its major tributaries: Boulder Creek, the Big Thompson River, Cherry Creek, Clear Creek, St. Vrain Creek, and the Cache la Poudre River (named by French trappers who hid gunpowder there).

The Arkansas River begins on the east side of Fremont Pass near Leadville and drains both the state's highest mountain (Mount Elbert) and its lowest point (near Holly). The Arkansas tumbles out of the Rockies through the 1,000-foot Royal Gorge just west of Canon City. Fountain Creek joins the Arkansas at Pueblo, where attempts at settlement began in 1842. Fountain Creek was originally named Fountaine-qui-bouille ("boiling spring") by French fur trappers, for the mineral hot springs around its headwaters at Manitou Springs.

Zebulon Pike explored the Arkansas River on his 1806–1807 expedition, and afterwards Santa Fe Trail traders and Bent's Fort travelers made the Arkansas the leading route into Colorado. During the 1849 California gold rush and the Civil War, traffic shifted north to the Platte River. The Santa Fe Railroad and U.S. Highway 50 later followed the Arkansas, helping establish it as Colorado's second most-populous valley of settlement.

The Rio Grande was called the Rio Grande del Norte ("Great River of the North") by Spaniards who followed it northward from Mexico. The Rio Grande originates in the San Juan Mountains and flows southward through the San Luis Valley. There along the Culebra ("snake") and Conejos ("rabbit") rivers, Mexicans founded settlements in the early 1850s that survive to this day.

The Colorado River, which carries more water out of the state than the three other major rivers combined—almost two-thirds of the state's total stream flow in an average year—originates in Rocky Mountain National Park. Major mountain tributaries include the Blue, Eagle and Roaring Fork rivers. The diversion of Colorado River water to thirsty Front Range cities is the most extensive and controversial rearrangement of Colorado waterways.

Until 1921 the Colorado River was called Grand River above its junction with the Green River. At Grand Junction the Colorado merges with the Gunnison River. The San Juan and Dolores rivers, which drain southwestern Colorado, join the Colorado River in Utah, as do the Green and White rivers, which drain parts of northwestern Colorado. After carving the Grand Canyon, and serving as the boundary between Arizona and California, the Colorado would flow into the Gulf of California. Since the 1980s, however, the waters of the Colorado have not reached the sea because it is waylaid by the many dams, diversions, and irrigation systems that make it the lifeblood of the Southwest.

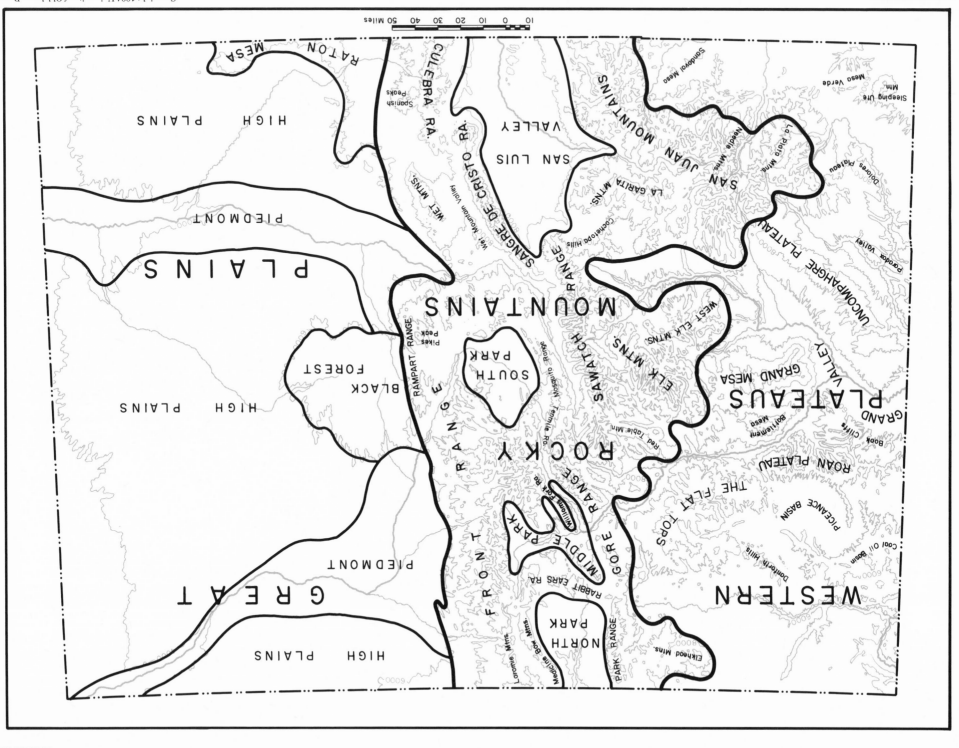

3. LANDFORMS

Tenderfeet often think of Colorado as mountains. They might more accurately think of it as five *p*s: peaks, plateaus, parks, plains, and piedmont.

The peaks of the Southern Rockies, Colorado's predominant landform, comprise the highest section of the Rockies between Canada and Mexico. They are a part of the vast mountain system that also includes the Andes of South America. In Colorado this cordillera is subdivided into numerous ranges, some of which are identified on this map.

The plateaus that prevail in western Colorado have been carved by the Colorado River and its tributaries. They range from 7,500-foot high Mesa Verde in the southwest to the 11,000-foot Flat Tops in the northwest. The higher plateaus catch more moisture and often are wooded, while bottomlands approach desert conditions. Settlement is largely confined to the canyons and valleys between the plateaus.

Parks are broad, relatively flat valleys surrounded by high mountains. The term is derived from *parc,* the French word for a game preserve. Once Colorado's grassy parks nourished many buffalo, deer, antelope, and other game animals, but cattle are the chief inhabitants today. With elevations ranging from 7,500 to 10,000 feet, Colorado's parks have a short growing season that has discouraged settlement and farming except for hay, cattle, and sheep ranching. North Park in north-central Colorado cradles the headwaters of the North Platte River and, like the river, spills into Wyoming. Middle Park is on the upper reaches of the Colorado River and its upper tributaries, including the Fraser and Blue rivers. South Park, on the headwaters for the South Platte River, is the highest park. The San Luis Valley, once known as San Luis Park, is the lowest, largest, and farthest south of these mountain valleys and produces cold-tolerant crops and livestock.

Plains prevail in the eastern half of Colorado. They are part of the Great Plains, which stretch from Canada to Mexico and gently slope from the Rockies to the Mississippi Valley. These high plains consist of sedimentary deposits built up by the erosion of the present Rockies and an ancestral range that wore away several hundred million years ago.

Colorado's high plains extend to the base of the mountains at an altitude of about 5,000 feet. Spectacular sandstone formations, such as the Garden of the Gods at Colorado Springs and Red Rocks at Morrison, are remainders of the sandy beaches left by an inland sea. The plains resemble a sea of grass except where overgrazing or farming of the land has cleared the way for sagebrush, thistles, tumbleweed, and bare dirt. Although they appear as level or rolling hills, the Colorado plains slope eastward at a rate of fifteen to eighteen feet per mile, descending to about 4,000 feet above sea level at the Kansas line.

Rivers formed largely by mountain snowmelt have carved out the piedmont (so called from the French for "foot of the mountain") along the South Platte and Arkansas rivers. This piedmont is divided by the Black Forest, a higher and wetter area noted for its thick growth of dark Ponderosa pines. Much of that forest was felled to build Denver and Colorado Springs.

Colorado's high plains and parks are sedimentary deposits atop ancient sea bottoms and are still reminiscent of seascapes, an illusion reinforced by the Great Sand Dunes National Monument in the San Luis Valley.

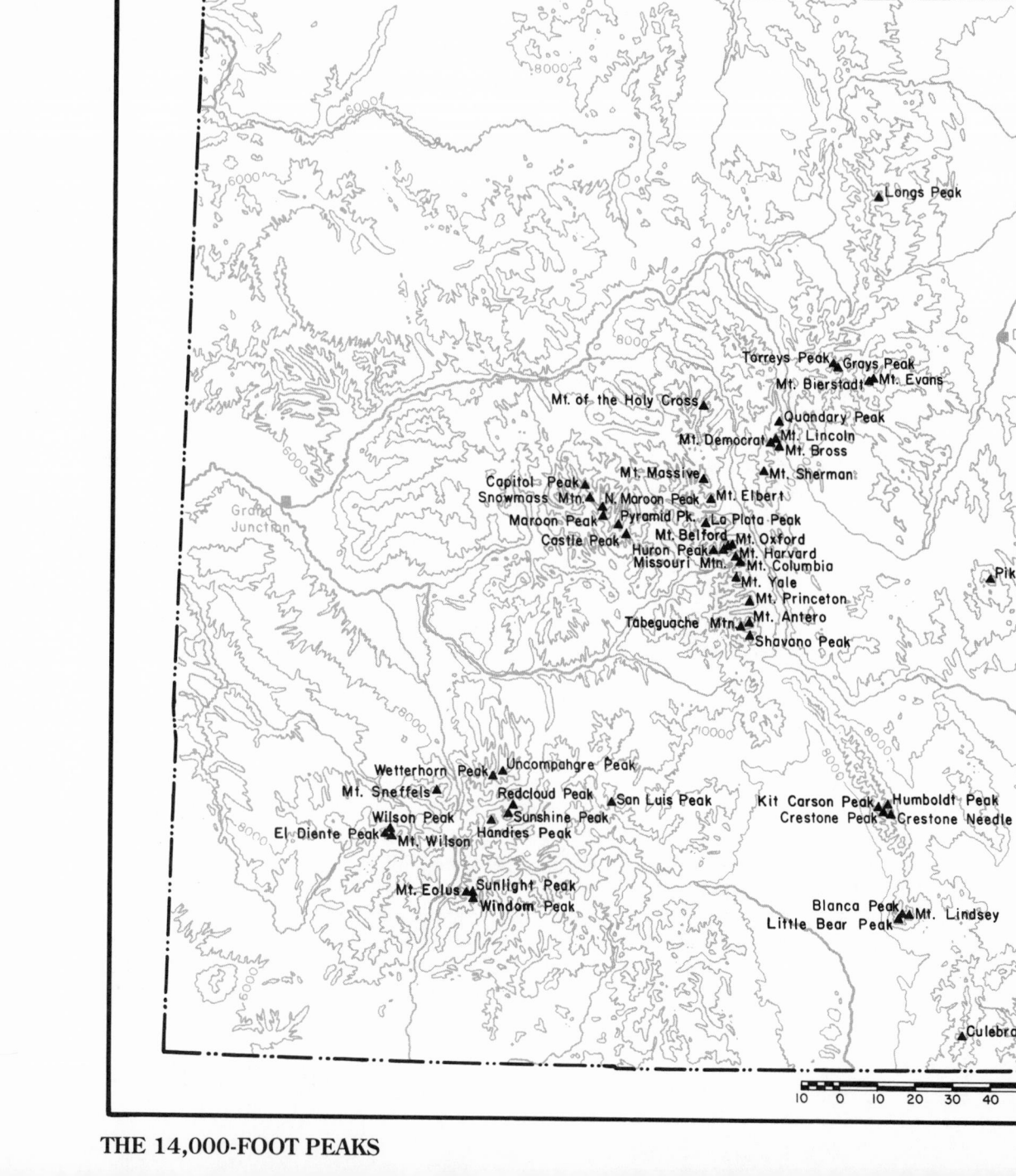

Longs Peak

Torreys Peak ▲ Grays Peak
Mt. Bierstadt ▲ Mt. Evans

Mt. of the Holy Cross ▲

Quandary Peak
Mt. Democrat ▲ Mt. Lincoln
Mt. Bross

Mt. Massive ▲ Mt. Sherman

Capitol Peak ▲
Snowmass Mtn. ▲ N. Maroon Peak ▲ Mt. Elbert
Pyramid Pk. ▲ La Plata Peak
Maroon Peak ▲
Castle Peak ▲ Mt. Belford ▲ Mt. Oxford
Huron Peak ▲ Mt. Harvard
Missouri Mtn. ▲ Mt. Columbia
Mt. Yale

Pikes Peak

Mt. Princeton
Tabeguache Mtn. ▲ Mt. Antero
Shavano Peak

Wetterhorn Peak ▲ Uncompahgre Peak
Mt. Sneffels ▲ Redcloud Peak ▲ San Luis Peak
Wilson Peak ▲ Sunshine Peak
El Diente Peak ▲ Handies Peak
Mt. Wilson

Kit Carson Peak ▲ Humboldt Peak
Crestone Peak ▲ Crestone Needle

Mt. Eolus ▲ Sunlight Peak
Windom Peak

Blanca Peak ▲ Mt. Lindsey
Little Bear Peak

Culebra Peak

Denver

Grand Junction

Pueblo

10   0   10   20   30   40   50 Miles

THE 14,000-FOOT PEAKS

4. THE 14,000-FOOT PEAKS

Of some nine thousand named mountains in Colorado, the fifty-three over 14,000 feet high excite the most interest. These lofty summits are favorite climbs, and each year people are officially honored by the Colorado Mountain Club for scaling them all.

The "fourteeners," as they are called, are the highest points remaining from a plateau that once covered much of the state. Typically, they are hard granite bulwarks that have resisted erosion. Exceptions include the scenic, if treacherous, Maroon Bells, which are of much softer sedimentary rock and provide more-dangerous footing.

Of the fourteeners, only Grays and Torreys peaks are on the continental divide. The other fifty-one are scattered on both sides. Thirty lie within fifty miles of Leadville, thirteen in the San Juan Mountains, and eight in the Sangre de Cristo Range. Pikes Peak, America's most-famous mountain, stands alone as a solitary sentinel overlooking the eastern plains. Atop this peak Katherine Lee Bates received the inspiration to write "America the Beautiful."

Native Americans probably climbed some of the fourteeners before Euro-Americans came to Colorado, but the first recorded ascent was by Dr. Edwin James, a member of the Long Expedition, who ascended Pikes Peak with some companions in 1820. Longs Peak, the second most-famous Colorado peak, was first scaled in 1868 by a party that included William N. Byers, the founding editor of the *Rocky Mountain News,* and Major John Wesley Powell, the illustrious, one-armed explorer. The last to be climbed was Crestone Peak, which was conquered by Albert R. Ellingwood and Eleanor S. Davis in 1916. The highest fourteener is Mount Elbert, at 14,433 feet; and the lowest is Sunshine, at 14,001. Mount Massive is more eye-catching than neighboring Mount Elbert, inspiring its fans to contemplate construction of a 13-foot rock pile on top to make it the highest peak.

Colorado's mountains have "grown" and "shrunk" over the years with measurements and remeasurements. In recent years Grizzly Peak was demoted from fourteener status. Mount Ellingwood, which some consider a fourteener, is officially considered a part of Mount Blanca. Many mountains come close to 14,000 feet, and more than six hundred Colorado peaks soar over 13,000 feet. To the chagrin of Coloradans, one peak in California is higher than Mt. Elbert. That is 14,495-foot Mount Whitney, which lost its title as the nation's highest when Alaska, with 20,300-foot Mount McKinley, became the fiftieth state.

Although many fourteeners are not challenging climbs for experienced mountaineers, they can be treacherous. Several people die on them each year. Trails often are narrow, with loose rock for footing and long drops. The fourteeners are notorious for sudden changes of weather: glorious mornings can turn into afternoon electrical storms with high winds, rain, sleet, and snow. Flatlanders not acclimated to lofty elevations may experience "mountain sickness" because reduced atmospheric pressure and thin air with less oxygen can cause dizziness, headaches, and nausea. To avoid violent afternoon electrical storms at the highest elevations, seasoned climbers start early in order to reach the summit by noon.

The climbing season for the fourteeners runs from July to September, when the peaks are relatively free of snow. Those planning their first high-peak climbs should seek experienced companions and leaders such as those provided by the Colorado Mountain Club. Less energetic sightseers wishing to conquer a fourteener may enjoy scenic automobile roads open in summer to the top of Mount Evans and Pikes Peak.

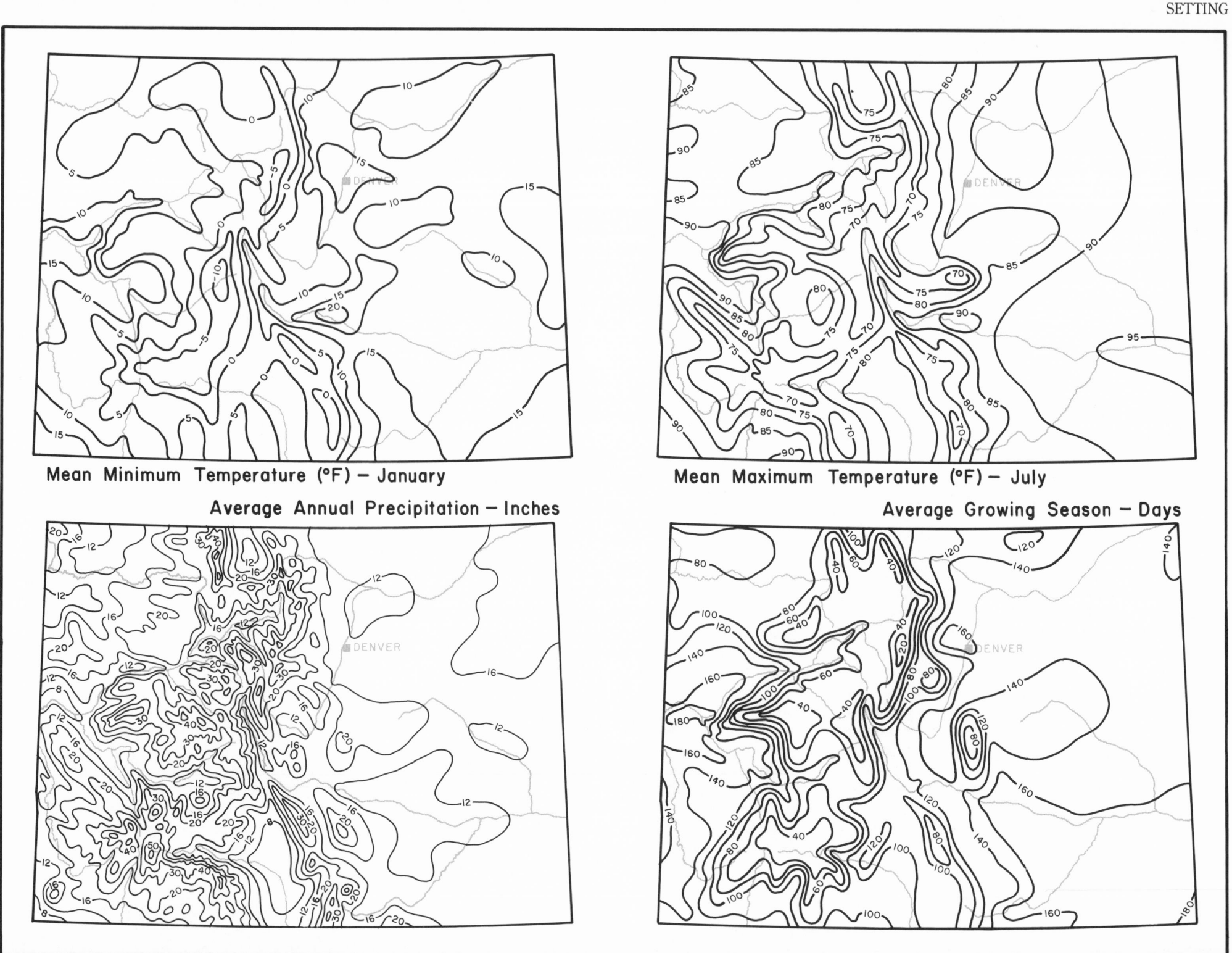

Mean Minimum Temperature (°F) — January

Mean Maximum Temperature (°F) — July

Average Annual Precipitation — Inches

Average Growing Season — Days

CLIMATE

5. CLIMATE

"If you don't like the weather, wait awhile. It'll change!" Many a state makes this claim, but Colorado's climate is particularly mercurial, with temperature and precipitation fluctuating wildly around a meaningless mean.

Colorado's weather is not moderated by any large body of water. The thin, dry air and intense solar radiation allow drastic temperature fluctuations, generally varying at least twenty-five degrees Fahrenheit within any twenty-four-hour period. The sudden encounter of a warm, humid front with a Canadian Polar front can drop temperatures abruptly by fifty degrees. A single storm can generate one-quarter of the average annual precipitation. In Colorado it is wise to prepare for extremes rather than means.

Colorado has three seasons—winter, summer, and fall. Spring is lost amid late winter snows that melt suddenly on hot summerlike days. Dry, sunny, mild weather often lingers into November. At lower altitudes this long, pleasant autumn colors the golden aspen, cottonwood, and willow, as well as the red scrub oak. Even in the mountain towns, snow usually does not become a winter-long blanket until December. Amid the western plateaus and on the eastern plains, snow rarely covers the earth for more than a week.

As the maps indicate, elevation greatly determines temperature, moisture, and the growing season. Note the mean January lows and the July highs when the mountains tend to be twenty-five degrees colder than the lowlands. The mean annual temperature difference between the summit of Pikes Peak and the lower Arkansas Valley towns one hundred miles away is thirty-five degrees Fahrenheit—the difference between Florida and Iceland. Generally, the higher you climb in elevation the colder and wetter it gets. For every one thousand feet up, temperatures drop about three degrees Fahrenheit, and the annual precipitation rate rises about three inches. Yet on winter days, when Canadian cold fronts bring subzero temperatures and blizzards to the plains, the foothills can be balmy thanks to warm chinook ("snow-eater") winds. Sometimes the mountains may be warmer than the plains because they wall out cold fronts.

Colorado's average temperature is forty-four degrees, but the records show an all-time high of 118 at Bennett, near Denver, and an all-time low of 61 below zero at Maybell, in Moffat County. Drastic temperature changes have brought snow and killing frosts to Denver as late as Memorial Day or as early as Labor Day. Summer highs over 90 are common along the Front Range; 100-degree days have been recorded at all the eastern plains weather stations.

Bitter cold grips every part of the state for at least a few days every year. Mountain-valley towns often have the dubious distinction of being the coldest in the contiguous forty-eight states. Gunnison led the nation in 1986: it was the coldest spot for eighty-one days, according to the February 1987 *Weatherwise Magazine*. Leadville and Alamosa ranked sixth and seventh in a 1986 "Icebox of the Nation" competition. Colorado's cold is often intensified by a high wind-chill factor. Winds, sometimes dangerously high, characterize all three regions of the state but especially the Front Range foothills. Denver's average wind speed, nine miles per hour, is something of a blessing when it blows away air pollution.

Throughout much of Colorado, winter days can be surprisingly warm, permitting golf, tennis, and other outdoor activities in January. Summer nights are cool because the dry, thin atmosphere rapidly loses heat after sunset. Colorado's dry, sunny climate once made it the leading state for tuberculosis victims chasing the "climate cure." Sadly, smog along the Front Range now may chase away people wanting to breathe easier. Overall, Colorado's cool, dry, sunny climate generally delights residents and visitors.

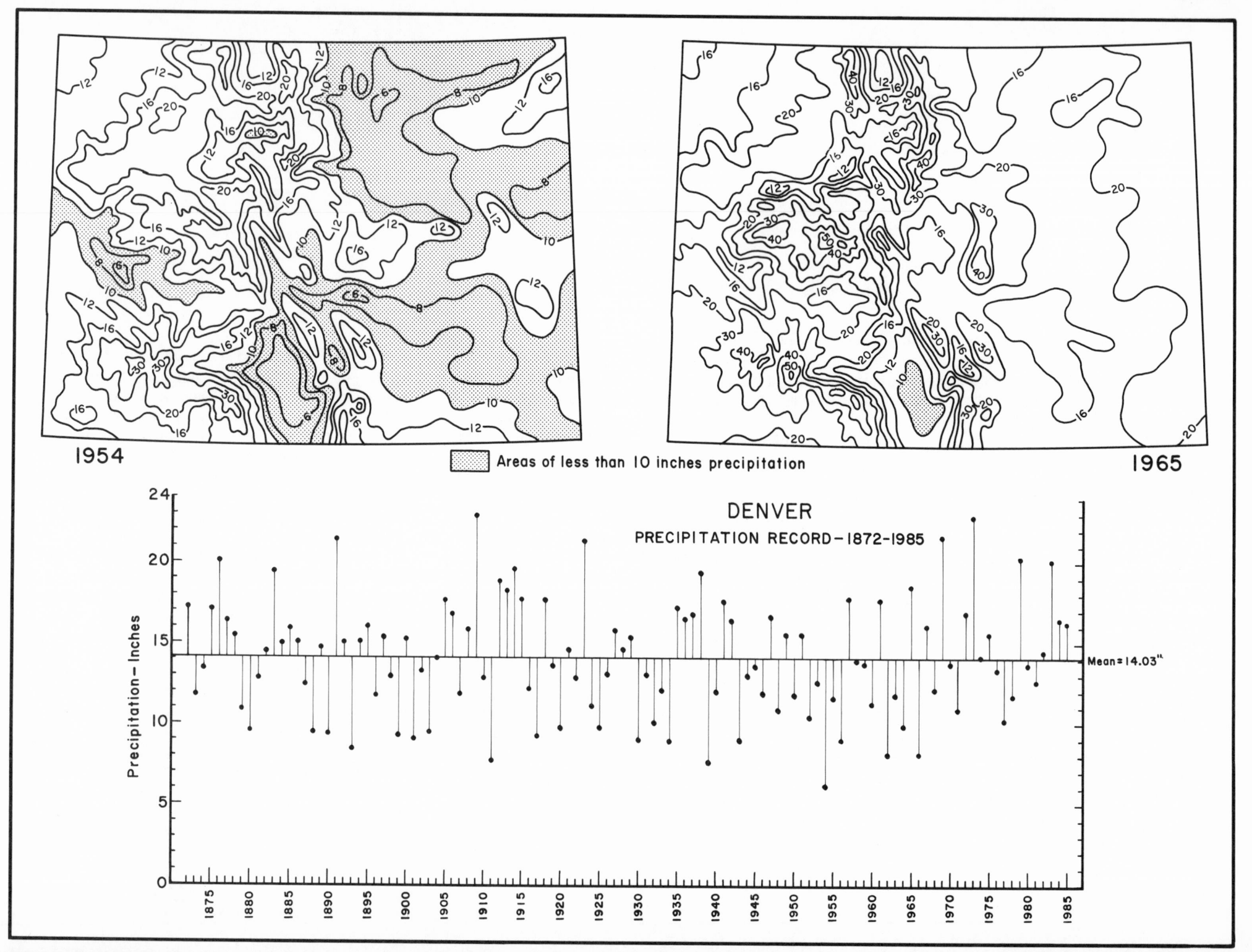

1954

Areas of less than 10 inches precipitation

1965

DENVER
PRECIPITATION RECORD-1872-1985

Precipitation-Inches

Mean = 14.03"

1875 1880 1885 1890 1895 1900 1905 1910 1915 1920 1925 1930 1935 1940 1945 1950 1955 1960 1965 1970 1975 1980 1985

WET AND DRY YEARS

6. WET AND DRY YEARS

Precipitation can vary widely from place to place and year to year. Colorado's average annual precipitation is seventeen inches, much of which comes as snow. The average annual snowfall on Wolf Creek Pass is more than 350 inches, while at Alamosa, fifty miles away, it is twenty-eight inches. The higher you climb, the wetter—and colder—it gets.

Precipitation reaches Colorado as rain, snow, sleet, graupel (granular snow pellets, or soft hail), mist, and hail. Hail is most frequent in northeastern Colorado where the South Platte Valley is called "hail alley." Hail has devastated crops, cars, property, and even people: hailstones the size of small grapefruit fell on Fort Collins on July 30, 1979, killing a three-month-old infant.

Snow, the principal form of precipitation in the central mountains, provides a year-around flow for the state's rivers and major creeks. Although the snow comes in fall, winter, and spring, it does not melt on the highest peaks until summer, providing water when the thirsty plains most need it. Snow, or "white gold," has become the greatest cash crop in Colorado, where skiing is now the major industry on the Western Slope of the Rockies. An abundance of this dry, powder snow makes Colorado "Ski Country U.S.A."

Water has been the subject of endless litigation, speculation, and study in Colorado. Despite many attempts to explain precipitation as cyclical, the historical pattern of wet and dry years defies generalizations. The Denver precipitation record from 1872 to 1985 disproves the common notion of severe droughts in the 1890s and 1930s. In both decades years of abnormally low rainfall were roughly balanced by years of above-average precipitation. Not until the 1950s did below-normal rainfall occur during eight out of ten years. Denver rainfall has varied from seven to twenty-three inches a year. From year to year, it generally fluctuates by four inches or more. Precipitation patterns vary widely within the state: farmers in a given locale may experience drought in a "wet" year.

The two maps, showing statewide rainfall in dry 1954 and wet 1965, further demonstrate the disparity between wet and dry years. One constant factor is the correlation of moisture to elevation. Year in and year out, the highest mountains receive about three times the moisture of the driest parts of the eastern plains and western plateaus. Moisture travels a long distance from the Pacific Ocean or the Gulf of Mexico to reach Colorado. If Pacific air finally reaches Colorado, the high Rockies drain what little moisture remains as the peaks poke holes in the clouds.

Few moisture-laden clouds from the West get across the Rockies to drop their liquid magic on the high plains, which are watered primarily by moisture from the Gulf of Mexico. A common high-plains phenomenon is "dry rain," or virga—trailing wisps of precipitation that evaporate before they reach the ground. The plains average fifteen inches of rain a year while the statewide average is about seventeen inches. Old-timers say it is so dry in eastern Colorado that the water is only wet on one side. Actually a few Western Slope valleys are the driest part of the state.

Rain tends to fall in sprinkles, in torrents, or not at all. Thus long droughts often end in flash floods. When rain finally does come, it is a glorious sight, described eloquently by naturalist Arthur Carhart in his book *Colorado:* "When fluffy white castellated thunderheads mount far in the blue and the banging roar of thunder gallops over the plains, the echo of old Indian drums may be hidden in those far-flung reverberations."

Indian rain dancers and modern meteorological scientists using cloud seeding have all tried to improve upon Colorado's scant and erratic precipitation. But no magic can change the basic fact that Colorado is a semiarid state where residents often look prayerfully to the heavens for moisture.

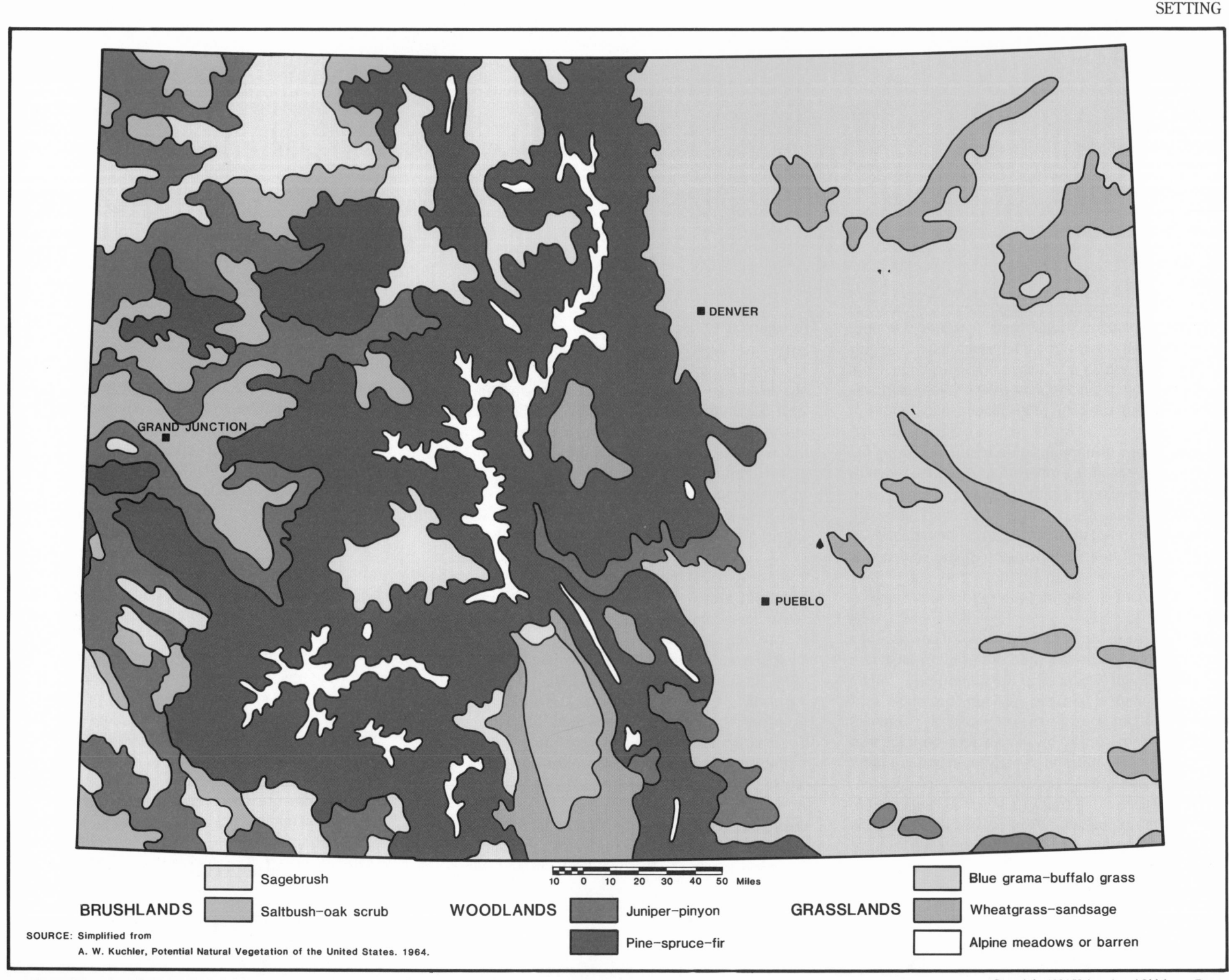

Sagebrush

BRUSHLANDS   Saltbush–oak scrub

WOODLANDS   Juniper–pinyon

Pine–spruce–fir

10   0   10   20   30   40   50   Miles

GRASSLANDS   Blue grama–buffalo grass

Wheatgrass–sandsage

Alpine meadows or barren

SOURCE: Simplified from
A. W. Kuchler, Potential Natural Vegetation of the United States. 1964.

NATURAL VEGETATION

7. NATURAL VEGETATION

Sparse moisture, temperature extremes, and high winds shape natural vegetation in the highest state. Human activities, notably stock grazing, farming, mining, and town building, have further modified the natural vegetation. Grasslands prevail on the eastern plains, woodlands in the central mountains, and brushlands on the central and western plateaus.

Grasslands of eastern Colorado are dominated by grasses such as buffalo grass *(Buchloë dactyloides)* and blue grama *(Bouteloua gracilis)*. Other common plants are the prickly pear *(Opuntia)*, sage *(Artemisia)* and wheatgrass *(Agropyron)*. Those plants have deep, probing roots that dig in to survive drought and high winds. Sunflowers *(Helianthus)*, yucca *(Yucca glauca)*, snow-on-the-mountain *(Euphorbia marginata)*, prairie evening primrose *(Oenothera)*, and other prairie flowers give the plains a subtle, unappreciated beauty. Although all of eastern Colorado is shown as grassland on this map, the area includes sandy wastes where little grows and, along watercourses, cottonwood thickets. Cottonwoods *(Populus)* are among the few trees native to the plains, along with the box elder *(Acer negundo)*, hackberry *(Celtis reticulata)*, and willow *(Salix)*.

Woodlands prevail in the foothills, which are adorned with ponderosa pine *(Pinus ponderosa)*, piñon pine *(Pinus edulis)*, juniper *(Juniperus)*, and scrub oak *(Quercus gambelii)*. At higher elevations you are more apt to encounter Douglas fir *(Pseudotsuga menziesii)*, blue spruce *(Picea pungens)*, and lodgepole pine *(Pinus contorta)*. Among the foothills wildflowers are the mariposa, or sego lily, called *Calochortus gunnisonii* in honor of Capt. John W. Gunnison's botanically minded 1853 expedition. Between about 8,000 feet and the timberline (10,500–11,500 feet), quaking aspen *(Populus tremuloides)* are common. Englemann spruce *(Picea engelmannii)* predominate at the highest elevations, where stunted, wind-sculpted individuals finally give way at the timberline to the alpine tundra. The bristlecone pines *(Pinus aristata)* found in a few timberline groves, notably on Mount Evans, are among the oldest trees in North America. Individual bristlecone pines may live for 4,000 years.

Parry's primrose *(Primula parryi)* adorns woodland streams and commemorates Charles C. Parry, who during the 1860s collected, studied, and wrote about Colorado vegetation. Relatively open forests and alpine meadows leave space for the wildflowers that bloom gloriously during the short summer season. These brightly colored floral carpets unfold within inches of melting snowdrifts. Above the tundra on the mountaintops, lichens and mosses decorate rocky summits.

Colorado forests have been subjected to tremendous changes during the past century. Lumbering, ski areas, road building, and above all, development have deforested many areas. Aspen trees, the first to emerge after an evergreen forest is lost, are now much more numerous. Aspen groves and lines on hillsides indicate where natural vegetation has been lost. One of the most dramatic such exhibits is in the San Juan Mountains where the Lime Creek Burn, sometimes blamed on the anger of dispossessed Utes, destroyed 26,000 acres in 1879. Terrible consequences resulted from massive cutting of spruce forests to feed charcoal smelters, timber mining shafts, and build Leadville, then the second largest city in Colorado. Instead of melting slowly in shady forests, the exposed snowfields melted rapidly and rushed down the Arkansas River in the deadly 1921 Pueblo flood.

Although the state tree, the Colorado blue spruce, has never been in danger of extinction, the state flower, the columbine, was almost loved to death. Wildflower excursion trains disgorged armies of tourists who picked every columbine in sight until lawmakers made this a finable offense.

Brushlands predominate in the driest parts of the state, especially on the Western Slope. Sagebrush *(Artemisia)* grows best above four thousand feet, and its mountain and plains varieties cover much of western Colorado. These brushlands, sometimes called a cold desert or a shrub steppe, also feature other woody shrubs such as rabbitbrush *(Chrysothamnus nauseosis)* and saltbush *(Atriplex canescens)*. Mountain brushlands harbor wild cherry *(Prunus)* and mountain mahogany *(Cercocarpus montanus)*.

Native vegetation can be seen in preserves such as the national parks, grasslands, and wilderness areas and the Plains Conservation Center southeast of Aurora. This map, however, shows natural vegetation as it is thought to have been before European settlement and intensive agriculture transformed the landscape.

PART TWO
BOUNDARIES

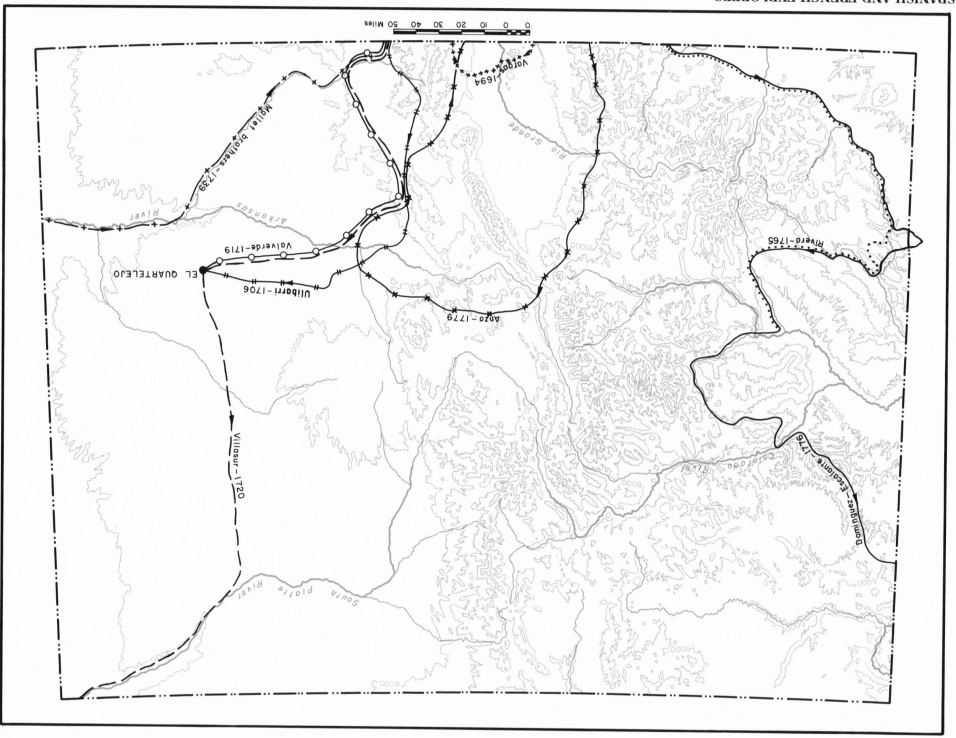

Valverde–1719

Villasur–1720

Mallet brothers–1739

EL QUARTELEJO

Ulibarri–1706

Anza–1779

Vargas 1694

Rivera–1765

Domínguez–Escalante–1776

Rio Grande

Arkansas River

South Platte River

Colorado River

River

50 Miles

0   0   10   20   30   40   50

8. SPANISH AND FRENCH EXPLORERS

A century after Columbus claimed America for Spain, the conquistadors had invaded Central America and were pushing into North and South America. In North America some of the remotest outposts of the Spanish empire were along the Rio Grande, which Don Juan de Oñate explored and began colonizing in 1598.

The famous 1540 expedition of General Francisco Vásquez de Coronado probably never entered what is now Colorado, where Juan de Archuleta led the first known Spanish excursion in 1664. Following an unknown route, he chased runaway Taos Pueblo Indians to El Quartelejo, an Apache settlement near the Arkansas River.

The first traceable Spanish expedition into Colorado came in 1694 when Don Diego de Vargas, the governor of New Mexico, followed the Rio Grande to a tributary, the Culebra River. Vargas skirmished with Ute Indians, marveled at a herd of five hundred buffalo in the San Luis Valley, and left a journal in which he mentioned existing names of Colorado rivers, creeks, and mountains, indicating that the Spanish had already explored parts of southeastern Colorado.

In 1706, Juan de Ulibarri and forty soldiers traveled north to the Arkansas River, skirting the Spanish Peaks. Like Archuleta, Ulibarri headed for El Quartelejo, the Apache settlement that had become a haven for Pueblo Indians fleeing Spanish rule. Ulibarri claimed the Rio Grande and Arkansas drainages for King Philip V of Spain. In officially claiming "the province of San Luis," Ulibarri's party first sang the *Te Deum Laudamus,* then he made a speech, cut the air in all four directions with his sword, and presided over a discharge of guns.

Antonio de Valverde, governor of New Mexico, became the next official visitor in 1719. He crossed the Raton Mountains and headed for El Quartelejo, where he apparently failed to build a planned fort and mission. In the following year Pedro de Villasur set out from Santa Fe with forty-five Spanish soldiers and about sixty Indian allies. Pushing beyond El Quartelejo into unknown territory, Villasur's party explored the South Platte, which he named the Rio Jesus y Maria. They camped near the junction of the North and South Platte rivers, where Pawnees, encouraged by the French, surprised the camp at dawn, killing Villasur and all but thirteen of his party.

In 1739 the brothers Paul and Pierre Mallet led the first recorded French expedition into Colorado. This was the earliest known crossing of the Great Plains from the Missouri River to Santa Fe. The eight-man Mallet party traveled up the Missouri to the Platte. Then they cut across the plains to the Arkansas River and followed its tributary, the Purgatoire, south, ultimately reaching Santa Fe.

Threatened by such French excursions into the Southwest, Spain pursued further exploration and settlement. Don Juan Maria de Rivera became the first recorded explorer of southwestern Colorado in 1765. Rivera skirted the San Juan Mountains and got as far as the Gunnison River near present-day Delta, where his troop carved a cross, a name, and the date into a tree.

After the French gave up their North American possessions in 1763, Spain concentrated on linking her New Mexico settlements with those in California. To find an overland route between Santa Fe and the West Coast, two Franciscan priests, Fathers Francisco Atanasio Dominguez and Silvestre Vélez de Escalante, set out from Santa Fe in 1776 for Monterey, the Spanish capital of California. In their ten-man party was Captain Don Bernardo y Pacheco Miera, an engineer and artist, who drew the first surviving, detailed map of Colorado. The Dominguez-Escalante party followed Rivera's route along the Dolores, San Miguel and Uncompahgre rivers to the Gunnison. Pushing westward into modern Utah, they reached Utah Lake before returning to Santa Fe via the Grand Canyon region. Escalante's diary and Captain Miera's map made this the most important Spanish expedition into Colorado.

In 1779 another governor of New Mexico, Juan Bautista de Anza, led 645 men on the last major Spanish thrust into Colorado. Marching through the San Luis Valley and over Poncha Pass, Anza's army reached South Park before turning east to corner Chief Cuerno Verde (Green Horn) and his Comanches, whom they routed on what is still called Greenhorn Creek. Other Spanish and Mexican explorations have gone unrecorded in a state that Hispanics were the first Europeans to explore and settle.

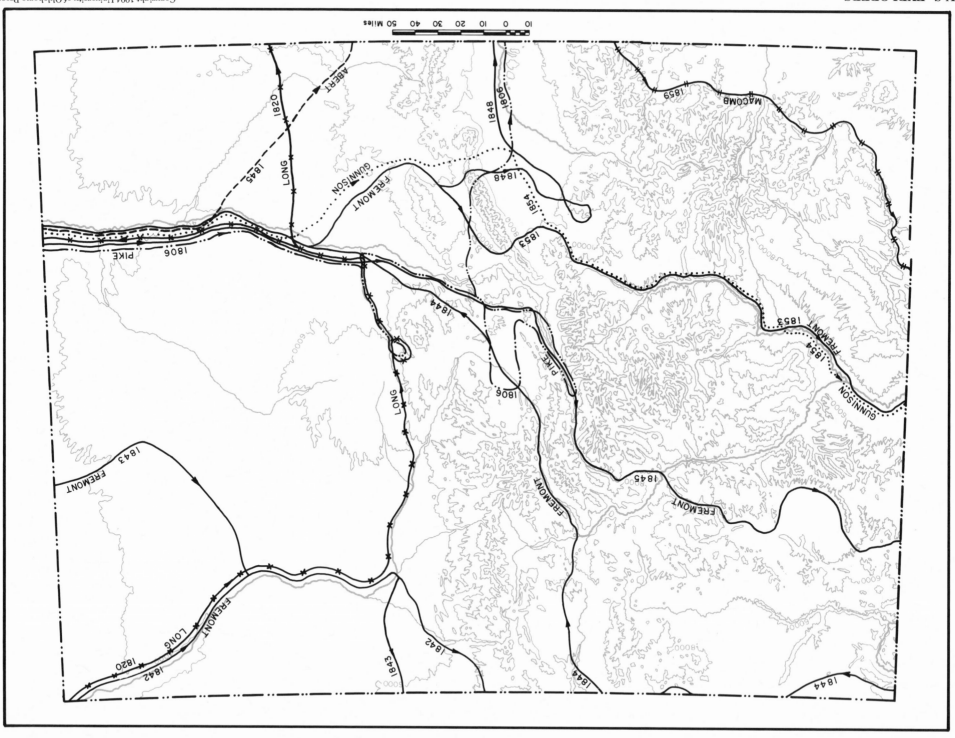

9. U.S. EXPLORERS

When Napoleon sold French Louisiana to President Thomas Jefferson in 1803, neither chief of state knew much about the vast tract, which included much of present-day Colorado. To learn more, Jefferson sent Capt. Meriwether Lewis and Lt. William Clark to explore the northern part of Louisiana. In 1806 Lt. Zebulon M. Pike and about seventy-five men, most of whom were Osage Indians, set out to investigate southwestern Louisiana.

Pike followed the Arkansas River west to Colorado and began looking for the Red River, which was then considered the boundary between Louisiana and Mexico. Pike became lost and confused, and built several small stockades in Colorado. He attempted to climb Pikes Peak, but was rebuffed by a November blizzard. After wandering from South Park into the San Luis Valley, Pike was captured by Spanish forces. Pike's party suffered many hardships in their travels, but they produced the first detailed report and maps of eastern Colorado. Pike returned to the United States, where he defended himself against charges of collaborating with the Spanish. He rose to the rank of general before being killed during the War of 1812.

The War of 1812 interrupted exploration of the West until 1819, when Maj. Stephen H. Long and his party headed west. To court the Native Americans, Long took six dozen mirrors and thirty pounds of vermilion face paint. His party followed the South Platte River into Colorado, camping on the future site of Denver on July 5, 1820. Failing to find a passage through South Platte Canyon, the expedition turned southward. Dr. Edwin James of the Long party, intrigued by the huge mountain jutting out onto the plains, led a soldier and wagonmaster to the top in the first recorded ascent of Pikes Peak. Long returned to Philadelphia, where he drew the map while Dr. James wrote the report, both published in 1823. Long's map labeled the High Plains as the "Great American Desert," and proclaimed it unsuitable for settlement.

The "Great American Desert" designation discouraged all but a few trappers, traders, and explorers from poking into Colorado. This changed after the 1846–48 Mexican War and the California gold rush in 1849, when many eyes turned west. Then California, held by a weak Mexican government, became a prize coveted by Britain, the United States, and Russia. The Yankees' success in claiming California was largely due to the explorations of Capt. John Charles Frémont. Frémont's father-in-law, the influential U.S. senator from Missouri, Thomas Hart Benton, backed Frémont's explorations. In turn, Frémont was predisposed to explore routes directly west of St. Louis. All five of his explorations passed through Colorado. His second expedition (1843–44) and his third expedition (1845) led to published reports and maps of Colorado's mountains and mountain parks. Frémont's works became popular reading, partly due to the writing and editing prowess of his wife, Jessie Benton Frémont.

When the Mexican War ended in 1848, Americans became more interested in paths across the "Great American Desert" and the western mountains. Expansionists argued that settling the West was America's "Manifest Destiny" and that a railroad should be built. Citizens of Chicago, St. Louis, and New Orleans all argued the merits of routes originating in their city. As a compromise, the president and congress asked the army to survey the competing routes.

Capt. John W. Gunnison surveyed the central route through Colorado in 1853, following the Arkansas River and then cutting southwest to enter the San Luis Valley via Sangre de Cristo Pass. After camping at Fort Massachusetts in the San Luis Valley, the party crossed Cochetopa Pass to follow what would be named the Gunnison River. It led them to the Colorado River and on into Utah, where Paiutes killed Gunnison and most of his command. Lt. E. G. Beckwith, the artist and topographer Richard H. Kern, and the expedition surgeon and geologist, Dr. James Schiel, survived to produce reports, illustrations, and the first good map of central Colorado. Their reports discouraged a Colorado rail route, not so much because of the mountains, but because of the broken terrain beyond them, including the spectacular Black Canyon of the Gunnison.

The Pike, Long, Frémont, and Gunnison expeditions, among others, produced detailed reports filled with maps, paintings, drawings, and encyclopedic treatments of not only the land but also its history and natural history, its flora and fauna, and its Native Americans.

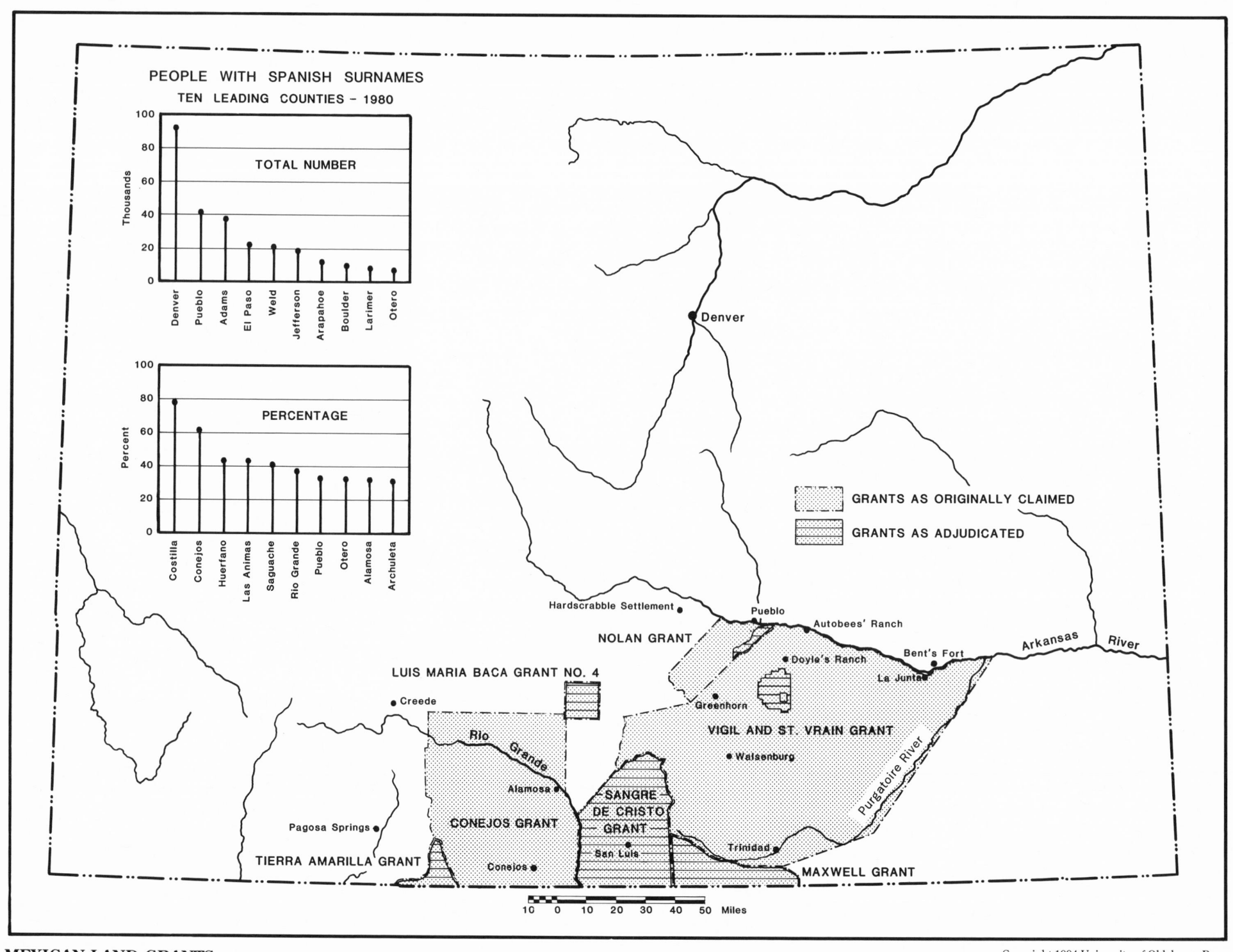

PEOPLE WITH SPANISH SURNAMES
TEN LEADING COUNTIES – 1980

TOTAL NUMBER

Thousands

Denver Pueblo Adams El Paso Weld Jefferson Arapahoe Boulder Larimer Otero

PERCENTAGE

Percent

Costilla Conejos Huerfano Las Animas Saguache Rio Grande Pueblo Otero Alamosa Archuleta

GRANTS AS ORIGINALLY CLAIMED

GRANTS AS ADJUDICATED

Denver

Hardscrabble Settlement

Pueblo

Autobees' Ranch

NOLAN GRANT

Doyle's Ranch

Bent's Fort

La Junta

Arkansas River

LUIS MARIA BACA GRANT NO. 4

Creede

Greenhorn

VIGIL AND ST. VRAIN GRANT

Rio Grande

Walsenburg

Purgatoire River

Alamosa

SANGRE
DE CRISTO
GRANT

CONEJOS GRANT

Pagosa Springs

Trinidad

San Luis

TIERRA AMARILLA GRANT

Conejos

MAXWELL GRANT

10 0 10 20 30 40 50 Miles

MEXICAN LAND GRANTS

10. MEXICAN LAND GRANTS

After winning independence from Spain in 1821, Mexico grew concerned about the northernmost limits of its territory, where it faced not only hostile Native Americans. Aggressive United States citizens had erected Bent's Fort just across the Arkansas River border between U.S. territory and Mexico.

To reinforce Mexican claims to what is now part of Colorado, Gov. Manuel Armijo of New Mexico made five land grants to attract settlers. The 1832 Tierra Amarilla grant along the Chama River went to Manuel Martinez, his eight sons, and several associates. Most of the area lay in New Mexico, but a small wedge protruded into parts of what became Archuleta and Conejos counties in Colorado.

In 1833 the Conejos grant was made at the request of certain citizens of Taos County, New Mexico. The large grant covered much of the western half of the San Luis Valley, including Conejos and Rio Grande counties in Colorado and some of New Mexico. An 1843 attempt to settle on the Conejos River was frustrated by hostile Utes. The town of Guadalupe was not established until 1854 (later it was absorbed by the nearby town of Conejos).

The Maxwell grant (also known as the Beaubien and Miranda) was awarded in 1841 to Charles Beaubien and Guadalupe Miranda. Lucien B. Maxwell, a son-in-law of Charles Beaubien, gained control of this vast New Mexico estate, which included a slice of the future Las Animas County in Colorado.

The 1843 grant to Cornelio Vigil and Ceran St. Vrain covered four million acres that stretched past the Purgatoire River on the south and east, roughly followed the Arkansas and Huerfano rivers on the north, and extended to the Sangre de Cristo Mountains on the west. Although St. Vrain, a trapper and trader, had been born a U.S. citizen in St. Louis, he became a naturalized Mexican. Charles Autobees, James P. Beckwourth, William Bent, Thomas O. Boggs, Kit Carson, Joseph B. Doyle, Lucien B. Maxwell, and Felix St. Vrain were among the early settlers on the Vigil and St. Vrain Grant, building adobe towns such as Greenhorn (1846), Hardscrabble (1840), and Pueblo (1842).

The Nolan grant to Gervacio Nolan, a French-Canadian living in Taos, was made by Governor Armijo a few days after the Vigil and St. Vrain grant in 1843. This Nolan tract along the St. Charles River included what is now South Pueblo. Nolan, an illiterate frontiersman, began planting corn on his grant in the 1840s, but he may have been a front man for Cornelio Vigil, who was legally entitled to only one claim.

The Sangre de Cristo grant, presented by Governor Armijo to Stephen Luis Lee and Narciso Beaubien in 1843, stretched from the crest of the Sangre de Cristo range westward to the Rio Grande, embracing all of what is now Costilla County and some of northern New Mexico. Although Lee and Beaubien, two residents of Taos, did not settle on their grant, others did. The town of San Luis, the oldest permanent settlement in Colorado, was established there in 1851. San Luis still uses its 1852 communal water ditch and La Vega, a 600-acre public commons.

The Luis Maria Baca grant number 4 in the San Luis Valley was made in 1860 when the U.S. government gave the 100,000-acre site to the Baca family in exchange for some of the original Baca grant in New Mexico.

These Mexican land grants suffered various fates after 1848, when Mexico surrendered this territory to the United States in the Treaty of Guadalupe Hidalgo, which ended the Mexican War. Although the treaty guaranteed property rights of Mexican settlers, much land was stripped away from the original owners. Complex and controversial circumstances surrounded the disposition of these vast grants. United States courts cast doubt upon the claims by citing an 1824 Mexican law forbidding government grants larger than eleven square leagues (a square league was about 4,400 acres). All of these Mexican grants were larger than that and thus could be construed as illegal. Under the terms of the original grants, settlement had to take place within a specified number of years or ownership would revert to the government. Thus lack of settlement became another legal cloud.

Many of the original grantees were dead or had disposed of their grants by 1891, when the U.S. Congress authorized settlement of the land-grant claims by the Court of Private Land Claims. This court threw out the Conejos grant, declaring that the land had not been settled within the time specified by the terms of the grant. The Vigil and St. Vrain grant was reduced from over 4 million acres to 97,390.95 acres in an 1860 U.S. court decision, which was upheld in 1898. The Maxwell, Sangre de Cristo, and Baca claims were upheld, but the Nolan grant was reduced to eleven square leagues.

Within the grants, individual settlers struggled to keep smaller lots. Sometimes U.S. courts threw out their claims for lack of written proof of ownership, a formality more important under Anglo than Hispanic law. Other Mexican-American pioneers were able to retain their property, but the land-grabbing legacy of conquest causes ill feeling to this day.

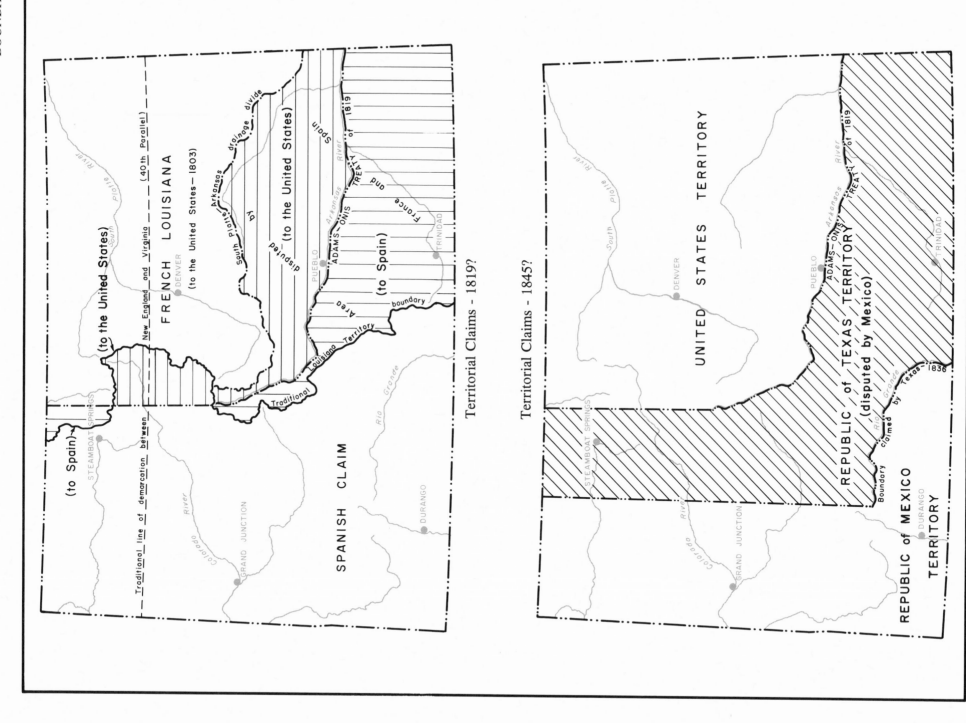

Territorial Claims - 1819?

FRENCH LOUISIANA

(to the United States)

(to the United States—1803)

New England and Virginia

(40th Parallel)

DENVER

drainage divide

Arkansas

South Platte

by

Friendship

(to the United States)

Spain

Arkansas River

ADAMS-ONIS TREATY of 1819

and

Spain

PUEBLO

France

TRINIDAD

(to Spain)

Louisiana Territory

Traditional

boundary

Area

Rio Grande

Platte River

South Platte River

STEAMBOAT SPRINGS

(to Spain)

Traditional line of demarcation between

Colorado River

GRAND JUNCTION

DURANGO

SPANISH CLAIM

Territorial Claims - 1845?

UNITED STATES TERRITORY

Platte River

South Platte River

DENVER

Arkansas River

ADAMS-ONIS TREATY of 1819

PUEBLO

REPUBLIC of TEXAS TERRITORY
(disputed by Mexico)

TRINIDAD

Rio Grande

Boundary claimed by Texas—1836

STEAMBOAT SPRINGS

Colorado River

GRAND JUNCTION

DURANGO

REPUBLIC of MEXICO
TERRITORY

For three centuries Colorado was a disputed border area claimed by Spain, England, France, the United States, Mexico, and the Republic of Texas. Between 1540 and 1848 all six nations claimed land within present-day Colorado. Some portions of the state changed hands nine times.

Spain was the first European nation to assert a title to Colorado, basing her case on the 1540 expedition of General Francisco Vásquez de Coronado and subsequent expeditions. Most authorities doubt that Coronado trod on Colorado soil during his expedition from Mexico City to what is now Kansas, but he came close enough to establish Spanish dominance.

Spain strengthened its claim in 1598 when Don Juan de Oñate, a wealthy mining man who had married the great-granddaughter of the Aztec emperor Montezuma, led a party of about one hundred soldiersettlers up the Rio Grande. Oñate formally claimed the entire Rio Grande drainage for Spain, announcing to astonished Indians that the king of Spain now had "the power of life and death over everything high and low, from the leaves of the trees to the stones and sands of the river."

Spaniards founded Santa Fe, New Mexico, in 1609 and soon established other settlements along the Rio Grande and its tributaries as far north as Taos. They never planted a colony in Colorado, and the Spanish settlements in New Mexico were small, remote frontier outposts, but they enhanced Spain's presence in the American Southwest. Pueblo Indians successfully revolted against Spanish control in 1680, only to be reconquered twelve years later by Don Diego de Vargas.

Spain's earliest challenge—a feeble one—came from England after British subjects planted colonies at Jamestown (1607) and Plymouth Rock (1620) on the Atlantic Coast. The English, believing the continent not to be smaller than it is, established colonies extending west to the Pacific Ocean. The major merit of these sea-to-sea boundaries, most of which the English never occupied, was to clearly mark boundaries and expansion spheres between the competing English colonies on the Atlantic Coast. The fortieth parallel, for example, separated Virginia's claims from those of the New England colonies. France presented the first serious challenge to

Spain. Robert Cavelier, sieur de La Salle, left French Canada in 1682 to explore the Great Lakes and the Mississippi River. When he reached the mouth of the Mississippi, La Salle claimed and named the entire Mississippi drainage for his king, Louis XIV. At the time no European nation had explored or mapped the western boundaries of Louisiana, but all were aware that the Mississippi River drainage extended to the Rockies along tributaries such as the Platte and Arkansas rivers.

The 1763 Treaty of Paris, ending the French and Indian War, awarded to Spain all French territory west of the Mississippi, including all of what is now Colorado. In 1800, however, Napoleon forced Spain to return Louisiana to France. Three years later Napoleon sold Louisiana to the U.S. for $15 million, giving the U.S. title to northeastern Colorado.

The boundary between Spanish territory and French Louisiana was vague. Initially Spain regarded the boundary as the divide between the South Platte drainage and the Arkansas drainage, until the Adams-Onís Treaty of 1819 established the Arkansas River as the boundary. Louisiana's western boundary was also disputed. Initially the continental divide north of the Arkansas was used, but later it became a line running due north from the headwaters of the Arkansas near Leadville, a boundary that was formalized in the 1819 treaty.

When Mexico gained its independence from Spain in 1821, she inherited Spanish claims to Colorado. Yet the Mexican government proved as weak as the Spanish by neglecting to send troops to establish forts, or to plant permanent settlements in southern Colorado and other parts of the Southwest. Thus Mexico was vulnerable when the Texans revolted and gained their independence in 1836. Texans claimed territory north and east of the Rio Grande, although Mexico disputed this. When the United States annexed the Republic of Texas in 1845, it also inherited the boundary disputes.

In 1848 the Treaty of Guadalupe-Hidalgo ended the Mexican War and awarded western and southern Colorado to the United States, which paid Texas to relinquish its claims to what is now eastern New Mexico and southeastern and central Colorado.

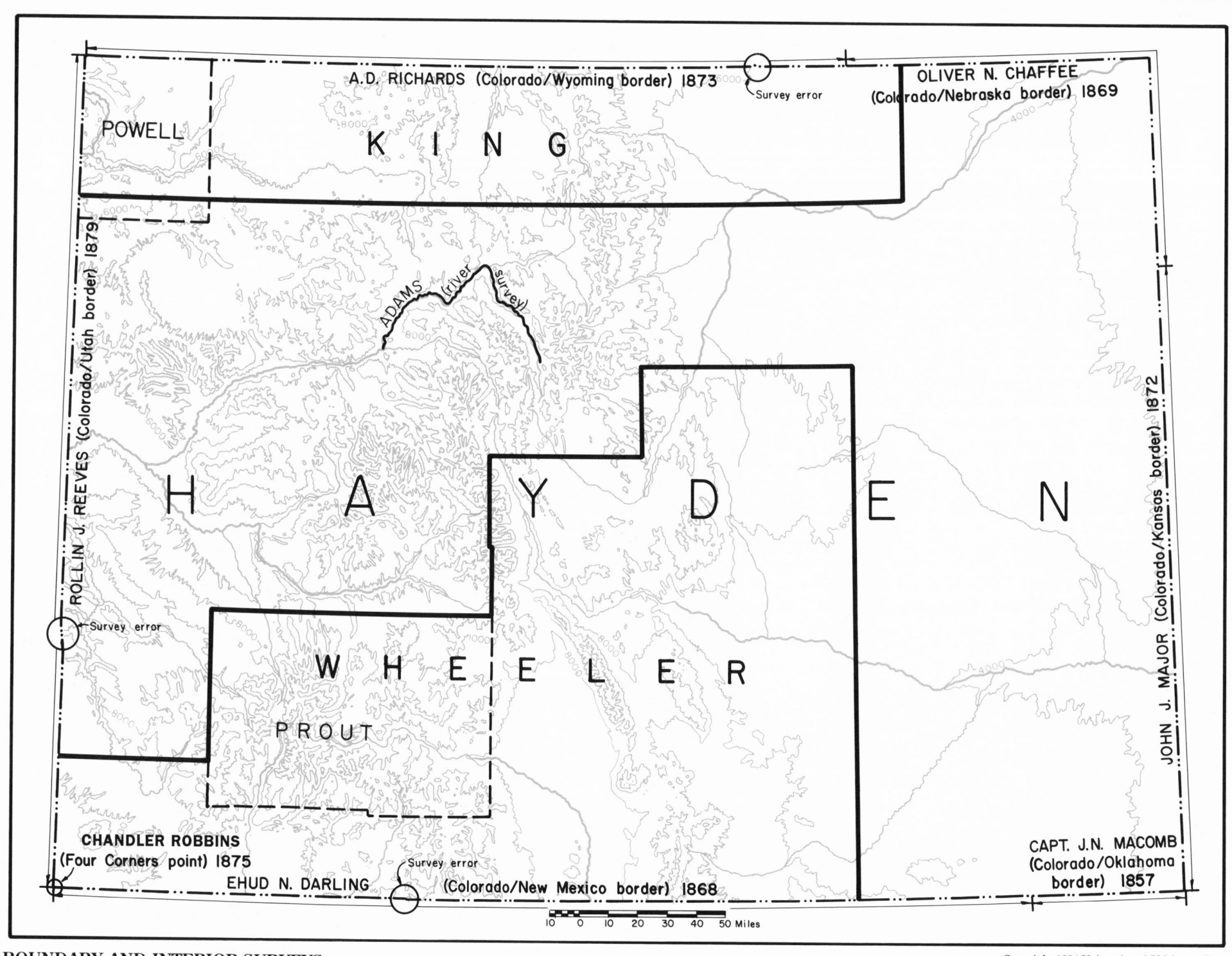

A.D. RICHARDS (Colorado/Wyoming border) 1873

Survey error

OLIVER N. CHAFFEE
(Colorado/Nebraska border) 1869

POWELL

K I N G

ROLLIN J. REEVES (Colorado/Utah border) 1879

ADAMS (river survey)

H A Y D E N

Survey error

W H E E L E R

PROUT

JOHN J. MAJOR (Colorado/Kansas border) 1872

CHANDLER ROBBINS
(Four Corners point) 1875

Survey error

CAPT. J.N. MACOMB
(Colorado/Oklahoma
border) 1857

EHUD N. DARLING   (Colorado/New Mexico border) 1868

10   0   10   20   30   40   50 Miles

BOUNDARY AND INTERIOR SURVEYS

12. BOUNDARY AND INTERIOR SURVEYS

The policy of the federal government until the 1930s was to make its land accessible to potential settlers. In order to inventory and dispose of the land, the government first had to survey it. The rectangular range and township system established by the Ordinance of 1785, however, proved hard to apply in Colorado's rugged landscape.

This tortured terrain caused problems in surveying the state's boundaries. At first glance, Colorado looks like a perfect rectangle. A closer look, however, reveals that only its eastern boundary is a straight line—the other three sides are crooked due to surveying errors. None of the corners are precise.

Capt. John N. Macomb's 1859 survey of what became the Colorado-Oklahoma boundary began the process of defining the territory. Ehud N. Darling completed the southern boundary survey in 1868, but in Archuleta County, near the tiny town of Edith, he ran awry. Darling's error led to a boundary dispute between Colorado and New Mexico that was not settled until 1960, when the U.S. Supreme Court held that an official boundary survey—even an erroneous one—was valid. Thus Darling's error persists, as do A. D. Richard's error, in his 1873 survey of the Wyoming border; Rollin J. Reeve's 1879 blunder, on the Utah border; and Chandler Robbins's 1875 mistake, in placing the Four Corners marker a half mile east of its true position. Oliver N. Chaffee surveyed the state's northeast corner and placed a limestone marker at the point where Colorado, Nebraska, and Wyoming meet.

The first interior survey of Colorado was more comedy than science. Capt. Charles Adams had navigated the lower Colorado River, and he decided to further explore its Rocky Mountain headwaters. After convincing ten men and a dog to join him, Adams set out in 1869 from Breckenridge in four small boats. The captain proposed that they descend the Blue River to the Colorado and then follow the Colorado to its mouth in the Gulf of California. His boats soon swamped, and some of his men jumped ship. By the time Adams had dissolved his Colorado navy in Eagle County, it had been reduced to ramshackle rafts and four sailors. The dog's fate is unknown.

The four great surveys of the American West were better equipped and better led by Ferdinand Hayden, Clarence King, John Wesley Powell, and George Wheeler—all of whom worked in Colorado. Henry G. Prout also did a small survey and produced the first good map of the San Juan Mountains, a map that helped federal officials sort out rival claims of miners and Ute Indians.

Maj. John Wesley Powell, a one-armed Civil War veteran, had done some exploring in Colorado as early as 1868, when he led the first recorded ascent of Longs Peak. Powell's most famous survey took place between 1869 and 1871 when he conducted a daredevil boat inspection of the Green and Colorado rivers. Clarence King's survey was chiefly concerned with the Union Pacific Railroad route through Nebraska and Wyoming, but included some of north-ern Colorado. King's report on what is still called Diamond Peak in Moffat County exposed the great diamond hoax of 1872.

Lt. George Wheeler surveyed southwestern Colorado as well as most of the American Southwest between 1871 and 1878. His *United States Survey West of the 100th Meridian* covered more terrain but offered less detail than the other surveyors.

The greatest of the Colorado surveyors was Ferdinand Vandeveer Hayden, a medical doctor turned geologist and explorer. His multivolume *United States Geological Survey of the Territories* focused first on Wyoming and fostered the creation of Yellowstone National Park. Between 1873 and 1876 Hayden supervised a detailed study of all of Colorado, each summer sending three parties of about seven men to systematically map the state from mountaintops and other high points. These surveyors were the first known Euro-Americans to climb and name many peaks.

Hayden's party was the first to provide reports, complete with expedition photographer William Henry Jackson's celebrated works, of such wonders as the Mancos Canyon cliff dwellings and the Mount of the Holy Cross. When Hayden's *The Atlas of Colorado* was published in 1877, he called it the finest atlas of any state and declared that Colorado would never have to be mapped again. He was essentially correct, as his work became the basis for subsequent mapping.

Principal Areas of Mining Claims

Mexican Land Grants

Land Office Survey Boundary

50 40 30 20 10 0 10 Miles

MAXWELL GRANT

Trinidad

SANGRE DE CRISTO GRANT

Durango

6th Standard Parallel South

9th Standard Parallel North

8th Standard Parallel North

5th Standard Parallel South

New Mexico

37
38
39
40

New Mexico Guide Mer.

10th Standard Parallel North

8th Guide Meridian

LUIS MARIA BACA GRANT NO. 4

2 3 4 5 6 7 8
Ranges East

1 2 3 4 5
Ranges West

42
43
44

4th Standard Parallel South

Pueblo

West of 6th Principal Meridian

New Mexico Principal Meridian

1st Guide Mer. West

11th Standard Parallel North

2 nd Aux. Guide Mer. West

2 nd Guide Mer. West

3rd Standard Parallel South

12th Standard Parallel North

Grand Junction

Ute Principal Meridian

2nd Standard Parallel South

R. 64 W.

31 32 33 34 35 36
30 29 28 27 26 25
19 20 21 22 23 24
18 17 16 15 14 13
7 8 9 10 11 12
6 5 4 3 2 1

T. 1 S.

1st Standard Parallel South

Denver

5
4
3
2
1

Townships South
Principal Meridian (Wichita, Kansas)

Baseline

9 th Guide Mer. West

10 th Guide Mer. West

11th Guide Mer. West

Craig

11th Aux. Guide Mer. West

12th Guide Mer. West

12 Aux. Guide Mer. West

6 th Guide Mer. West

(40° North Latitude)

7 th Guide Mer. West

57 58 59 60 61 62 63 64 66 67 68 69 70 71 72
Ranges West

2
3
4
1

Townships North

1st Standard Parallel North

2nd Standard Parallel North

13. THE PUBLIC DOMAIN

With the federal land ordinances of the 1780s, the United States continued to put its vast landholdings in the hands of its citizenry. Federal land was either given away or sold at a nominal cost in order to promote settlement and exploitation of natural resources. Not until 1935 did Pres. Franklin D. Roosevelt close public land sales, changing the federal policy from distribution to conservation and leasing.

Colorado Territory was part of the public domain with the exception of the Mexican land grants (Map 10) and the Indian reservations (Map 45). From the time of the creation of Colorado Territory in 1861 to the closing of the public domain in 1935, about two-thirds of Colorado was transferred from the federal government to other owners.

Miners were among the first Coloradans concerned with land claims. Initially, since no effective federal, territorial, or local laws regulated mineral claims, miners formed mining districts and claim clubs to record and govern their property. During its first session in 1861 the Colorado Territorial Legislature recognized the mining-district law that had been developed in California during the 1850s. The federal government followed suit with its first mining law, passed in 1866 and refined in 1872. The Federal Mining Law of 1872, which is still in effect, continues to indulge mineral seekers on federal lands.

Types of claims varied with the types of mining. If minerals were to be taken from the surface or from a stream bed, the miner filed a placer claim. The size of placer claims varied over the years and from district to district. After 1872, however, placer claims were restricted to a minimum of 20 acres and a maximum of 160 acres.

While placer claims covered surface minerals, lode claims applied to underground mineral deposits. Most lode claims were between 100 and 300 feet wide, although Colorado law ultimately allowed a maximum width of 600 feet and a length of 1,500 feet along a vein. A miner had to stay within the limits of his claim on the surface, but underground he could follow a mineral vein wherever it went.

Miners could also file mill claims to acquire additional land on which to build a mill or other ore-processing plant. If the miner surveyed his claim, published legal notices, paid a patent fee, and spent a minimum of $500 on improvements (such as building a shaft or a residence), his title could be patented. A patented claim gave the miner full legal ownership as well as underground mineral rights.

While mining claims are a notable exception, most of Colorado was dispensed in accordance with the basic Land Ordinance of 1785, which provided for rectangular surveys dividing the land into townships six miles square. These townships were then subdivided into thirty-six sections of 640 acres (one square mile). Within each township one section was set aside as income property for public schools. As a result of the 1785 ordinance, the West was surveyed in a grid pattern, without regard for terrain or water sources.

Federal surveyors laid out townships by measuring from guide meridians and baselines established to keep up with westward migration. The first surveyors came to Colorado in 1858 to establish the New Mexico Principal Meridian, which was used to survey southwestern Colorado. When settlement leaped westward with the Pikes Peak gold rush, new meridians were established. To expedite surveying, the Eighth Guide Meridian ran north and south from a point on the fortieth parallel near Brighton. In 1880 another guideline, the Ute Meridian, was established near Grand Junction.

The Federal Land Office sold land at $1.25 an acre and also offered special grants for mining, railroads, townsites, homesteads, and war veterans. In Colorado two large grants were made to the Denver Pacific and the Kansas Pacific railroads to subsidize their construction. Both railroad grants consisted of alternate square-mile sections twenty miles wide on either side of the track, creating a checkerboard of federal and railroad lands.

The Homestead Act of 1862 allowed settlers 160 acres for their homes, farms, and ranches. Homestead claimants were required to make improvements and live on the land for five years before title was conveyed to them from the federal government.

Since 1812 the United States has allowed townsite claims of 320 acres. Boulder, Denver, Pueblo, Georgetown, and Golden were originally townsite claims, as were many now-vanished towns. Towns laid out under townsite claims are often distinguished by a grid pattern aligned along a creek or a railroad.

Until 1935 the federal government's goal was to get the public domain into the hands of settlers who would use it. Partly because of fraud, legal loopholes, and bank foreclosures on mortgaged land, property gravitated to large landowners, companies, and banks. Only an estimated one-third of all homesteaders ultimately secured full title and long-term ownership. Nevertheless, the distribution of roughly two-thirds of Colorado's public domain did help many Coloradans to realize the American dream of land ownership.

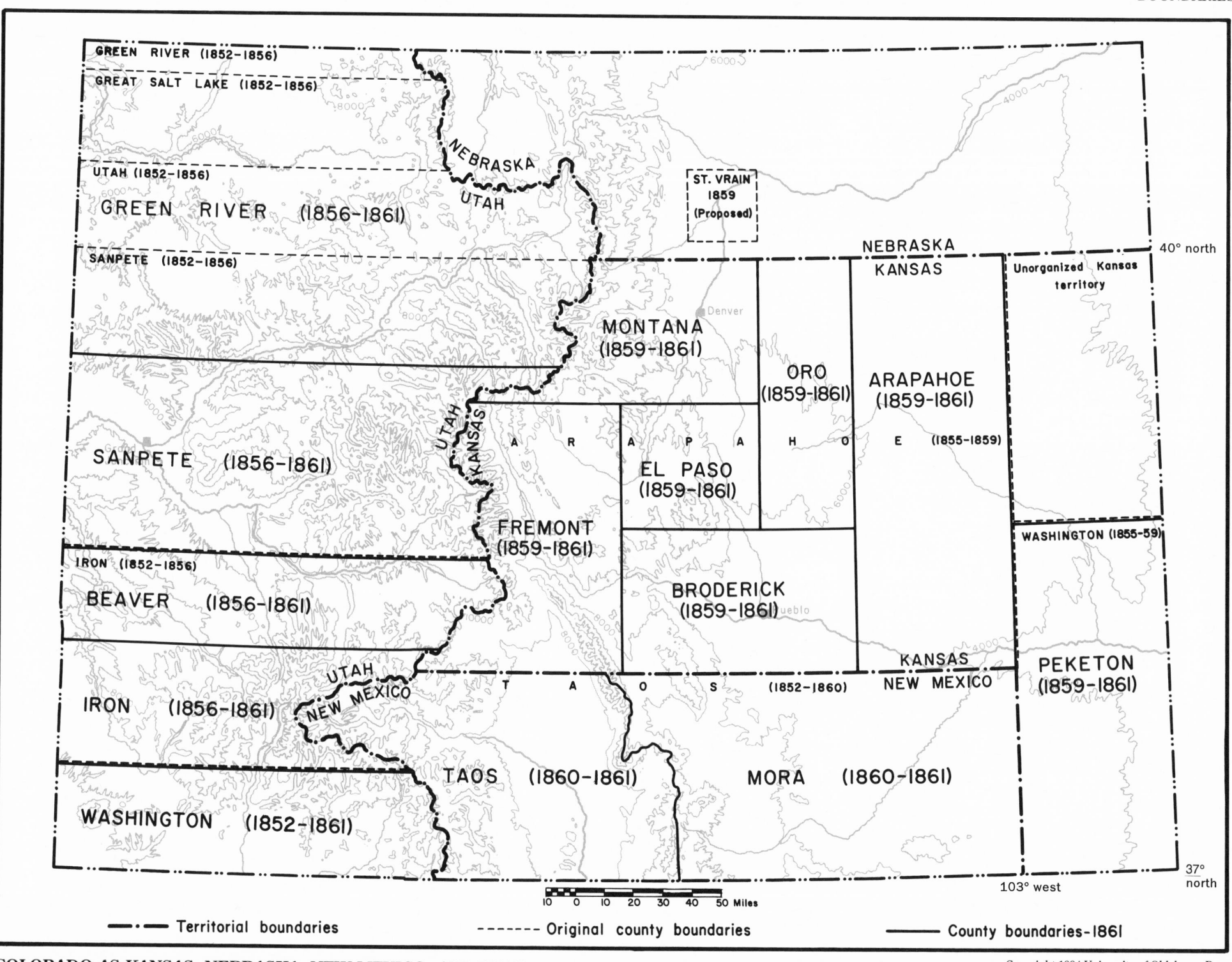

GREEN RIVER (1852-1856)

GREAT SALT LAKE (1852-1856)

NEBRASKA
UTAH

UTAH (1852-1856)

GREEN RIVER (1856-1861)

ST. VRAIN
1859
(Proposed)

NEBRASKA
40° north
SANPETE (1852-1856)

KANSAS

Denver

Unorganized Kansas
territory

MONTANA
(1859-1861)

ORO
(1859-1861)

ARAPAHOE
(1859-1861)

SANPETE   (1856-1861)

A   R   A   P   A   H   O   E   (1855-1859)

UTAH
KANSAS

EL PASO
(1859-1861)

FREMONT
(1859-1861)

WASHINGTON (1855-59)

IRON (1852-1856)

BEAVER   (1856-1861)

BRODERICK
(1859-1861)

Pueblo

KANSAS
NEW MEXICO

PEKETON
(1859-1861)

UTAH
NEW MEXICO

T   A   O   S   (1852-1860)

IRON   (1856-1861)

TAOS   (1860-1861)

MORA   (1860-1861)

WASHINGTON   (1852-1861)

37°
north
103° west

10 0 10 20 30 40 50 Miles

—·—·— Territorial boundaries   -------- Original county boundaries   ——— County boundaries-1861

COLORADO AS KANSAS, NEBRASKA, NEW MEXICO, AND UTAH

14. COLORADO AS KANSAS, NEBRASKA, NEW MEXICO, AND UTAH

When Colorado Territory was created in 1861, it was carved out of the four surrounding territories. Utah Territory, which had been organized in 1850, included all of Colorado west of the continental divide. This part of Utah Territory was initially carved into six counties in 1852. Thus the mining camps that sprang up before 1861 near Breckenridge and elsewhere on the Western Slope were in Utah.

East of the continental divide, Nebraska, Kansas, and New Mexico territories each included sections of modern-day Colorado. New Mexico Territory, which had been organized three months after Utah Territory in 1850, included Colorado below the 38th parallel between the continental divide on the west and the 103d meridian on the east (which served as the eastern boundary of New Mexico). Several decades before the Colorado gold rush and settlement of northern Colorado, this area of New Mexico had been settled by Hispanics and a few Yankees in the San Luis Valley, the Arkansas River Valley, and the Trinidad area. Southeastern Colorado was initially in Taos County, which was formed on January 9, 1852. In 1860 the part of Taos County lying east of the Sangre de Cristo Mountains became Mora County.

The territories of Nebraska and Kansas were created in 1854 by a single act of the U.S. Congress. Nebraska consisted of all the area north of the forti-eth parallel between the Missouri River and the crest of the Rocky Mountains. As the map shows, this encompassed much of northeastern Colorado, including all of Boulder, Larimer, and Weld counties. Nebraska Territory did not attempt to establish counties in its part of Colorado, even after settlers near old Fort St. Vrain petitioned for a county of St. Vrain.

Kansas Territory stretched across eastern Colorado to the crest of the Rockies between the fortieth parallel on the north and the thirty-eighth parallel on the south. Arapahoe County, Kansas Territory, was formed in 1855 and included all of Kansas Territory in present Colorado except for the land east of the 103d meridian. The latter in 1855 was partly unorganized and partly Washington County (renamed Peketon County from 1859 to 1861), in Kansas Territory. As the map shows, Arapahoe County, Kansas Territory, was divided up into six counties in 1859. Kansas became a state on January 29, 1861, a month before the birth of Colorado Territory. Thus eastern Colorado was briefly a part of the state of Kansas.

The territorial and county boundaries shown here were not much more than lines on a map. Except for the attempts of Kansas Territory, few efforts were made to provide law enforcement or governmental services in the wild new gold regions. Coloradans, who numbered 38,500 in the 1860 census, eagerly pushed for their own territorial government. Albert D. Richardson visited Colorado in 1859, and in his book *Beyond the Mississippi,* remarked: "Congregate a hundred Americans anywhere beyond the settlements, and they immediately lay out a city, frame a state constitution and apply for admission into the Union, while twenty-five of them become candidates for the United States Senate."

Pikes Peakers convened on November 5, 1858, to elect a delegate to Washington who would lobby for the establishment of a new territory. When Washington took no action, the frontiersmen met in Uncle Dick Wootton's Tavern on Cherry Creek on April 15, 1859, to form Jefferson Territory. This proposed territory, a huge chunk of land bounded by the 102d and 110th meridians between the 37th and 43d parallels, was approved by voters on October 24, 1859. Although Jefferson Territory was never recognized by the federal government and remained extralegal, factious, and semieffective, its existence helped pave the way for Colorado Territory, which was created by Congress and approved by Pres. James Buchanan on February 28, 1861. The name Colorado was chosen after Republican congressman rejected Jefferson, not wanting to honor the founder of the Democratic Party.

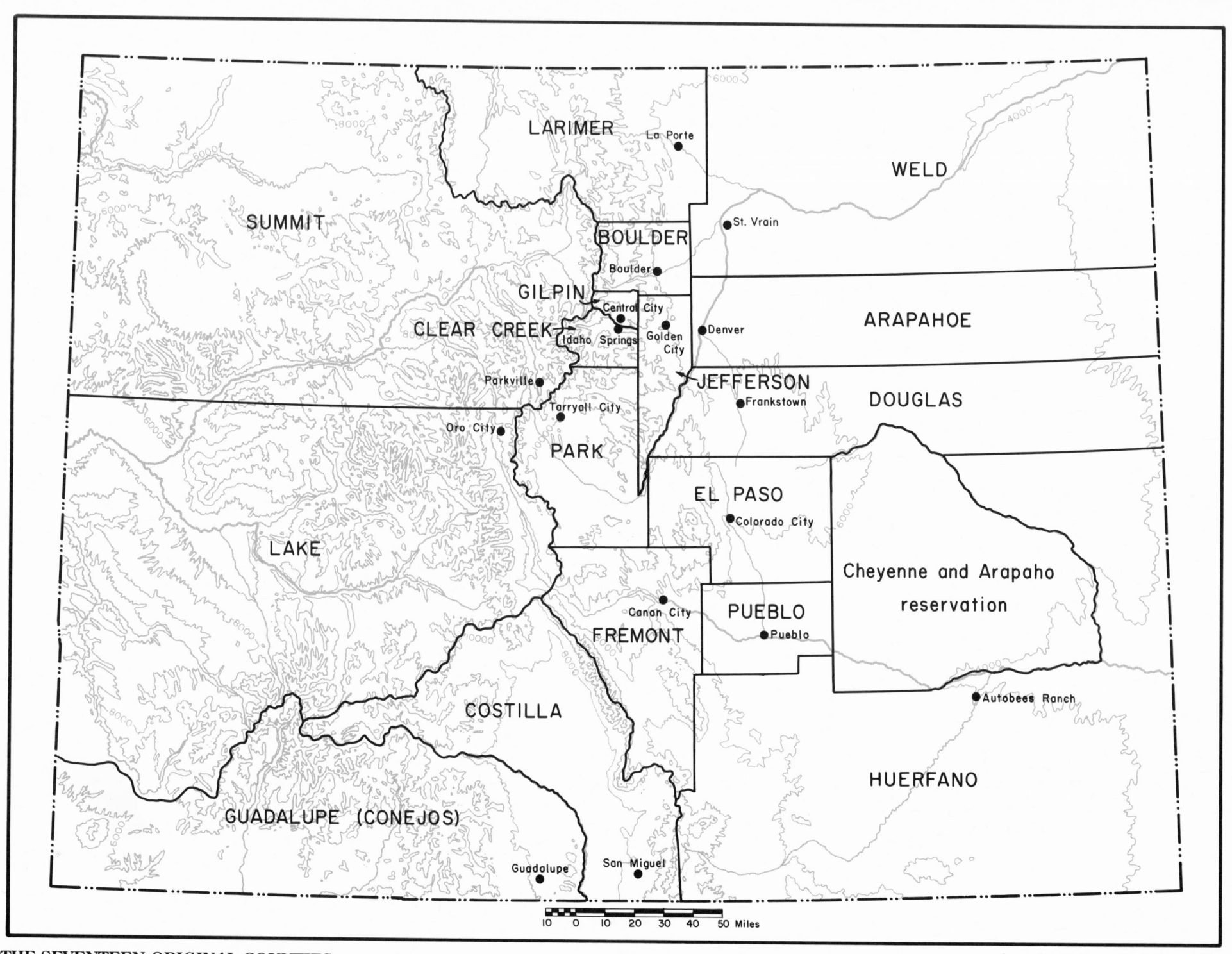

LARIMER
La Porte
WELD
SUMMIT
St. Vrain
BOULDER
Boulder
GILPIN
Central City
CLEAR CREEK
Idaho Springs
Golden City
Denver
ARAPAHOE
Parkville
JEFFERSON
Frankstown
DOUGLAS
Tarryall City
Oro City
PARK
EL PASO
Colorado City
LAKE
Cheyenne and Arapaho reservation
Canon City
PUEBLO
FREMONT
Pueblo
COSTILLA
Autobees Ranch
GUADALUPE (CONEJOS)
HUERFANO
Guadalupe
San Miguel

10 0 10 20 30 40 50 Miles

THE SEVENTEEN ORIGINAL COUNTIES

15. THE SEVENTEEN ORIGINAL COUNTIES

Colorado Territory was established the year after the federal census of 1860 showed that the area had a population of 38,500. The gold-rush population clogged the mining regions along Boulder Creek, Clear Creek, the Arkansas River, and the South Platte River.

Although most of that territory was unoccupied except by Native Americans, Gov. William Gilpin asked the new territorial legislature to extend county boundaries across the entire territory. It quickly obliged, passing an act to create seventeen counties on November 1, 1861. The original counties were concentrated in the Front Range and foothills, where mining activity was heaviest. The legislature carved the sparsely settled western and eastern outskirts of the territory into larger counties. Only the Arapahoe and Cheyenne Reservation in southeastern Colorado was left outside the new county lines.

In shaping the seventeen original counties, the legislators had two problems. First, they had to describe boundaries in a territory that had just begun to be surveyed on the east and remained largely unexplored on the west. Second, they had to decide where to locate the county seats. They worked through the first problem with only a few difficulties. The second was to haunt them for decades.

Surveyors drawing the initial county boundaries relied on the 1858 New Mexico Guide Meridian and the Eighth Guide Meridian that ran just east of Denver. Part of the Eighth Guide Meridian served as a western boundary for Weld, Arapahoe, Douglas, and Huerfano counties. A problem arose at the northwest corner of El Paso County where a few acres were given to Jefferson County, an error not corrected until 1908. In the same area the pointed tip at the southern end of Jefferson County was later ceded to Park County.

The boundary between Jefferson, Gilpin, and Clear Creek counties was at the confluence of the north fork of Clear Creek with the main stream. The rugged surrounding canyon made that a difficult spot from which to survey, leading to future uncertainties. The western boundary of Larimer County was described as the Snowy Range without clarifying whether that meant the continental divide or the crest of the Medicine Bow Range. When valuable minerals were discovered in North Park, both Larimer County and Grand County (Map 17) claimed the area. In 1886 the Colorado Supreme Court declared the disputed land a part of Larimer County (and in 1909 it became Jackson County). The Colorado high court also ultimately settled the Lake–Summit county boundary dispute in 1919. The Mosquito Range was a jagged and confusing boundary, and when fabulously rich molybdenum deposits were found on Bartlett Mountain, both counties claimed it.

Establishing county seats led to numerous squabbles. Ideally, county seats should be located in large and stable communities. Yet mining towns, even if they were relatively large, were rarely stable. Trading centers such as Boulder, Canon City, Denver, Golden, and Pueblo proved more durable. Colorado City, the trading center that became the El Paso County seat, was later eclipsed and annexed by nearby Colorado Springs. In the mining counties only Central City has persisted from the beginning as a county seat. Tarryall, Oro City, and Parkville became ghost towns, while Idaho Springs lost the Clear Creek County seat to Georgetown. Agricultural towns could be just as ephemeral as mining towns. Witness the demise of the onetime county seats at Autobees Ranch, Guadalupe, La Porte, San Miguel, and St. Vrain.

At first, county boundaries often were little more than lines on a map. County commissioners rarely met and had little business to conduct. In Larimer County, for example, commissioners reported that there was no privately held land—only homestead claims on government land. With no private property to tax, counties had little to spend. In the mining regions, county government replaced the claim clubs that had tried to regulate mining claims and otherwise impose law and order. Although county government developed slowly, the county seat was a coveted point of prestige that evolved into a source of jobs and government contracts.

Arapahoe County, created in 1855 as a much-larger county in Kansas Territory, was named in honor of the actual residents, a friendly tribe who were quickly dispossessed. Boulder County prospered as a mining and farming area. Douglas, Fremont, Gilpin, Larimer, and Weld counties were named for popular politicians of the day, while Pueblo was named for a preexisting town. In Spanish-speaking southern Colorado, Costilla, Guadalupe (or Guadaloupe), and Huerfano counties were formed from Mexican land grants. Six days after the February 26, 1861, act creating Colorado Territory, the name of Guadalupe County was changed to Conejos. The rest of western Colorado was divided into the two giant counties of Lake and Summit. Of the seventeen original counties, only Boulder, Clear Creek, and Gilpin retain their original boundaries. The other fourteen were changed as subsequent settlement led to the creation of forty-six more counties.

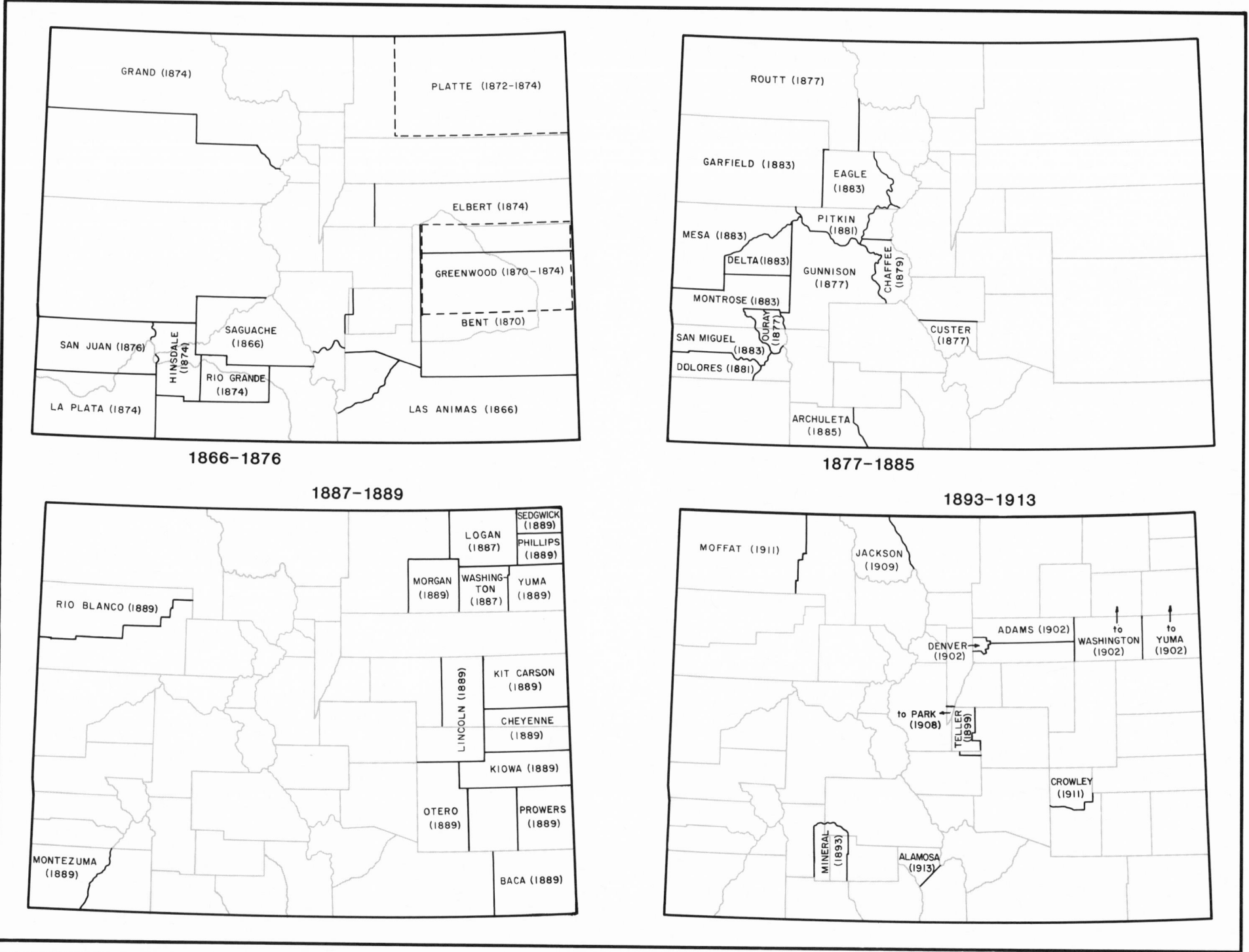

1866–1876

GRAND (1874)

PLATTE (1872–1974)

ELBERT (1874)

GREENWOOD (1870–1874)

BENT (1870)

SAN JUAN (1876)

HINSDALE (1874)

SAGUACHE (1866)

RIO GRANDE (1874)

LA PLATA (1874)

LAS ANIMAS (1866)

1877–1885

ROUTT (1877)

GARFIELD (1883)

EAGLE (1883)

MESA (1883)

PITKIN (1881)

DELTA (1883)

GUNNISON (1877)

CHAFFEE (1879)

MONTROSE (1883)

CUSTER (1877)

SAN MIGUEL (1883)

OURAY (1877)

DOLORES (1881)

ARCHULETA (1885)

1887–1889

SEDGWICK (1889)

LOGAN (1887)

PHILLIPS (1889)

MORGAN (1889)

WASHINGTON (1887)

YUMA (1889)

RIO BLANCO (1889)

LINCOLN (1889)

KIT CARSON (1889)

CHEYENNE (1889)

KIOWA (1889)

OTERO (1889)

PROWERS (1889)

MONTEZUMA (1889)

BACA (1889)

1893–1913

MOFFAT (1911)

JACKSON (1909)

ADAMS (1902)

to WASHINGTON (1902)

to YUMA (1902)

DENVER (1902)

to PARK (1908)

TELLER (1899)

CROWLEY (1911)

MINERAL (1893)

ALAMOSA (1913)

COUNTY EVOLUTION

16. COUNTY EVOLUTION

These four maps show how additional counties were carved from the original seventeen. The first additions reflected a growth in agricultural areas that led to the creation of Saguache and Las Animas counties in 1866; Bent and Greenwood, in 1870; Platte, in 1872; and Elbert, in 1874. Greenwood showed early promise as a rail center, but was bypassed by both the Kansas Pacific and the Santa Fe Railroad. It was dissolved in 1874, and the land ultimately was divided between Bent and Elbert counties. Platte County, created in 1872 to separate most of Weld County from the influence of Utopian colonizers in Greeley, was abandoned two years later when voters squelched the idea. Greenwood and Platte were the only counties to be abolished.

Western Colorado was reserved for the Ute Indians until palefaces found gold and silver there. Then the Utes signed the Brunot Agreement, opening up the San Juan Mountains to a mining rush that led to the creation of Hinsdale, La Plata, and Rio Grande counties in 1874 and San Juan in 1876, while Grand County was carved out of Summit County in 1874.

After Colorado became a state in 1876, a rash of counties emerged on the map: twenty-nine of Colorado's sixty-three counties were created between 1877 and 1889. The mining counties of Custer, Gunnison, Ouray, and Routt were established in 1877. Fabulous silver strikes around Leadville led to fur-

ther subdivision of the original Lake County as Chaffee (1879) and Pitkin (1881). The Ute removal of 1881 opened up northwestern Colorado, leading to the 1883 formation of Delta, Eagle, Garfield, Mesa, and Montrose counties. The San Juan mining boom continued, resulting in the new counties of Dolores (1881), San Miguel (1883), Archuleta (1885), and Montezuma (1889).

Large counties, occupied primarily by ranchers and farmers, prevailed on the eastern plains. Stockgrowers generally opposed the formation of new counties, reckoning that the convenience of a closer courthouse was not worth the cost of building and staffing it. Furthermore, many rural folk reasoned that creation of a county government only attracted politicians, lawyers, and other undesirables.

Railroads steaming westward into Colorado during the 1880s promoted heavier settlement of the plains by farmers who would become customers both as passengers and as shippers of grain and livestock (see Maps 28 and 29). With that in mind, railroads provided cheap or free trips for settlers and energetically promoted the dry, dusty, drab high plains as a Garden of Eden. To convince skeptics that the Great American Desert could be made fruitful, railroads established agricultural experiment stations to promote dry-land and irrigated farming. The Atchison, Topeka, and Santa Fe Railroad line through the Arkansas Valley led to the creation of Baca, Otero, and

Prowers counties in 1889. The Union Pacific built along the South Platte River through northeastern Colorado, sparking formation of Logan, Morgan, Phillips, Sedgwick, Washington, and Yuma counties in the late 1880s. The Burlington, the Missouri Pacific, the Rock Island, and the Union Pacific also laid tracks through the central eastern plains, encouraging the establishment of Cheyenne, Kiowa, Kit Carson, and Lincoln counties in 1889.

A silver strike at Creede gave life to Mineral County (1893), and the last and greatest gold rush, at Cripple Creek, led to the creation in 1899 of Teller County from what had been western El Paso and the northeast tip of Fremont. When the Moffat Railroad reached northwestern Colorado in 1911, a county was named in honor of rail tycoon David Moffat. Development of lumbering, mining, and ranching led to the formation of Jackson County from Larimer in 1909.

Passage of a state home-rule amendment permitted the city and county of Denver to be carved from Arapahoe County in 1902. Further dismemberment of the once-vast Arapahoe County created Adams County (1902) and gave rural, eastern chunks of the county to Washington and Yuma. The last two counties formed were Crowley (1911) and Alamosa (1913), two agricultural areas. Since 1913, Colorado's 63-county configuration has been stable.

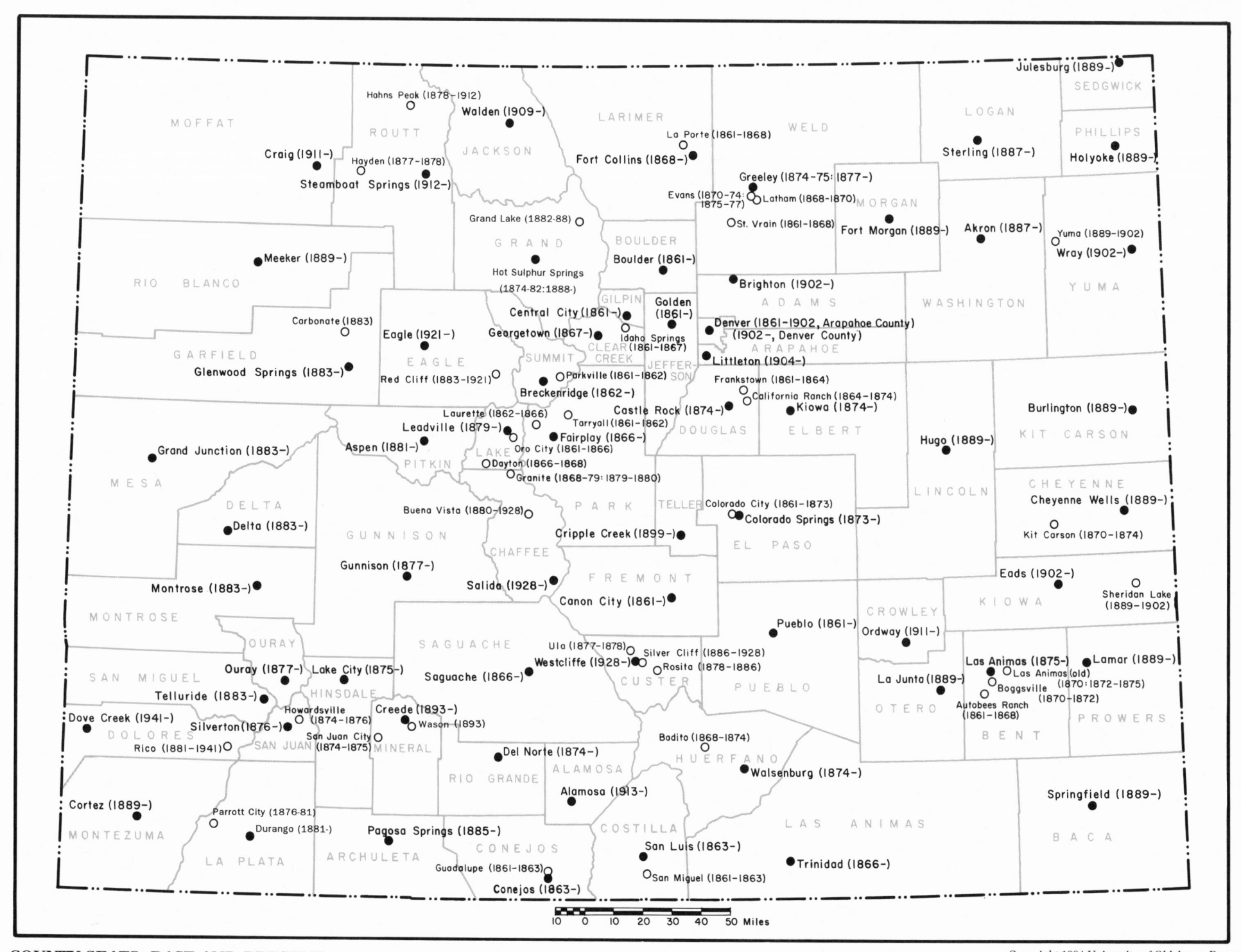

Julesburg (1889–)

SEDGWICK

Hahns Peak (1878–1912)

Walden (1909–)

LARIMER

La Porte (1861–1868)

WELD

LOGAN

PHILLIPS

Craig (1911–)

ROUTT

Hayden (1877–1878)

JACKSON

Fort Collins (1868–)

Sterling (1887–)

Holyoke (1889–)

Steamboat Springs (1912–)

Greeley (1874–75: 1877–)

Evans (1870–74: 1875–77)

Latham (1868–1870)

MORGAN

Grand Lake (1882–88)

BOULDER

St. Vrain (1861–1868)

Fort Morgan (1889–)

Akron (1887–)

Yuma (1889–1902)

Wray (1902–)

Meeker (1889–)

GRAND

Boulder (1861–)

ADAMS

WASHINGTON

YUMA

RIO BLANCO

Hot Sulphur Springs
(1874–82: 1888–)

Brighton (1902–)

Carbonate (1883)

GILPIN

Central City (1861–)

Golden (1861–)

Denver (1861–1902, Arapahoe County)
(1902–, Denver County)

Eagle (1921–)

Georgetown (1867–)

Idaho Springs
(1861–1867)

GARFIELD

EAGLE

SUMMIT

CLEAR CREEK

JEFFER SON

ARAPAHOE

Glenwood Springs (1883–)

Red Cliff (1883–1921)

Parkville (1861–1862)

Frankstown (1861–1864)

Littleton (1904–)

Breckenridge (1862–)

California Ranch (1864–1874)

Burlington (1889–)

Laurette (1862–1866)

Castle Rock (1874–)

Kiowa (1874–)

Leadville (1879–)

Tarryall (1861–1862)

DOUGLAS

ELBERT

KIT CARSON

Aspen (1881–)

Fairplay (1866–)

Hugo (1889–)

Grand Junction (1883–)

Oro City (1861–1866)

LAKE

Dayton (1866–1868)

PITKIN

Granite (1868–79: 1879–1880)

PARK

TELLER

CHEYENNE

MESA

DELTA

Buena Vista (1880–1928)

Colorado City (1861–1873)

Cheyenne Wells (1889–)

LINCOLN

Delta (1883–)

GUNNISON

Colorado Springs (1873–)

Kit Carson (1870–1874)

Cripple Creek (1899–)

EL PASO

CHAFFEE

FREMONT

Eads (1902–)

Gunnison (1877–)

Sheridan Lake
(1889–1902)

Salida (1928–)

KIOWA

Montrose (1883–)

Canon City (1861–)

MONTROSE

CROWLEY

Pueblo (1861–)

Ordway (1911–)

OURAY

SAGUACHE

Ula (1877–1878)

Silver Cliff (1886–1928)

Las Animas (1875–)

Lamar (1889–)

Ouray (1877–)

Lake City (1875–)

Westcliffe (1928–)

Rosita (1878–1886)

Las Animas (old)
(1870: 1872–1875)

SAN MIGUEL

HINSDALE

Saguache (1866–)

CUSTER

La Junta (1889–)

Boggsville
(1870–1872)

Telluride (1883–)

PUEBLO

Autobees Ranch
(1861–1868)

PROWERS

Dove Creek (1941–)

Creede (1893–)

OTERO

BENT

Silverton (1876–)

Howardsville
(1874–1876)

Wason (1893)

DOLORES

Rico (1881–1941)

San Juan City
(1874–1875)

SAN JUAN

MINERAL

Badito (1868–1874)

Del Norte (1874–)

HUERFANO

Cortez (1889–)

RIO GRANDE

ALAMOSA

Walsenburg (1874–)

Springfield (1889–)

Parrott City (1876–81)

Alamosa (1913–)

MONTEZUMA

Durango (1881–)

Pagosa Springs (1885–)

COSTILLA

LAS ANIMAS

BACA

ARCHULETA

CONEJOS

San Luis (1863–)

Guadalupe (1861–1863)

San Miguel (1861–1863)

Trinidad (1866–)

LA PLATA

Conejos (1863–)

10 0 10 20 30 40 50 Miles

COUNTY SEATS, PAST AND PRESENT

17. COUNTY SEATS, PAST AND PRESENT

Becoming the county seat brought a town prestige and government jobs, but it was a contested honor that sometimes led to squabbles, burned courthouses, and even murder. Upstart towns often tried to take the county seat from their fading elders. The first county seats were particularly vulnerable. Autobees was only a ranch, Frankstown little more than a sawmill. St. Vrain was a crumbling fur-trade post. Parkville buried itself in its own mine tailings, leaving only the cemetery gravemarkers above ground. Most ghostly of all the former county seats is San Miguel in Costilla County. Even its exact location is a mystery.

County capitals were moved for various reasons. In Conejos County the seat was moved to Conejos because floods plagued Guadalupe. Higher ground was also the reason why Larimer County transplanted its offices from La Porte to Fort Collins. When James Frank Gardner, the founder of Frankstown, moved four miles south to California Ranch, he took the Douglas County records with him. There they stayed until the county seat relocated at the rail town of Castle Rock.

Railroad construction determined the location of many county seats. Huerfano County moved its headquarters from Badito to the rail town of Walsenburg. Railroads gave Evans, then Greeley, preeminence in Weld County, where Latham earlier had

captured the county seat because of its stage stop. The Denver and Rio Grande bypassed three county seats—Colorado City, Howardsville, and Parrott City—in favor of towns that it founded which subsequently became county seats: Colorado Springs, Silverton, and Durango.

In the mining counties the dominant mining town at the time the county was formed generally became the seat. Oro City, briefly a booming county seat of several thousand residents, was nearly a ghost town by 1866, when Dayton took the title. When Dayton declined two years later, the county government moved to Granite. A decade later fabulous silver strikes made an instant city of Leadville, which almost overnight became the second largest city in Colorado and acquired the Lake County government for good. Granite consoled itself by becoming the county seat of newly formed Chaffee County, only to lose the honor to Buena Vista and finally Salida. Idaho Springs lost the Clear Creek seat to silver-rich Georgetown in 1867. Two one-time seats of Park County, Tarryall and Laurette (renamed Buckskin Joe in 1865), became ghost towns, while Fairplay survived with the help of county jobs. Most violent among the county-seat squabbles was the struggle between Grand Lake and Hot Sulphur Springs in Grand County, culminating in a July 4, 1883, shootout that ended the lives of four men.

Miners and agriculturalists frequently fought over placement of the seat of county power. Hayden, an agricultural hub, served as the first Routt County seat until voters moved it to the boomtown of Hahns Peak. For years that mining town, despite its decline, clung to the honor because rivals Craig and Steamboat Springs could not muster a majority of the county vote. In 1911, Moffat County was split off with Craig as the seat, allowing Steamboat Springs to claim the honor in Routt. The mining town of Carbonate became the first seat of Garfield County in 1883, but when it proved to be a flash in the pan promoted with salted mines, Glenwood Springs took the title. In Dolores County, the mining town of Rico did not lose out to Dove Creek, an agricultural center, until 1941. The process was reversed in Mineral County, where the ranch of Martin Van Buren Wason was rejected by miners in favor of Creede.

Four communities in agricultural Baca County fought for the title until the state legislature designated Springfield, where bitter losers burned down the first county courthouse. In Weld County the location of the county seat changed six times, a record among Colorado counties. County seats are now well entrenched, with no changes since 1941. Mapped here are the 106 county seats, past and present, that have served Colorado's sixty-three counties since 1861.

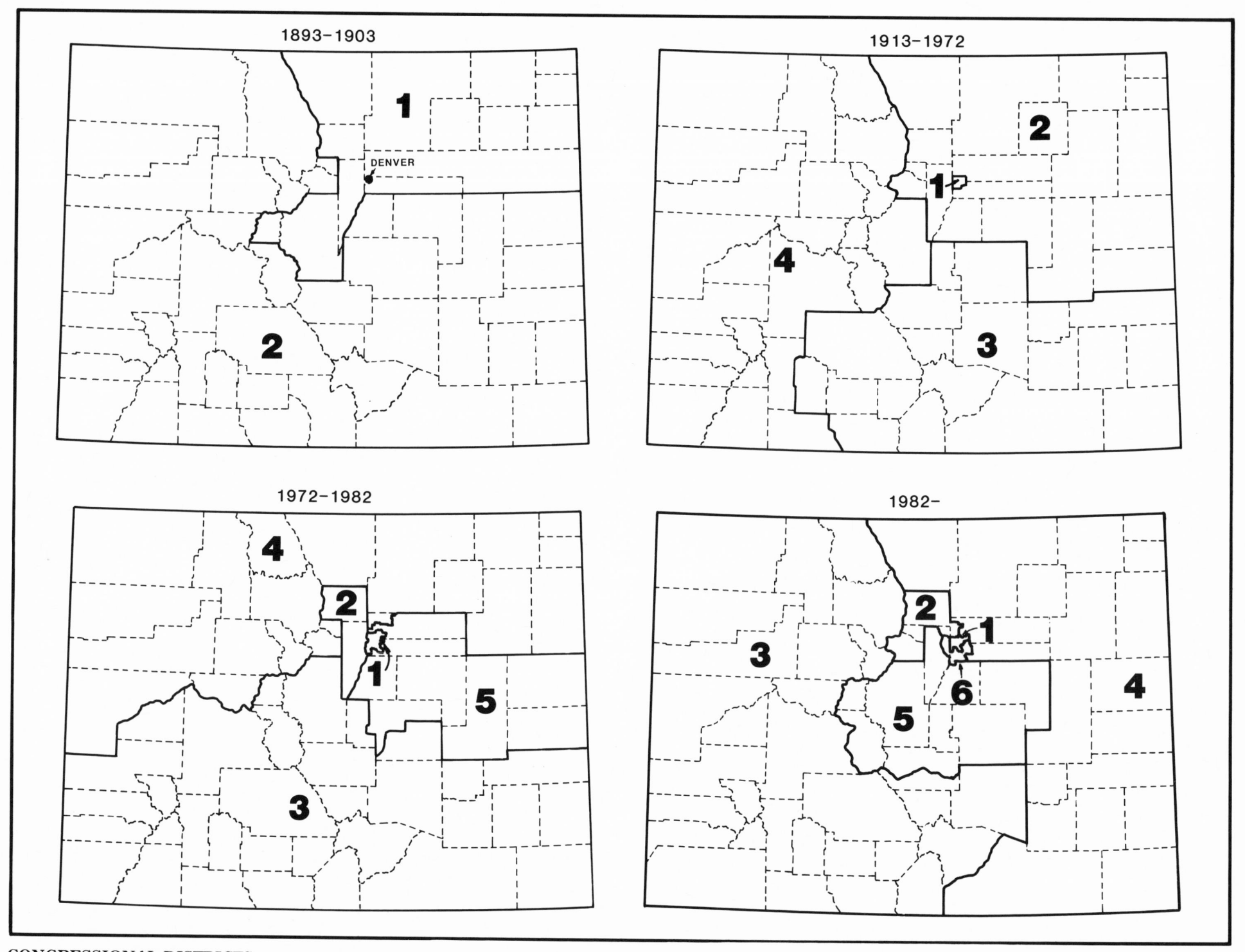

1893–1903

1913–1972

1972–1982

1982–

CONGRESSIONAL DISTRICTS

18. CONGRESSIONAL DISTRICTS

Settlers in the Rocky Mountains soon sent representatives to the national capital. In 1858, a few months after the initial gold discovery, pioneers dispatched Hiram J. Graham to Washington to lobby for territorial status. After Colorado Territory was created in 1861, the territory elected Hiram P. Bennet its delegate to Washington.

Bennet was followed by Allen Bradford, George Chilcott, Jerome Chaffee, and Thomas Patterson during the territorial period. Patterson, the first Democrat to hold territorywide office, helped persuade Democrats in Congress to support statehood for Colorado even though it was a Republican state. With statehood in 1876, Colorado gained the right to elect two senators, Jerome Chaffee and Henry M. Teller, and a representative, James B. Belford.

Colorado started with only one representative because its population did not justify a second until 1891, when the second congressional district was created. The second representative was seated in 1893, when both Coloradans were members of the Populist Party protesting the national failure to subsidize the silver industry and agriculture. The First District included urbanized Denver and Leadville (Lake County) and the northeastern counties of the state. The Second District encompassed southern Colorado (including Colorado Springs and Pueblo) and the Western Slope.

In 1903, Colorado elected a third congressman as a statewide, at-large representative. Republicans, who controlled both districts and a statewide majority, favored this arrangement rather than creation of a new district that might vote Democratic. Continuing population gains entitled Colorado to a fourth representative in 1913. The statewide, at-large position was dropped in the 1914 election with the creation of four congressional districts. The City and County of Denver comprised the first seat; northeastern Colorado, the second; southeastern Colorado, the third; and the Western Slope, the fourth. In 1921 the Colorado General Assembly slightly modified the county alignment of the four districts, which would not change again until 1964. During that time the representation became unequal: while District Four, the Western Slope, served fewer than 200,000 people, District Two, in northeastern Colorado, represented over 600,000.

Overrepresentation of rural areas at the expense of fast-growing urban centers was common throughout the United States. Such inequities were not rectified until 1962, when the U.S. Supreme Court ruled that federal courts could require reapportionment in the state legislatures to equalize representation. In 1964 the Supreme Court extended the "one person, one vote" principle to federal congressional districts, forcing Colorado to redraw its districts.

Colorado politicos resisted redistricting because the lightly populated Fourth District had been regularly electing a popular and powerful conservative Democrat, Wayne Aspinall. When the state was awarded a fifth congressional district in 1972, however, it had to redesign congressional districts along more reasonable lines. This was done by consolidating southern Colorado's Eastern and Western slopes in District Three and placing rural northern Colorado in District Four. Most of Denver remained in District One, but its northwestern suburbs were put into District Two, while the southeastern suburbs became the new District Five.

As Colorado's population climbed past three million in the 1980s, a sixth district was established in 1982. Instead of assigning whole counties to the Sixth District, it was formed of major Denver suburbs—Aurora, Englewood, Lakewood, Littleton, and Wheat Ridge—in a crescent shape wrapped around District One. District One's Representative Patricia Schroeder, who has been repeatedly re-elected after her 1973 election, emerged as Colorado's senior and most powerful congressperson. The *New York Times* dubbed her "the most powerful woman in Washington."

The Western Slope was reunited as the new District Three, with Pueblo and a few other south-central counties added to provide the population support. Fast-growing Colorado Springs and its environs gained a separate representative, from District 5. Under the 1982 realignment, the Western Slope has District 3 mostly for its own, Denver has its own representative from District 1, the rapidly developing Denver suburbs have their own spokesperson from District 6, and rural farmers of the eastern plains have their own District 4. Most Coloradans seemed happy with the boundaries drawn to reflect communities of interest as well as similar-sized populations.

PART THREE
AGRICULTURE

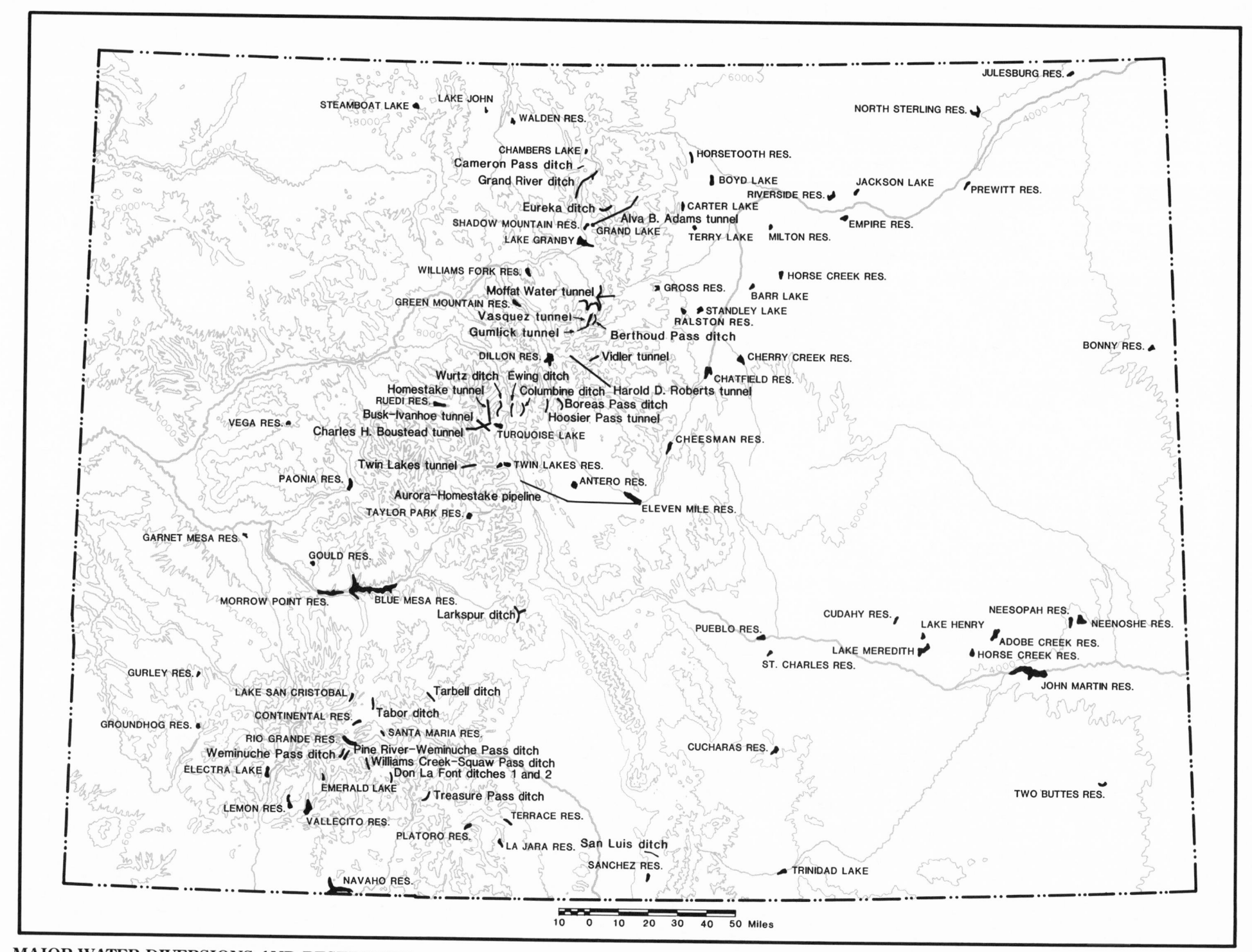

JULESBURG RES.

STEAMBOAT LAKE   LAKE JOHN
                                            NORTH STERLING RES.
        WALDEN RES.

    CHAMBERS LAKE   HORSETOOTH RES.
Cameron Pass ditch   JACKSON LAKE
 Grand River ditch   BOYD LAKE   PREWITT RES.
                                         RIVERSIDE RES.
    Eureka ditch   CARTER LAKE
SHADOW MOUNTAIN RES.   Alva B. Adams tunnel   EMPIRE RES.
                    GRAND LAKE
    LAKE GRANBY   GRAND LAKE   TERRY LAKE   MILTON RES.

WILLIAMS FORK RES.   HORSE CREEK RES.

    Moffat Water tunnel   GROSS RES.
GREEN MOUNTAIN RES.   BARR LAKE
    Vasquez tunnel   STANDLEY LAKE
    Gumlick tunnel   Berthoud Pass ditch
                                RALSTON RES.

                              Vidler tunnel   CHERRY CREEK RES.
DILLON RES.   BONNY RES.
    Wurtz ditch   Ewing ditch   CHATFIELD RES.
Homestake tunnel   Columbine ditch Harold D. Roberts tunnel
    RUEDI RES.   Boreas Pass ditch
    Busk-Ivanhoe tunnel   Hoosier Pass tunnel
VEGA RES.   Charles H. Boustead tunnel
                        TURQUOISE LAKE   CHEESMAN RES.

    Twin Lakes tunnel   TWIN LAKES RES.
PAONIA RES.   ANTERO RES.
        Aurora-Homestake pipeline
TAYLOR PARK RES.   ELEVEN MILE RES.

GARNET MESA RES.

        GOULD RES.

MORROW POINT RES.   NEESOPAH RES.
    BLUE MESA RES.   CUDAHY RES.   LAKE HENRY
        Larkspur ditch   NEENOSHE RES.
                        PUEBLO RES.   ADOBE CREEK RES.
GURLEY RES.   LAKE MEREDITH   HORSE CREEK RES.
                    ST. CHARLES RES.
LAKE SAN CRISTOBAL   Tarbell ditch   JOHN MARTIN RES.
    CONTINENTAL RES.   Tabor ditch
GROUNDHOG RES.   SANTA MARIA RES.   CUCHARAS RES.
    RIO GRANDE RES. Pine River-Weminuche Pass ditch
Weminuche Pass ditch   Williams Creek-Squaw Pass ditch
ELECTRA LAKE   Don La Font ditches 1 and 2   TWO BUTTES RES.
        EMERALD LAKE   Treasure Pass ditch
LEMON RES.   TERRACE RES.
    VALLECITO RES.   TRINIDAD LAKE
        PLATORO RES.
            LA JARA RES. San Luis ditch
                    SANCHEZ RES.
    NAVAHO RES.

10 0 10 20 30 40 50 Miles

MAJOR WATER DIVERSIONS AND RESERVOIRS

19. MAJOR WATER DIVERSIONS AND RESERVOIRS

In many parts of the world agricultural water is provided by rain and taken for granted except during a drought. In Colorado, where precipitation averages only about seventeen inches a year, water for both agriculture and domestic consumption is scarce. To cope with dry years, providers have constructed numerous diversions (ditches, canals, and tunnels) and storage reservoirs.

Colorado's first farmers were Native Americans such as those who lived on and around Mesa Verde. These early-day agrarians built dams and canals to divert water to their corn, bean, and squash fields. Later Hispanic settlers, steeped in a Spanish tradition of dryland and irrigated farming, also brought irrigation systems to Colorado. Indeed, the oldest working system in the state is the People's Ditch, built by Spanish-surnamed pioneers in the town of San Luis in 1852.

After the 1858–59 gold rush, irrigation ditches were dug in the Denver area. The first recorded success came in 1859 on David K. Wall's farm in Golden. Denver's 1865 City Ditch has been designated by the Denver Landmark Preservation Commission as "the oldest working thing in Denver." Another early ditch, the Highline Canal, still carries water to the Denver area from the mouth of South Platte Canyon. Much of its cottonwood-shaded bank has been converted to a paved urban hike-bike trail.

Greeley, Colorado's first great agricultural colony, constructed a community canal that brought water from the Cache la Poudre. Boosters of Greeley and other agricultural colonies claimed that western irrigation was safer and more productive than eastern agriculture relying on natural rainfall.

During dry years ditches and canals often ran out of water. To solve this problem, settlers began looking for water storage reservoirs. At first, natural lakes were used, but they were soon augmented with artificial reservoirs created by dams such as the Terry Lake built near Longmont in 1890. Many reservoirs double as recreation areas for boating, fishing, and swimming. Water also is stored in huge above-ground tanks, which have become the most prominent landmarks in many Colorado communities.

As droughts dried up even artificial reservoirs, Eastern Slopers began eyeing the Western Slope, which had about twenty percent of the population and eighty percent of the stream flow. The first transbasin ditch, Cameron Pass Ditch (1882), was followed by larger ones such as the Grand River Ditch, which was dug through what is now Rocky Mountain National Park.

To carry more water from the Western to the Eastern Slope, tunnels became a major tool after 1911, when the Laramie-Poudre Tunnel opened. The Gunnison Tunnel, America's first U.S. Bureau of Reclamation tunnel, diverted the waters of the Gunnison River to the Uncompahgre Valley. This $3 million, 5.8 mile-long tunnel was proclaimed the world's longest when it opened in 1910. Subsequent Reclamation Bureau efforts have reshaped Colorado water flow with massive projects such as the Colorado–Big Thompson, a $160 million scheme completed in 1959 to water northeastern Colorado. In southeastern Colorado another giant Reclamation Bureau project, Fryingpan-Arkansas, has created Pueblo, Ruedi, Turquoise, and Twin Lakes reservoirs as well as several smaller ones.

The other agency that has drastically altered stream flow is the Denver Water Department, proprietor of Antero (1924), Cheesman (1905), Dillon (1964), Eleven Mile (1932), Gross (1954), and Ralston (1937) reservoirs, as well as Gumlick (1940), Moffat (1937), Roberts (1964), and Vasquez (1958) tunnels. Despite opposition from the Western Slope, much of its water is diverted eastward toward Denver. Water, some quip, flows uphill toward money. Eastern Slopers, on the other hand, fret that almost two-thirds of Colorado's stream flow is claimed by other western states, most notably Arizona and California.

This disruption of natural stream flow is promoted by Colorado water law, the so-called Doctrine of Prior Appropriation. It holds that the first person to divert water to beneficial use has a permanent right to it. This law, which was upheld by the U.S. Supreme Court, promotes endless water wars and litigation, excessive use to protect allotments, and a first-come, first-served approach to water. Interstate squabbling over Colorado water has been largely resolved by regional compacts between the states involved. But Mexico complains that by the time the Colorado River and the Rio Grande reach its borders the water is greatly diminished and badly polluted.

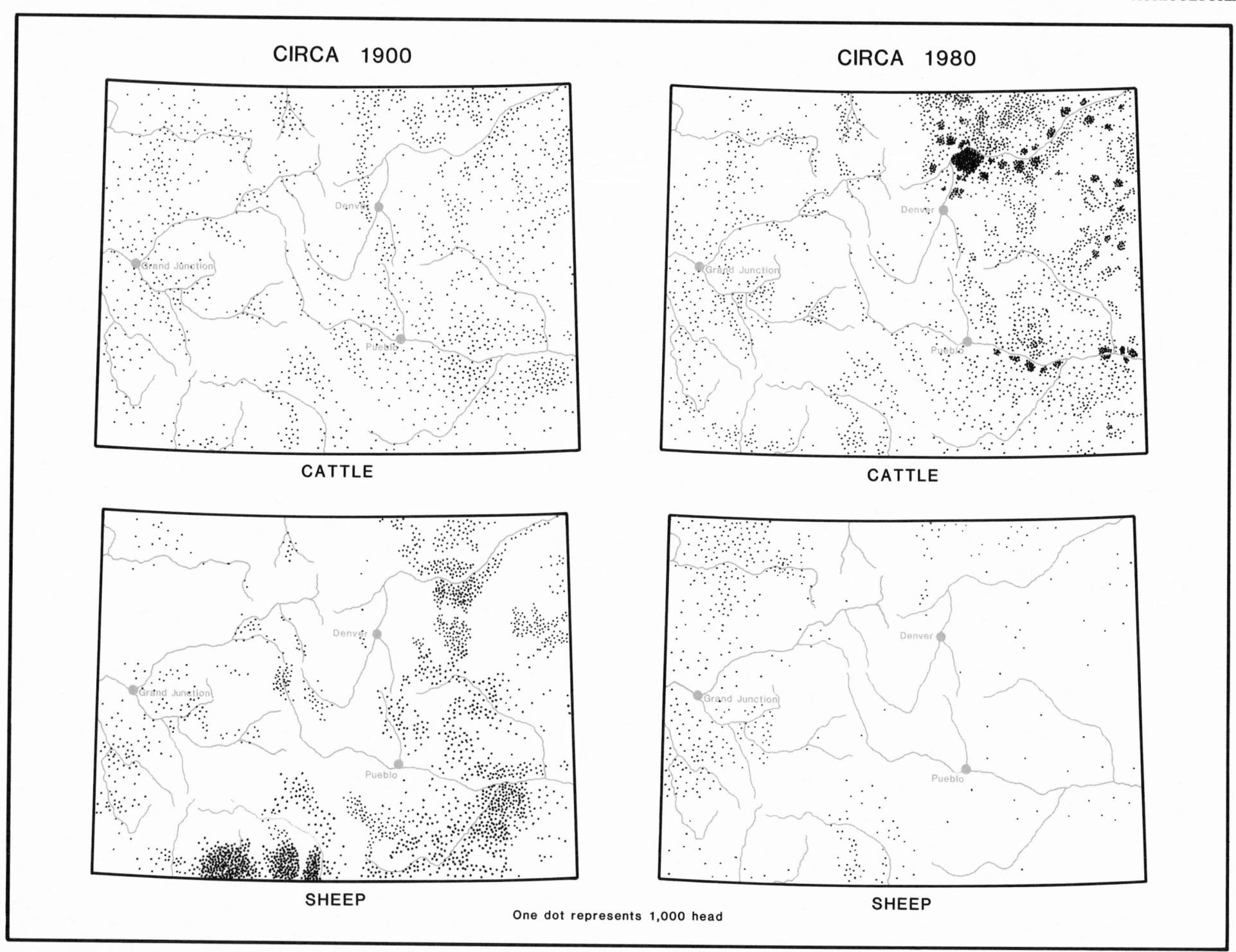

CIRCA 1900

CATTLE

SHEEP

CIRCA 1980

CATTLE

SHEEP

One dot represents 1,000 head

20. LIVESTOCK

Vast buffalo herds convinced pioneer settlers that Colorado could be a haven for grazing animals. Hispanic settlers successfully raised horses, cattle, sheep, hogs, and chickens in the San Luis Valley. But not until the mass migration of the gold rush did livestock become a large industry. Ever since, livestock raising has been a basic Colorado industry and financially more important than crop raising.

Some of the early Euro-American settlers, without barns and hay, left their cows and horses outdoors in winter. To the surprise of many, the animals grew fat on the gramma and buffalo grasses, a natural hay drying on the stalk. Hordes of miners arrived in the spring to pay premium prices for fresh beef, encouraging some to take up ranching.

John Wesley Iliff built up a huge cattle kingdom on the South Platte River, while John W. Prowers became a cattle baron in the Arkansas River Valley. Iliff, who got his start buying up footsore and crippled cattle from immigrants, offered premium prices for wild Texas longhorns. This inspired Charles Goodnight to bring the first Texas herd up in 1868, establishing the Goodnight-Loving Trail along the Front Range of Colorado. Goodnight later reminisced about the cattle industry that had made the cowboy America's folk hero: "We were solitary adventurers in a great land as free and new as a spring morning, and we were free and full of the zest of darers."

Iliff, Goodnight, and Prowers flooded Colorado with huge longhorn herds, which could be rounded up wild or bought cheaply in Texas. Meanwhile, Samuel Hartzel of South Park introduced shorthorn Hereford cattle to Colorado in 1864. The cattle industry boomed during the 1870s and early 1880s, supplying hungry towns, mining camps, rail construction crews, military posts, and Indian reservations.

The Colorado Stockgrower's Association, formed in 1867 to register brands and crack down on rustling, established the Denver Union Stockyards in 1886. At the stockyards huge Armour, Swift, and Cudahy packinghouses prepared fresh Colorado beef and lamb for transport in refrigerated railcars to dinner tables from California to New York. The cattle industry changed the American diet, making the United States a nation of beefeaters, a society raised on beefsteak and hamburgers.

Englishmen and easterners invested heavily in the Colorado cattle industry, and initially they profited royally. The bust came during the winter of 1885–86 when blizzards wiped out whole herds. Survivors had to deal with a new 1885 federal law that forbade fencing of the public domain, a practice cattlemen had frequently used to enlarge their grazing territory. Overgrazing also became a major problem, resulting in the degradation of once-lush prairie grassland with sagebrush, cactus, thistles, and dirt blowouts.

As sodbusters moved onto the plains, the days of open-range cattle drives ended. Cattlemen settled down on ranches, although many continued to drive herds to high-country pasture every summer. Ranchers bitterly fought conservationists attempting to preserve public lands, but accepted the 1934 compromise, the Taylor Grazing Act. This national legislation, introduced by Colorado Congressman Edward Taylor of Glenwood Springs, allowed ranchers, for a minimal fee, to graze their herds on public lands.

To celebrate the livestock industry, and to provide an auction, exhibitions, a rodeo, and a trade show, Denver in 1905 inaugurated its annual National Western Stock Show. The stock show and the live-

stock industry thrived during much of the twentieth century. Feedlots became ever more common and were clustered, as the 1980 cattle map shows, in the South Platte and Arkansas river valleys. The Monfort Cattle Company claims its huge feedlots near Greeley are the world's largest.

Cattle were not the only form of livestock. A herd of swine was brought from Missouri in 1861, and a swarm of bees was brought across the plains in 1862, launching major industries in Colorado. Chickens, the most common form of livestock over the years, reached a peak of 5.3 million in 1944. After the 1885–86 setback for the cattle industry, sheep became more important. In 1900 the state was home to about 2 million sheep, with the count rising close to 3 million between 1914 and 1945. Indeed, sheep were more numerous than cattle between 1900 and 1950. As the 1900 and the 1980 maps reveal, however, the cattle industry was thriving in 1980, while sheep were less numerous than in 1900.

Conflicts between sheepmen and cattlemen are legendary—and also real—particularly in southern Colorado, where Texas trail herds invaded the traditional Hispanic sheep range. Sheep, which once blanketed the San Luis Valley, are now confined primarily to southwestern Colorado. Cattle have increased to over 3 million while sheep now number less than 500,000. Chickens outnumber all other livestock, however. Hogs and pigs hold fourth place, followed by dairy cows, horses, and mules. Since the 1980s llamas have become popular in Colorado. Another exotic creature, the alligator, has been successfully introduced into the San Luis Valley, where a farmer found that gators fancy the natural hot springs.

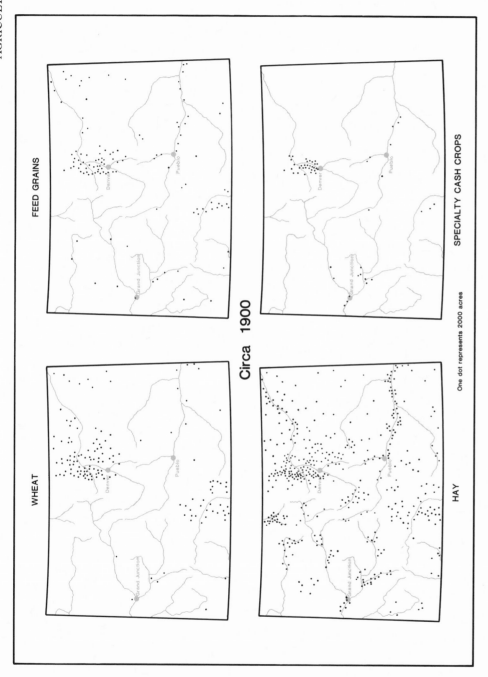

FEED GRAINS

WHEAT

Denver

Pueblo

Grand Junction

Denver

Pueblo

Grand Junction

Circa 1900

SPECIALTY CASH CROPS

HAY

Denver

Pueblo

Grand Junction

Denver

Pueblo

Grand Junction

One dot represents 2000 acres

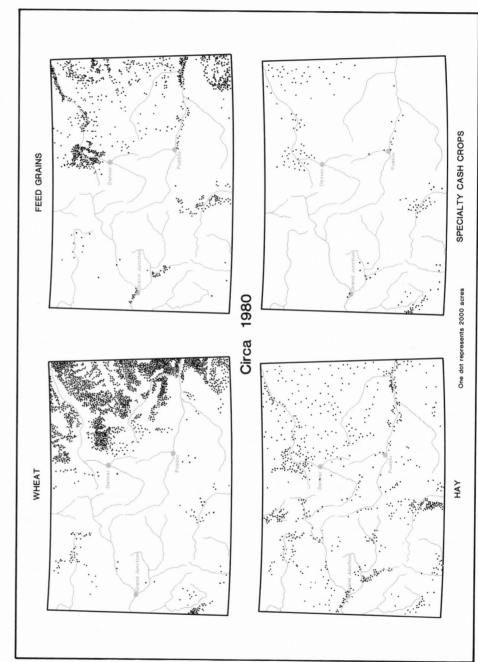

FEED GRAINS

WHEAT

Denver

Pueblo

Grand Junction

Denver

Pueblo

Grand Junction

Circa 1980

SPECIALTY CASH CROPS

HAY

Denver

Pueblo

Grand Junction

Denver

Pueblo

Grand Junction

One dot represents 2000 acres

AGRICULTURAL CROPS

21. AGRICULTURAL CROPS

Maj. Stephen H. Long reported after his 1820 expedition that the Colorado region was "almost wholly unfit for cultivation." Yet after the 1858–59 gold rush the tremendous expense of importing food inspired some farmers to see what crops might grow in what Long had labeled the Great American Desert.

Native Americans had grown corn, beans, and squash in various locations, and Mexican Americans cultivated the high, dry San Luis Valley, using irrigation to grow corn, peas, onions, peppers, and wheat. During the 1850s corn and wheat mills were established in the San Luis Valley, which exported grain to the mining regions. During the gold rush tremendously inflated food prices inspired farmers like Denver's Rufus ("Potato") Clark. He capitalized on prices as high as sixteen dollars for a bushel of potatoes.

Colorado's number one crop, wheat, has always been important but difficult to grow. As hot, dry, windy summers often toasted wheat plants, farmers learned early to cultivate winter wheat. They planted varieties such as Turkey Red in the fall, allowing winter snows to nourish plants that were harvested in late spring. Wheat farmers concentrated in the South Platte Valley and the eastern plains and more sporadically in the Colorado and Arkansas river drainages. Lesser amounts of wheat were raised in the Rio Grande Valley, where Hispanics had first introduced to Colorado the "staff of life."

Not only early settlers but also their livestock needed nourishment, and those needs promoted a large feed-grain industry. As the maps show, hay was grown throughout Colorado, becoming the most common crop by 1900. Other feed grains included alfalfa, barley, corn, oats, and rye. Such operations often clustered where the settlements and the livestock were, notably in Denver and the settled river bottoms around the state. During the twentieth century the feed-grain business grew in importance with the cattle feedlots (see Map 20).

Hay has remained a major crop, grown throughout the state, even at high elevations. Hay, be it alfalfa, clover, field peas, grasses, timothy, or wild hay, cures quickly in Colorado's dry climate. Many ranchers got their start by providing the hay that was desperately needed in Colorado's instant cities and mining towns to feed horses, mules, and other livestock.

Colorado's major specialty crop has been sugar beets. The McKinley (1890) and Dingley (1897) tariffs on imported sugar boosted the domestic sugar-beet business. Several giant firms—Great Western, Holly, and National—transformed the South Platte Valley and other areas into beet kingdoms. By 1926 sugar beets replaced wheat as Colorado's number-

one cash crop. For decades Colorado led the nation in beet-sugar production, until the industry turned sour in the 1960s.

Since 1900 other specialty cash crops have become important. These include apples, asparagus, barley, beans, carrots, celery, cherries, corn, lettuce, mushrooms, onions, peaches, pears, plums, raspberries, sprouts, squash, and tomatoes. Fruit growing has been heaviest in the Colorado River Valley around Grand Junction. In Mesa and Delta counties valleys are protected by high plateaus and mountains, although early and late freezes may still devastate orchards.

Potatoes, a mainstay of farmers in the San Luis Valley and other higher, cooler regions, had become a major crop by 1900 and a leading commodity in "meat and potatoes" mining towns. The Arkansas Valley has become famous for its Rocky Ford cantaloupes, first developed in the 1870s by George W. Swink. Firms such as D. V. Burnell Seed Company, founded in Rocky Ford in the 1860s, have made the Arkansas Valley a major source of flower and fruit seeds. Colorado floriculturists, specializing in carnations and roses, thrived after World War II, but have faded in recent decades due to foreign competition.

Irrigated farming, in which Colorado acreage has been second only to California, greatly expanded agricultural production. Dryland farming also flourished, especially on the eastern plains. Between 1890 and 1917 cultivated acres grew from 4.6 million to 23.7 million. After slumping during the 1930s depression and dust storms, farm acreage climbed to 40 million during the 1950s. Since then the development of high-volume pumps and center-pivot irrigation has triggered a new boom in irrigated farming—and greatly diminished underground aquifers.

Many Colorado communities celebrate their specialty cash crops with harvest festivals such as Melon Day in Rocky Ford, where revelers have gorged themselves on free watermelons, honeydew melons, and cantaloupes since 1878. Glenwood Springs has staged Strawberry Days since 1898. Grand Junction celebrates Peach Day, Greeley commemorates Potato Day, Longmont glories in its Pumpkin Pie Day, and Platteville savors its Pickle Day.

Many specialty crops were grown near cities by truck farmers. During the 1980s the old farmers' markets made a comeback in Aurora, Boulder, Denver, Fort Collins, and many other cities and towns, reintroducing Coloradans to farm-fresh crops and the cries of produce vendors: "Fresh pascal celery!" "Vine-ripened tomatoes!" "Organic squash!" and "Strawberries fresh picked this morning!"

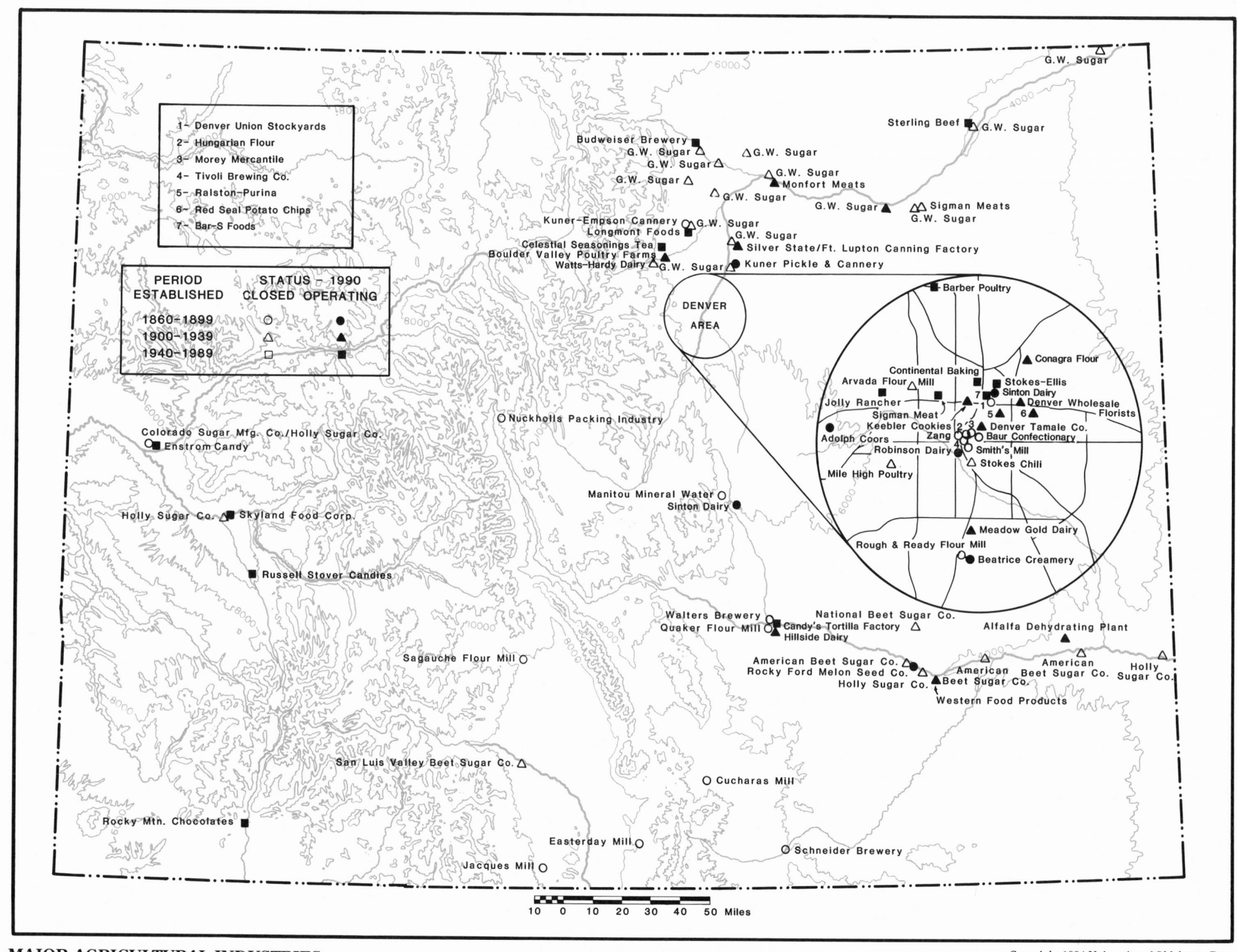

1– Denver Union Stockyards
2– Hungarian Flour
3– Morey Mercantile
4– Tivoli Brewing Co.
5– Ralston–Purina
6– Red Seal Potato Chips
7– Bar-S Foods

PERIOD
ESTABLISHED

STATUS – 1990
CLOSED   OPERATING

1860–1899   ○   ●
1900–1939   △   ▲
1940–1989   □   ■

G.W. Sugar

Sterling Beef   G.W. Sugar

Budweiser Brewery
G.W. Sugar   △ G.W. Sugar
G.W. Sugar △
G.W. Sugar △   △ G.W. Sugar
                     Monfort Meats
                △ G.W. Sugar
G.W. Sugar △   G.W. Sugar ▲   △ Sigman Meats
                                    G.W. Sugar

Kuner-Empson Cannery ○ G.W. Sugar
Longmont Foods
                     G.W. Sugar
Celestial Seasonings Tea   Silver State/Ft. Lupton Canning Factory
Boulder Valley Poultry Farms
Watts-Hardy Dairy △ G.W. Sugar   ● Kuner Pickle & Cannery

DENVER
AREA

Barber Poultry

▲ Conagra Flour

Continental Baking
Arvada Flour △ Mill   Stokes-Ellis
                           Sinton Dairy
Jolly Rancher   7   ▲ Denver Wholesale
Sigman Meat   1   Florists
               2 3 5 6
Keebler Cookies   ▲ Denver Tamale Co.
Adolph Coors   Zang   Baur Confectionary
    Robinson Dairy   Smith's Mill
Mile High Poultry   △ Stokes Chili

Nuckholls Packing Industry

Colorado Sugar Mfg. Co./Holly Sugar Co.
○ Enstrom Candy

Meadow Gold Dairy

Rough & Ready Flour Mill

Beatrice Creamery

Manitou Mineral Water ○
Sinton Dairy ●

Holly Sugar Co. ▲ Skyland Food Corp.

Russell Stover Candies

National Beet Sugar Co.
Walters Brewery
Quaker Flour Mill ○ Candy's Tortilla Factory △   Alfalfa Dehydrating Plant ▲
                    Hillside Dairy

American Beet Sugar Co.   △   American
Rocky Ford Melon Seed Co.   △   American   Beet Sugar Co.   △ Holly
    Holly Sugar Co.   ▲ Beet Sugar Co.   Sugar Co.

Western Food Products

Sagauche Flour Mill ○

San Luis Valley Beet Sugar Co. △

Cucharas Mill ○

Rocky Mtn. Chocolates ■

Easterday Mill ○

Schneider Brewery ○

Jacques Mill ○

10 0 10 20 30 40 50 Miles

MAJOR AGRICULTURAL INDUSTRIES

Coloradans not only raised crops and livestock but also developed industries to process the state's agricultural products for the marketplace. Milling, brewing, meat processing, dairying, sugar-beet refining, canning, and other agricultural industries have been concentrated in Denver, Pueblo, and other urban areas.

Grain has been processed for at least two thousand years by Colorado's Native Americans, who grew corn and hand ground it with stone manos and metates. Wheat and barley, as well as corn, were grown by early Hispanic settlers, who used the sharp hooves of sheep, as well as stones, to grind the grains into meal. A short-lived mill, opened at Greenhorn in 1847, was followed in 1856 by Jose Marie Jacques's mill at Guadalupe. Other early southern-Colorado mills included H. E. Easterday's at San Luis (1859), J. M. Francisco's Cucharas Mill (1865) at La Veta, and Otto Mears's mill (1873) at Saguache.

The Rough and Ready Mill opened in Littleton in 1867 and was followed by others in and around Denver. Several early mills were ultimately acquired by John K. Mullen, an Irish immigrant, who began milling as a boy and later in life loved to show off his calloused hands, which were embedded with stone chips from flour mills. Mullen assembled a vast empire of mills, grain elevators, and wheatfields throughout the Rockies and the high plains. His huge Colorado Milling and Elevator Company, now part of the Conagra conglomerate, marketed the still-popular Hungarian High Altitude Flour.

This pattern of local, then regional and national consolidation is also reflected in the history of another leading Colorado firm, the Merchants Biscuit Company, which has been bought by a national cookie and cracker maker, the Keebler Company. A rare relic of the hometown mill days is Arvada's restored Flour Mill Museum (Map 57).

Living not by bread alone, Coloradans founded at least one hundred breweries, mostly short-lived, small, local firms. The first brewery, Rocky Mountain (1859) in Denver, evolved into the Zang Brewing Company, the largest preprohibition beer maker in the Rockies. The national trend toward consolidation was exacerbated by Prohibition, which dried up most of the breweries. Four Colorado firms survived the Prohibition dry spell (1916–1934): Adolph Coors, in Golden; the Tivoli, in Denver; Walters, in Pueblo; and Schneider, in Trinidad.

By 1970 Coors was the sole survivor. Begun by a German immigrant in a Golden tannery in 1873, Coors has become the nation's third most-popular brew and Colorado's largest single industrial plant. After Coors chief rival, Anheuser-Busch, opened a giant plant in Fort Collins, Colorado became the nation's number-one beer-producing state in 1991.

Besides beer and bread, Coloradans fancied meat. Most communities had meat-processing facilities of some kind, ranging from butcher shops to packing plants. Colorado, one of the prime livestock-raising states, initially shipped animals east to Kansas City and Chicago stockyards. This changed after development of the Denver Union Stockyards in the 1880s. Meat packing became a major industry. Monfort Meats, headquartered in Greeley, is one of the nation's largest feedlot and meat-packing operations, moving cattle "from the range to the range."

Hundreds of dairies sprang up throughout Colorado. Among the oldest and best known are Sinton Dairy, which started in 1880 in Colorado Springs; Robinson Dairy (1885), in Denver; Meadow Gold Dairies, in Englewood; and Hillside Dairy, in Pueblo. Although Coloradans began experimenting with sugar beets in the 1860s, the state's first important processing plant did not open until after 1900. In that year Charles Boettcher, John F. Campion, and others founded the Great Western Sugar Company. This corporate giant built most of the state's beet-sugar plants, of which only the Fort Morgan plant is still humming. Higher labor costs, disputes between the growers and the sugar companies, and cheaper imported cane sugar doomed what was once the state's mightiest food industry. The Holly Sugar Company built plants at Holly, Delta, and Swink; the American Beet Sugar Company located at Lamar, Las Animas, and Rocky Ford; and the National Beet Sugar Company settled at Sugar City.

Beet-sugar production encouraged the rise of candymakers such as Baur's, in Denver; Jolly Rancher, in Wheat Ridge; Enstrom's, in Grand Junction; Rocky Mountain Chocolates, in Durango; and Russell Stover's, which moved from Denver to Montrose in 1973. Many smaller firms also cater to sweet lovers in a food industry that still boasts small, local manufacturers.

Colorado's cornucopia of fruits and vegetables flowed to large local canneries. At first, canning and bottling were confined mostly to pickles, preserves, and ketchup. The development of inexpensive tin cans around 1900 gave rise to giants such as Kuner, which started out pickling in Denver in 1872 and merged in 1927 with the J. H. Empson and Company. Major canneries are Skyland, headquartered in Delta since 1943, and Stokes, which started out in Colorado Springs, specializing in chili. They and most of the food processors mapped here have generally carved out a statewide, if not a regional, market. A few giants, most notably Coors, have captured national markets.

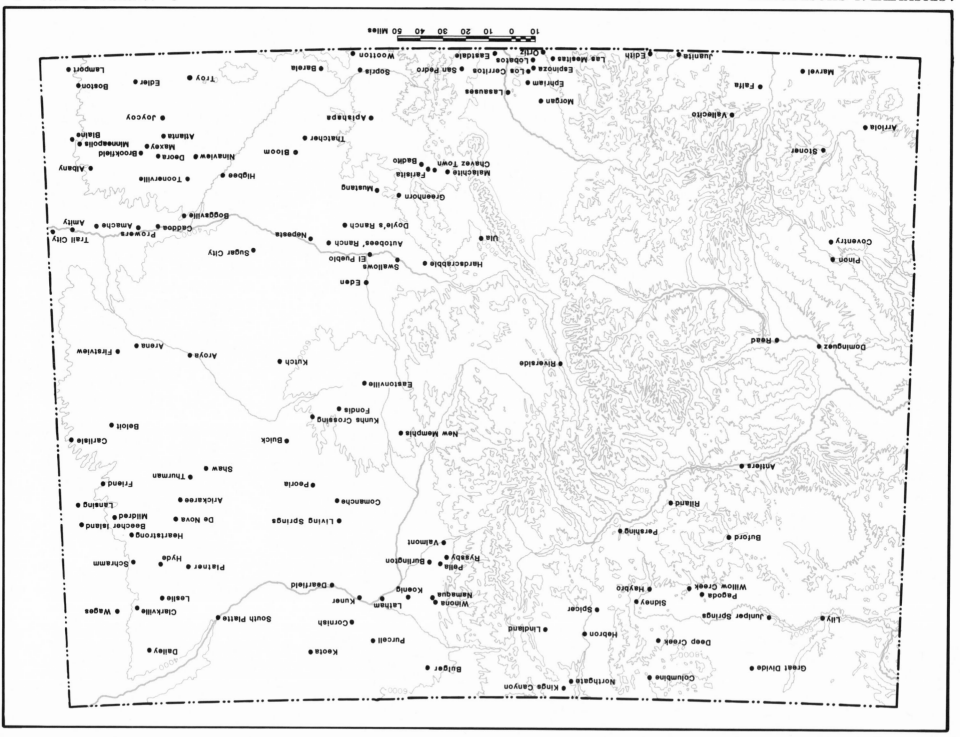

23. AGRICULTURAL GHOST TOWNS

Colorado's mining booms and busts left the mountains littered with more than three hundred ghost towns that fascinate both locals and tourists. Far fewer folks realize that the eastern plains and western canyonlands are also haunted by more than two hundred dead towns.

The agricultural ghosts include antique Mexican plaza towns dating back to the 1830s, pre–gold rush Anglo-American villages, stage stops, cowtowns, ethnic settlements, and utopian communities. Started with high hopes, these towns withered away. Townsfolk vanished after enduring droughts, dust storms, high winds, and scorching heat, as well as shaky grain and livestock prices. Abandoned by the railroads and ignored by new highways, communities died as their people migrated to larger towns and cities.

This map shows some of the better-known ghost towns no longer on the Colorado Highway Department map. Nearly all of them once had a post office, closure of which is the best evidence that a town has expired. Some were sizable places of several hundred people. Five of the dead towns—Autobees, Badito, Boggsville, Latham, and Ula—were once county seats. Some—like tiny Chavez Town—died leaving few traces, remembered only by a few old-timers. Chavez Town epitomizes the many Hispanic settlements that have disappeared, victims perhaps of not only the usual mishaps but also the dominant Anglo culture. Crumbling adobe churches, neglected graveyards, and broken-down haciendas mark the sites of the oldest non-Indian ghost towns in Colorado (see Map 44 for Native American ghost towns such as those of Mesa Verde).

Other notable now-defunct ethnic communities include Amache, a World War II Relocation Center, where 7,657 Japanese-Americans were illegally imprisoned between 1942 and 1945. Dearfield was the Utopian dream town of African Americans hoping to establish their economic and ethnic independence. The Swedish Lutherans who settled Ryssby are remembered today because of the lovely stone chapel they left behind.

Autobees, Boggsville, Doyles, and Namaqua are among the oldest settlements of the state, established before the gold rush by pioneers Charles Autobees, Thomas Boggs, Joseph Doyle, and Mariano Medina. Among the Utopian communities founded as communal efforts with idealistic goals was Amity, established by the Salvation Army as a haven for city-weary urbanites and those hoping to graduate from skid row. Coventry and Pinon were havens on the Western Slope, where the nearby socialist experiment of Nucla survives after switching to capitalism. Eastdale and Ephriam were two of the Mormon colonies in the San Luis Valley. Boston, Trail City, and Minneapolis were cattle towns, miniature versions of Abilene, Dodge City, and Wichita.

Other agricultural ghost towns were the predecessors of later and larger settlements. These include the 1840s settlement of El Pueblo, which was destroyed by Ute Indians on the site where Pueblo was founded in 1860; old Burlington, which became Longmont; and New Memphis (or Citadel), which became Castle Rock.

Agricultural ghost towns characteristically had a church, a cemetery, a school, and a post office. Sometimes the churches are still used, but the tiny, local schoolhouses were closed during the 1950s and 1960s when Colorado's public schools were consolidated. Towns typically had a general store, a café, and a gas station–garage that often was descended from an earlier livery stable–blacksmith shop. Officially recognizing that a community had become a town, the federal government established a post office. In a town's infancy or its dying years, many of those functions might be combined in a single, multipurpose store–café–gas station–post office.

Abandoned general stores, wireless telephone poles, and creaky old windmills guard approximately two hundred Colorado ghost towns where the "Great American Desert" has repossessed what was once puffed as a new Garden of Eden for farmers, ranchers, and townbuilders.

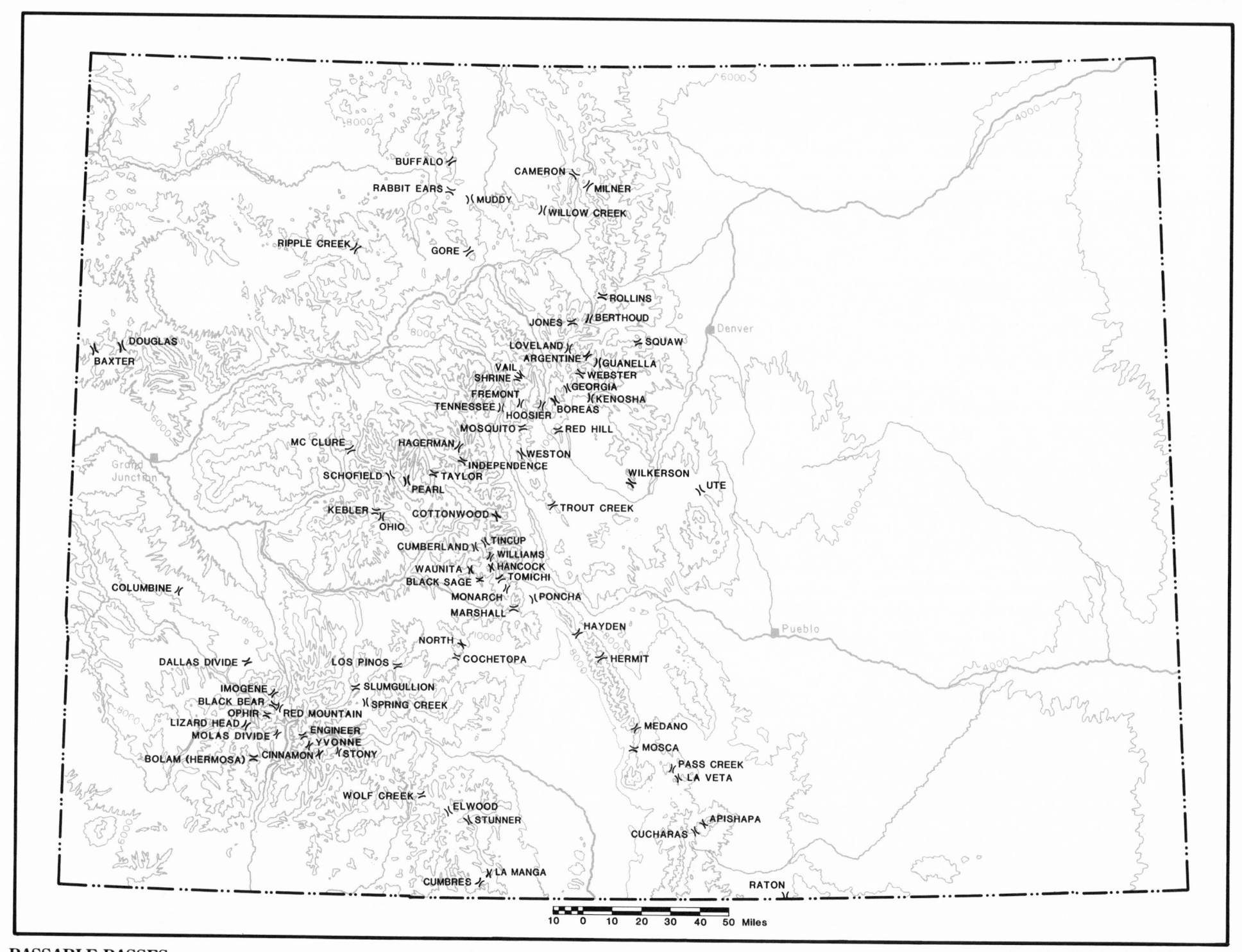

BUFFALO)(
CAMERON)(
RABBIT EARS)( )(MILNER
)(MUDDY
)(WILLOW CREEK

RIPPLE CREEK)(
GORE)(

)(ROLLINS
JONES)( )(BERTHOUD
Denver
LOVELAND)( )(SQUAW
ARGENTINE)( )(GUANELLA
VAIL)(WEBSTER
SHRINE)( )(GEORGIA
FREMONT)( )(KENOSHA
TENNESSEE)( )( )(BOREAS
HOOSIER
MOSQUITO)( )(RED HILL
MC CLURE)( )(WESTON
HAGERMAN)(
Grand INDEPENDENCE)(WILKERSON
Junction SCHOFIELD)( )(TAYLOR
PEARL)(UTE
KEBLER)(COTTONWOOD)(
OHIO)(TROUT CREEK
)(TINCUP
CUMBERLAND)( )(WILLIAMS
WAUNITA)( )(HANCOCK
BLACK SAGE)( )(TOMICHI
MONARCH)( )(PONCHA
MARSHALL)(
COLUMBINE)(HAYDEN)(
NORTH)(HERMIT
DALLAS DIVIDE)(LOS PINOS)( )(COCHETOPA
IMOGENE)( )(SLUMGULLION
BLACK BEAR)( )(SPRING CREEK
OPHIR)(RED MOUNTAIN
LIZARD HEAD)(MEDANO)(
MOLAS DIVIDE)(ENGINEER)(MOSCA)(
BOLAM (HERMOSA))(CINNAMON)(YVONNE)(PASS CREEK)(
)(STONY LA VETA)(
WOLF CREEK)(
ELWOOD)(APISHAPA)(
STUNNER)(CUCHARAS)(
CUMBRES)(LA MANGA)(RATON)(

Pueblo

10 0 10 20 30 40 50 Miles

PASSABLE PASSES

24. PASSABLE PASSES

Penetrating Colorado's two-mile-high Rocky Mountain barrier preoccupied Indians, explorers, trappers, traders, miners, and railroad and road builders. All of them sought passes—the lowest places to cross high country dividing two watersheds.

Native Americans first found these gateways, a fact commemorated by names such as Arapahoe Pass and Ute Pass. Early Spanish explorers such as Juan de Ulibarri probed Colorado for passages through the southern Rockies. Zebulon Pike in 1806 became the first U.S. citizen of record to cross a Colorado pass when he entered South Park, possibly via Kenosha Pass. The next major U.S. explorer to traverse Colorado divides was John C. Frémont, who publicized numerous mountain crossings. John W. Gunnison, an explorer investigating possible rail routes through Colorado, surveyed Mosca and Cochetopa passes, neither of which was ever saddled by a railroad.

While explorers and trappers discovered many of the passes, road builders strove to make them passable for wheeled vehicles. Otto Mears, "Pathfinder of the San Juan," built 382 miles of toll roads through the rugged, remote San Juan Mountains. He and other private entrepreneurs developed wagon roads later used by railroads.

Railroad builders found it difficult to conquer the high country. Most of the "Pacific" railroads ran out of steam trying to build over or under Colorado's notorious passes. For example, a fall blizzard chased Union Pacific Chief Engineer David C. Dodge off Berthoud Pass, prompting him to recommend a Wyoming route instead. The Denver, South Park, and Pacific became the first railroad to tunnel under the continental divide via Alpine Tunnel near Williams Pass. Another narrow-gauge pass climber, the Denver and Rio Grande, built over La Veta, Marshall, and Cumbres passes. The Moffat Road built over Rollins Pass before burrowing under it through the Moffat Tunnel. The Colorado Midland dug two tunnels under what is today Hagerman Pass. Some railroad passes still have the old water tanks, which testify to the thirst of steam locomotives puffing up the divides.

Most of the passes on this map defied railroad builders, but nearly all were wagon routes. Colorado history flowed over such historic divides as Raton Pass, which straddles the New Mexico border. This "Pass of the Rat" served as Colorado's southern gateway on the Mountain Branch of the Santa Fe Trail, the Goodnight-Loving Cattle Trail, the Santa Fe and Amtrak passenger railroads, and Interstate 25.

Since its 1973 opening, the most important pass through Colorado is not a pass at all. It is the Eisenhower-Johnson Tunnel underneath the continental divide on Interstate-70. Although winter storms may close stretches of I-70 for a few hours, it is the most reliable east-west route Colorado has ever had. On weekends, however, the busier of the twin two-lane tunnels often becomes a bottleneck clogged with traffic.

Authorities have never agreed on the number of passes in Colorado. Some passes have no name, and others have two or more. Multiple strands of a trail passing over a high divide may all bear the same name or separate names. At least a hundred passes remain unnamed. In the first, and still the most comprehensive, published treatment of Colorado passes, Clyde and Chloe Edmondson counted 278 named passes. Ed and Gloria Helmuth of Buena Vista, Colorado, had catalogued 468 named passes by 1993 in their research.

At least thirty-three of the passes shown on this map are open all year. Over two hundred passes not shown on this map are accessible only by foot. Rocky Mountain National Park, for example, has twenty-seven named foot passes as well as the paved roads over Fall River and Milner passes. Many crossings are closed in winter, cutting off access between the east and west slopes.

This map shows routes that are generally passable—in good weather after the snow melts—by regular automobiles or four-wheel-drive vehicles. Conditions change rapidly, and any route may be closed at any time by natural or unnatural happenings. These include avalanches, flash floods, mud slides, rockslides, snowstorms, serious traffic accidents, or the apprehensions of the Colorado Highway Patrol.

Elevation and weather determine when the gates through the mountains are open. Imogene Pass in the San Juans, at 13,365 feet, may remain blocked by snow all year. On the other hand, 6,100-foot Gypsum Pass in the desert between Dove Creek and Naturita is so gentle that few notice that it is a pass.

Driving, bicycling, hiking, running, and cross-country skiing over Colorado's passes are challenging and popular sports. Like the bear who went over the mountain to see what he could see, Coloradans and visitors alike find the passable passes a splendid way to see what they can see in the Highest State.

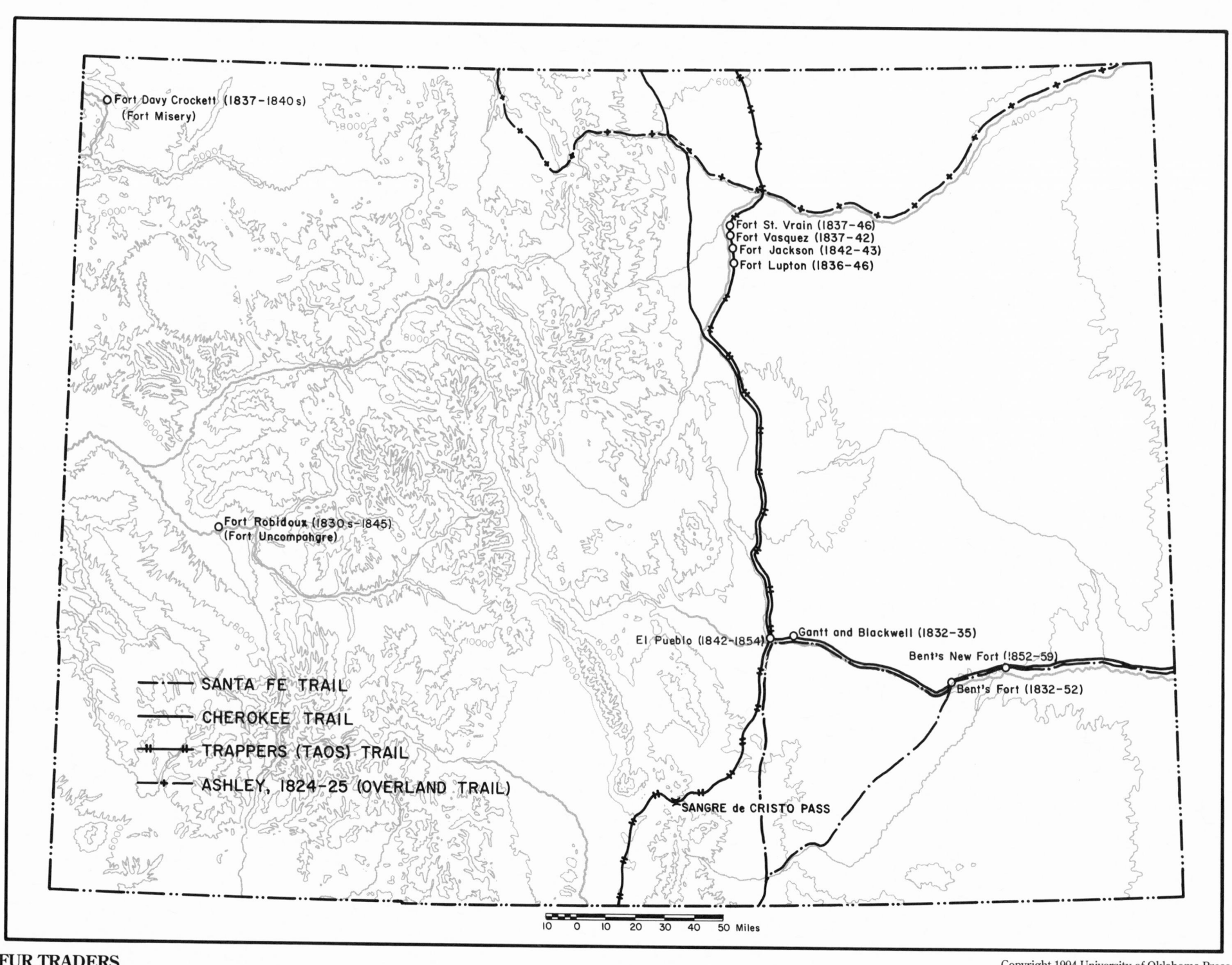

Fort Davy Crockett (1837–1840s)
(Fort Misery)

Fort St. Vrain (1837–46)
Fort Vasquez (1837–42)
Fort Jackson (1842–43)
Fort Lupton (1836–46)

Fort Robidoux (1830s–1845)
(Fort Uncompahgre)

Gantt and Blackwell (1832–35)

El Pueblo (1842–1854)

Bent's New Fort (1852–59)

Bent's Fort (1832–52)

SANTA FE TRAIL

CHEROKEE TRAIL

TRAPPERS (TAOS) TRAIL

ASHLEY, 1824–25 (OVERLAND TRAIL)

SANGRE de CRISTO PASS

10 0 10 20 30 40 50 Miles

FUR TRADERS

Copyright 1994 University of Oklahoma Press

25. FUR TRADERS

Many of the first Euro-Americans to reach Colorado came in search of beaver pelts, which sold in the East and Europe for as much as thirty dollars a piece—at a time when many lived on a monthly salary of thirty dollars or less. After beaver hats went out of style in the 1830s, the fur trade faded, although traffic in buffalo bones and robes continued until the bison, like the beaver, was almost extinct.

Lone wolves like the mountain man James Purcell had poked into Colorado as early as 1805, but not until 1815 did Auguste P. Chouteau and Julius De Munn introduce a large-scale, organized fur trade. They brought fifty men to trap and trade with the Native Americans. Trade fairs and rendezvous were held at various places, including Bear Creek in what is now southwest Denver. At the confluence of Fountain Creek and the Arkansas River, Hugh Glenn and Jacob Fowler began trading in 1821 with Native Americans and Mexicans at the outpost that became El Pueblo.

By the 1830s fur traders and trappers had prowled into even the remotest parts of Colorado, finding paths and passes that would later be used by settlers. In 1824–25, William Ashley, a founder of the Rocky Mountain Fur Trade Company, explored the Platte River route that became the Colorado branch of the Overland Trail. Frequent traffic between Fort Laramie in Wyoming and Taos in New Mexico created the Trappers, or Taos, trail. From Taos this route extended northward along the Rio Grande through the San Luis Valley, then cut over Sangre de Cristo Pass to the Front Range.

The Cherokee Trail, named for the Oklahoma tribe who developed it as a route to the California goldfields, followed the Arkansas River to Bent's Fort and El Pueblo, then cut north along the Trappers Trail to the Overland Trail. Although the Over-land Trail went through Wyoming, a southern branch followed Ashley's route through northern Colorado. The Santa Fe Trail along the Arkansas River connected St. Louis with Santa Fe, becoming the most heavily traveled and most famous of the early pathways through Colorado. Its Mountain Branch led west from Bent's Fort to El Pueblo, then south over Raton Pass to Santa Fe.

In 1832 brothers Charles and William Bent, and Ceran St. Vrain, erected Bent's Fort, the most important outpost of the southwestern fur trade, on the north side of the Arkansas River boundary between the U.S. and Mexico. Measuring 180 by 135 feet, the fort had adobe walls 4 feet thick and 15 feet high. Inside, the Bents welcomed Plains Indians, Mexicans, French Canadians, and mountain men of mixed pedigree. Bent's Fort became the hub of the fur trade in the southern Rockies before its destruction in 1852, apparently by the Bents. During the 1970s the National Park Service restored this prairie fortress as a living museum. Today visitors may once again explore the dining room, billiard room, shops, corrals, trade rooms, and quaint privies.

Eighty miles west of Bent's Fort, John Gantt and Captain Blackwell built a trading post near the confluence of Fountain Creek and the Arkansas River in 1832. There the African American James Beckwourth and others constructed in 1842 the adobe fort known as El Pueblo, on the future site of Pueblo.

Louis Vasquez, a French-Spanish trader from St. Louis, established in 1832 a small, short-lived post at the confluence of Vasquez Creek (now called Clear Creek) and the South Platte in what is now metropolitan Denver. Five years later, Vasquez and Andrew Sublette erected a second, better-known Fort Vasquez a mile south of Platteville. This adobe fort has been reconstructed as a fur-trade museum by the Colorado Historical Society. Ten miles south on the Platte, Lancaster P. Lupton constructed a trade fort in 1837. Although the fort, like most of the fur posts, was abandoned during the 1840s, the town of Fort Lupton sprang up nearby. Six miles north of Fort Lupton, Henry Fraeb and Peter A. Sarpy in 1842 built Fort Jackson, named for Pres. Andrew Jackson. A fourth fort on the South Platte was Fort St. Vrain, named for Ceran St. Vrain, who operated it between 1837 and 1846 as a branch of Bent's Fort.

In western Colorado, Antoine Robidoux of the St. Louis fur-trade clan opened in the 1830s a log fort and trading post on the Uncompahgre River, near its confluence with the Gunnison. Known as Fort Robidoux or Fort Uncompahgre, this outpost five miles southwest of modern-day Delta survived until 1846, when the Utes reduced it to ashes. The only other known western Colorado fur-trade outpost was Fort Davy Crockett, constructed around 1837 in Brown's Hole on Vermillion Creek at its confluence with the Green River. Disappointed patrons of this crude log structure renamed it Fort Misery before it disappeared during the 1840s.

The life of fur traders and trappers—the celebrated mountain men—was difficult, dangerous, and often short. Most died young, but some survived to guide gold seekers and immigrants westward. Jim Bridger lived to age seventy-seven, Kit Carson to fifty-nine, James Beckwourth to sixty-six. The mountain men generally got along well with the Native Americans, Hispanics, and French, often intermarrying. Modern, urbanized Coloradans owe much to these first, wild, courageous traders and trappers who spearheaded U.S. settlement.

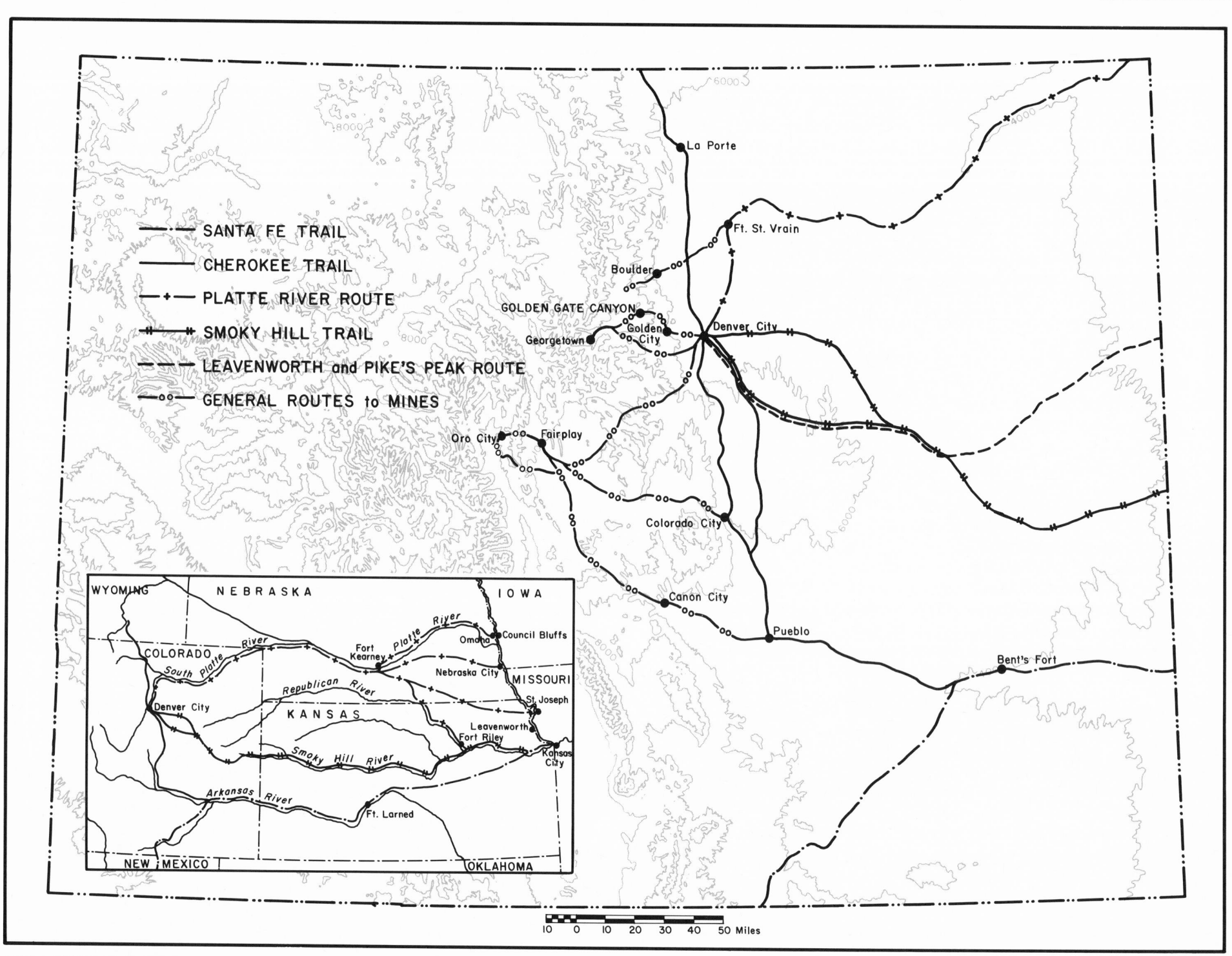

SANTA FE TRAIL

CHEROKEE TRAIL

PLATTE RIVER ROUTE

SMOKY HILL TRAIL

LEAVENWORTH and PIKE'S PEAK ROUTE

GENERAL ROUTES to MINES

La Porte

Ft. St. Vrain

Boulder

GOLDEN GATE CANYON

Golden City

Georgetown

Denver City

Oro City   Fairplay

Colorado City

Canon City

Pueblo

Bent's Fort

WYOMING   NEBRASKA   IOWA

COLORADO

South Platte   River

Platte River

Fort Kearney

Omaha   Council Bluffs

Nebraska City   MISSOURI

Republican River

Denver City

KANSAS

St. Joseph

Leavenworth
Fort Riley

Kansas City

Smoky Hill River

Arkansas River

Ft. Larned

NEW MEXICO   OKLAHOMA

10 0 10 20 30 40 50 Miles

GOLD RUSH ROUTES

Golden rumors drifted out of the Rockies for three centuries before the gold rush. Rumor did not become reality until the summer of 1858 when William Green Russell and some sidekicks found color in the sands of the South Platte.

Gold fever spread quickly to the Missouri River frontier towns of Atchison, Council Bluffs, Independence, Kansas City, Leavenworth, Omaha, and St. Joseph. These supply towns outfitted the argonauts and encouraged them with numerous guidebooks that prescribed supplies and routes and described the fabulous fortunes to be made. Thousands set out in 1859 for the vaguely labeled "Pike's Peak Diggings." Two-thirds of this mass migration would become disappointed "go-backs."

Gold seekers faced a 700-mile trek across "the Great American Desert." To be sure of water and grass for their livestock, most stuck to the routes along rivers—the Arkansas, the Platte, the Republican, and the Smoky Hill. Those following the Republican and the Smoky Hill found that those streams dwindled into sandy wastes with only a few waterholes. The Leavenworth and Pike's Peak Express Company started stagecoaching on the Republican River route in May 1859, but soon shifted to the surer South Platte River route.

Argonauts were advised to take not mules or horses but the slower, steadier oxen. While oxen carried their goods in wagons, most travelers walked alongside, making perhaps twenty miles a day. Emigrants stuffed their wagons with cherished possessions from their former homes—heirlooms, keepsakes, choice pieces of furniture, and perhaps seed potatoes and lilac slips. For the women, emigration often seemed to be a particularly unsettling process in which the familiar and the comfortable—relatives, friends, possessions, and surroundings—were exchanged for an uncertain new future.

Horace Greeley, who saw the 1859 rush, claimed that "the very mothers who bore them would hardly recognize their sons now toiling across the Plains, and staggering into this place [Denver] hideously hirsute, recklessly ragged, barefoot, sun-browned, dust-covered, and with eyes shielded (where they have them) by goggles from the glare of the prairie sun, reflected from the desert clay."

Ominously, dead livestock, broken wagons, and crude gravestones marked the trail. Although Indian attacks were most feared, the biggest problems were lack of water and food, disease, and accidents. Indeed, supposedly hostile Indians often proved friendly, as Daniel Blue discovered on the Smoky Hill Trail. Lost, disoriented, and starving, he had survived by dining on his two brothers. Arapaho Indians rescued him, nursed him into recovery, and then guided him to Denver to tell his macabre tale.

After the Civil War cut off the southern routes feeding into the Santa Fe Trail along the Arkansas River, the Platte River route (which also served the California, Mormon, Oregon, and Overland trails) became the most popular. The shift to the northern route led to a decline in the Arkansas Valley settlements at Bent's Fort, Pueblo, and Canon City, which had aspired to be the regional trade and political centers.

Gold rush routes converged on Boulder, Denver, Golden City, Colorado City, Pueblo, and Canon City along the Front Range. In those supply centers travelers lingered to repair themselves and their equipment. There they could find food, drink, and lodging, livestock boarding and sales, and fresh news and rumors about the latest bonanzas. Commercial and residential real-estate possibilities in the thriving supply towns persuaded some of the fifty-niners to settle and open businesses to exploit the emigrants and miners. This usually proved easier and more profitable than wading through icy mountain streams with picks and pie pans, looking for elusive "color."

From the supply towns, steeper, narrower trails led westward up Front Range streams through the foothills and into the mountains. From Denver, for example, major trails led up the Golden Gate, Clear Creek, and South Platte canyons. In South Park, branches of the Platte River road from Denver and the Colorado City road converged. The main Arkansas route led to the gold strike at Oro City on the river's headwaters. North-south travelers along the Front Range continued to use the old fur-trade routes—the Cherokee and Trappers trails.

An estimated 100,000 set out for Colorado in 1859, but federal census takers in the spring of 1860 found a population of only 39,864 in what would become Colorado Territory the following year. One of the great mass migrations in history had attracted settlers from nearly every territory, state, and nation. Within a few years the gold rush had transformed one of America's most rugged and remote regions into an urbanized, industrialized mining territory, to the dismay of the Native Americans and Hispanic farmers. Although often denounced as a hoax, the 1859 rush paid off in hundreds of mining discoveries between 1858 and the 1890s. The strikes made Colorado, briefly at least, the nation's leading producer of gold, silver, and certain other minerals.

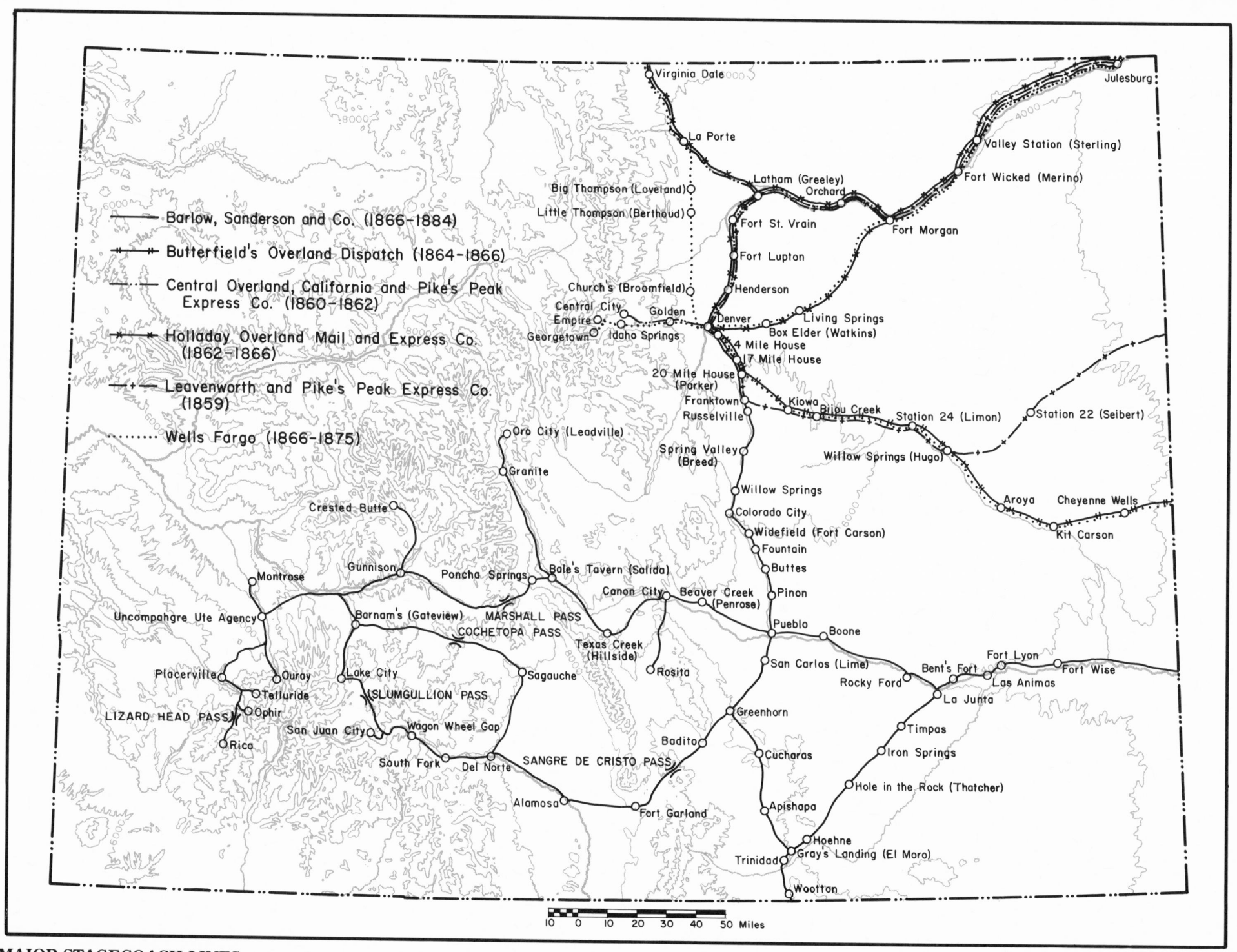

Legend:
- ———— Barlow, Sanderson and Co. (1866–1884)
- ╫╫╫ Butterfield's Overland Dispatch (1864–1866)
- ·–·–· Central Overland, California and Pike's Peak Express Co. (1860–1862)
- ✕✕✕ Holladay Overland Mail and Express Co. (1862–1866)
- —+— Leavenworth and Pike's Peak Express Co. (1859)
- ········ Wells Fargo (1866–1875)

Virginia Dale · Julesburg · La Porte · Valley Station (Sterling) · Latham (Greeley) · Fort Wicked (Merino) · Orchard · Big Thompson (Loveland) · Little Thompson (Berthoud) · Fort St. Vrain · Fort Morgan · Fort Lupton · Church's (Broomfield) · Henderson · Central City · Golden · Empire · Denver · Living Springs · Georgetown · Idaho Springs · Box Elder (Watkins) · 4 Mile House · 17 Mile House · 20 Mile House (Parker) · Franktown · Kiowa · Bijou Creek · Station 24 (Limon) · Station 22 (Seibert) · Russelville · Oro City (Leadville) · Spring Valley (Breed) · Willow Springs (Hugo) · Granite · Willow Springs · Aroya · Cheyenne Wells · Crested Butte · Colorado City · Widefield (Fort Carson) · Kit Carson · Fountain · Gunnison · Buttes · Montrose · Bale's Tavern (Salida) · Poncha Springs · Pinon · Canon City · Beaver Creek (Penrose) · Uncompahgre Ute Agency · Barnam's (Gateview) · MARSHALL PASS · Pueblo · Boone · COCHETOPA PASS · Texas Creek (Hillside) · San Carlos (Lime) · Bent's Fort · Fort Lyon · Placerville · Ouray · Lake City · Sagauche · Rosita · Rocky Ford · Las Animas · Fort Wise · Telluride · SLUMGULLION PASS · La Junta · Ophir · Greenhorn · Timpas · LIZARD HEAD PASS · San Juan City · Wagon Wheel Gap · Badito · Iron Springs · Rica · South Fork · Del Norte · SANGRE DE CRISTO PASS · Cucharas · Hole in the Rock (Thatcher) · Alamosa · Fort Garland · Apishapa · Hoehne · Gray's Landing (El Moro) · Trinidad · Wootton

10 0 10 20 30 40 50 Miles

MAJOR STAGECOACH LINES

27. MAJOR STAGECOACH LINES

On May 7, 1859, the first stages—they traveled in pairs for safety—rumbled into Denver. They were greeted by a crowd of pioneers wearing slouched hats, tattered woolen shirts, buckskin trousers, and belts sagging with knives and pistols. These Leavenworth and Pike's Peak Express Company coaches had traveled 687 miles from "the States" to the Pike's Peak gold regions. The company had invested an estimated $250,000 in fifty-two Concord stages, one thousand mules, stage stops at 25-mile intervals, and "sober, discreet, and experienced drivers."

The six large stagecoach outfits mapped here grew by absorbing small, local lines, a pattern followed later by American railroads and airlines. Of many stage lines once criss-crossing Colorado, most were short-lived due to the extreme distances, raw climate, bandits, and the intense competition to capture federal mail subsidies. The federal mail contracts, along with passenger, freight, and express service, could make stagecoaching profitable.

Most lines used the sturdy coaches made in Concord, New Hampshire, by the Abbott-Downing Company. The white-oak carriage, reinforced by iron and suspended on broad leather straps, was, as Mark Twain wrote in *Roughing It,* "a great swinging and swaying stage, of the most sumptuous description—an imposing cradle on wheels."

The Leavenworth and Pike's Peak stage, after operating for a month along the Republican River and Cherry Creek, switched to the South Platte River route into Denver. In the spring of 1860 the high-plains freighting company of Russell, Majors, and Waddell reorganized the L & PP as the Central Overland California and Pike's Peak Express Company (COC & PP). This firm cut the travel time from Leavenworth to Denver to six days, reduced the Leavenworth-to-Denver fare from $200 to $75, and extended service to Central City and on to California via the Central Overland Trail. Still, the COC & PP, dubbed the "Clean Out of Cash & Poor Pay," suffered the same financial woes as its predecessor.

Ben Holladay, king of western stagecoaching, purchased the remaining assets of the COC & PP at auction in the spring of 1863. The Holladay Overland Mail and Express Company continued to use the South Platte River route into Denver, but saved a day's travel by using the Fort Morgan cutoff. Holladay's Overland reigned until 1865, when David A. Butterfield established the Butterfield's Overland Dispatch stage between Atchison, Kansas, and Denver via the Smoky Hill Trail. In 1866, Holladay bought out Butterfield and sold all the Holladay lines to Wells Fargo and Company. Wells Fargo, the western branch of the American Express Company, came to dominate western stagecoaching. In Colorado the San Francisco–based firm operated South Platte, Smoky Hill, and mountain routes until it abandoned all Colorado stage operations in 1875.

While Russell, Majors, and Waddell; Ben Holladay; the Butterfields; and Wells Fargo fought for control of interstate lines, numerous local firms built feeder stage lines within Colorado. By the early 1860s the Denver and South Park Stage Line tapped the gold-mining towns of Fairplay, Tarryall, and Buckskin Joe in South Park and crossed Boreas Pass to Breckenridge. Other lines were built over the Golden Gate Canyon–Guy Hill and the Mount Vernon Canyon–Floyd Hill routes to Black Hawk, Central City, Idaho Springs, and Georgetown. Ten years later local lines had pushed over Berthoud Pass into Grand County, over the Loveland and Argentine passes into Summit County, and over Weston Pass to Leadville. During winter some high-country stagecoachers substituted runners for wheels, turning stages into sleds.

Colorado's most-enduring and important stage empire, Barlow, Sanderson, and Company, was created in 1866. Bradley Barlow and Jared L. Sanderson were two veterans of Santa Fe Trail freight, mail, express, and passenger services. Their Southern Overland Mail and Express Company operated between Kansas City and Santa Fe on the Mountain Branch of the old Santa Fe Trail, using the ruins of Bent's Fort as one station. Another branch continued up the Arkansas River to Pueblo and Canon City. In 1870, Barlow and Sanderson added the Denver and Santa Fe stage to their growing network, and in 1876 they opened the first major line into the San Juan Mountain mining region of southwestern Colorado. Stages from Pueblo crossed Sangre de Cristo Pass into the San Luis Valley via Fort Garland and Alamosa, then followed the Rio Grande westward to Del Norte and on to Lake City. Another route pushed up the Arkansas River to the silver city of Leadville. By 1880 Barlow and Sanderson had extended lines over Marshall Pass into Gunnison. While railroads replaced stages in eastern Colorado after 1870, stages continued to operate in the San Juans as late as the 1880s, serving Rico, Telluride, and Montrose.

After 1870 stagecoaches retreated as railroad construction advanced. While many stage lines went out of business, others survived by connecting railheads to remoter regions. A few stagecoach runs survived until the 1900s and the advent of the "motorcoach."

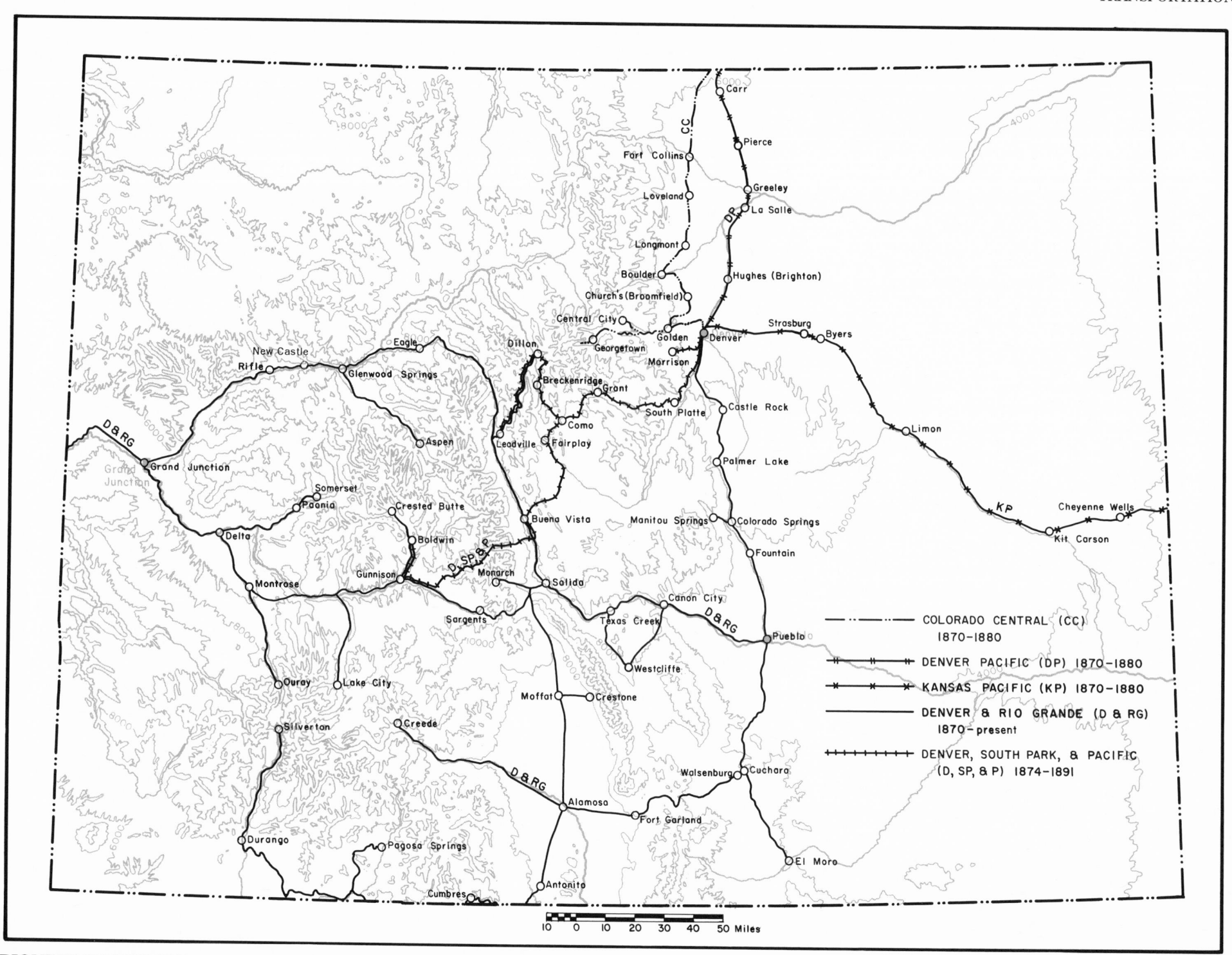

Carr
Pierce
Fort Collins
Greeley
Loveland
La Salle
Longmont
Boulder
Hughes (Brighton)
Church's (Broomfield)
Central City
Strasburg
Golden
Byers
Denver
Georgetown
Morrison
Eagle
Dillon
New Castle
Breckenridge
Rifle
Grant
Glenwood Springs
Como
Castle Rock
South Platte
Limon
Aspen
Fairplay
Leadville
Palmer Lake
Grand Junction
Somerset
Paonia
Crested Butte
Buena Vista
Manitou Springs
Colorado Springs
Cheyenne Wells
Delta
Baldwin
Fountain
Kit Carson
Gunnison
Monarch
Montrose
Salida
Canon City
Sargents
Texas Creek
Ouray
Lake City
Westcliffe
Pueblo
Moffat
Crestone
Silverton
Creede
Walsenburg
Cuchara
Alamosa
Durango
Pagosa Springs
Fort Garland
El Moro
Antonito
Cumbres

COLORADO CENTRAL (CC)
1870–1880

DENVER PACIFIC (DP) 1870–1880

KANSAS PACIFIC (KP) 1870–1880

DENVER & RIO GRANDE (D & RG)
1870–present

DENVER, SOUTH PARK, & PACIFIC
(D, SP, & P) 1874–1891

10 0 10 20 30 40 50 Miles

PIONEER RAILROADS

28. PIONEER RAILROADS

As a stagecoach territory, Colorado stagnated. The slow, expensive, and uncomfortable stage travel discouraged visitors and would-be settlers. Mining also suffered; only the highest-grade ores could be shipped east by wagon for profitable refinement. If only Colorado had railroads, a New York assayer reported, it would "rival or supersede California and Australia, and become the El Dorado of the West."

Coloradans tried to coax railroads across the seven hundred miles of sparsely settled prairies separating them from the Missouri River frontier towns. When the Union Pacific Railroad (UP) skirted Colorado's Rocky Mountain barrier by building the first transcontinental route through Wyoming, Denverites decided to build their own railroad. John Evans, William Byers, and other entrepreneurs incorporated the Denver Pacific Railway (DP) in 1867. Three years later the DP completed a 106-mile steel lifeline between Denver and the UP tracks at Cheyenne.

Railroads did more than enable existing towns to survive and prosper; they became the principal vehicle of town building. The Denver Pacific, for instance, created Hughes (Brighton), Evans, Pierce, and Carr—towns named for railroad officials. Greeley's townsite was purchased from the DP by the Union Colony and promoted by Horace Greeley, editor and owner of the *New York Tribune*. Like many other rail towns, Greeley sprouted as an instant community whose pioneer buildings were dumped onto the site from railroad flat cars.

Golden also boasted a railroad incorporated during the 1860s, the Colorado Central (CC). The CC built a narrow-gauge line up Clear Creek to Central City in the Gilpin County gold regions, then up the south fork of Clear Creek to the first silver mining center, Georgetown. The CC constructed standard-gauge branches to Denver and to Cheyenne, the Wyoming rail hub, via Boulder, Longmont, Fort Collins, Berthoud, and Loveland, the last two being named for the railroad's chief engineer and president. In 1884 the Georgetown, Breckenridge, and Leadville (a creature of the UP, which had acquired the CC) completed its famous Georgetown Loop to Silver Plume.

In 1870 the Kansas Pacific (KP) completed its line between Kansas City and Denver. To create business along its tracks, the KP attempted to convince prospective settlers that "the Great American Desert" was actually a Garden of Eden. The railroad established an agricultural experiment station at Cheyenne Wells and promoted dry-land farming and stock raising. The KP helped plant the towns of Strasburg and Limon, which were both named for section foremen. Another town was named for William N. Byers, the founder and editor of the *Rocky Mountain News*, who moonlighted as a sales agent for KP lands.

The Denver and Rio Grande (D & RG), biggest and best known of all the Colorado railroads, was incorporated in 1870 by William J. Palmer and some associates. Palmer introduced a narrow-gauge track 3 feet wide that could be installed for about two-thirds the cost of the standard 4 feet 8-1/2 inch gauge. It could also tackle tighter curves and steeper grades. Palmer's baby road initially headed south, creating the towns of Castle Rock, Palmer Lake, Colorado Springs, and El Moro along the Front Range. After silver was discovered in Leadville, the D & RG built a line up the Arkansas River canyon from Pueblo to the silver city. Another western extension was built from Walsenburg to the San Juan Mountains, where the D & RG platted towns such as Alamosa, Antonito, and Durango. The D & RG became the first railroad to cross Colorado and reach Utah, beating rivals through the Arkansas, Colorado, and Gunnison river canyons. In western Colorado the D & RG promoted the tourist mecca of Glenwood Springs and helped establish the fruit-growing centers of Paonia, Delta, and Grand Junction, as well as coal towns of New Castle and Somerset.

The Denver, South Park, and Pacific (DSP & P), another narrow-gauge line, originated in Denver in 1872. Wriggling up the South Platte River canyon, the South Park spawned towns such as South Platte, Grant, and Como. From Como one branch crossed Boreas Pass to Breckenridge, Dillon, and Leadville. Another ran southeast to Fairplay and Buena Vista and then burrowed through Alpine Tunnel, the first passage under the continental divide. Ultimately this line reached Gunnison—still far away from its nominal goal, the Pacific Ocean. Many other small "Pacific" railroads ran out of steam trying to build across the Rockies.

These pioneer railroads carried out minerals and other raw materials and brought in goods and supplies, tourists, and new residents. Colorado's population grew 500 percent during the 1870s, reaching 413,149 by 1890. In a single generation, railroads helped transform a remote frontier territory into a state noted for industry, agriculture, and tourism, not just for its silver and gold.

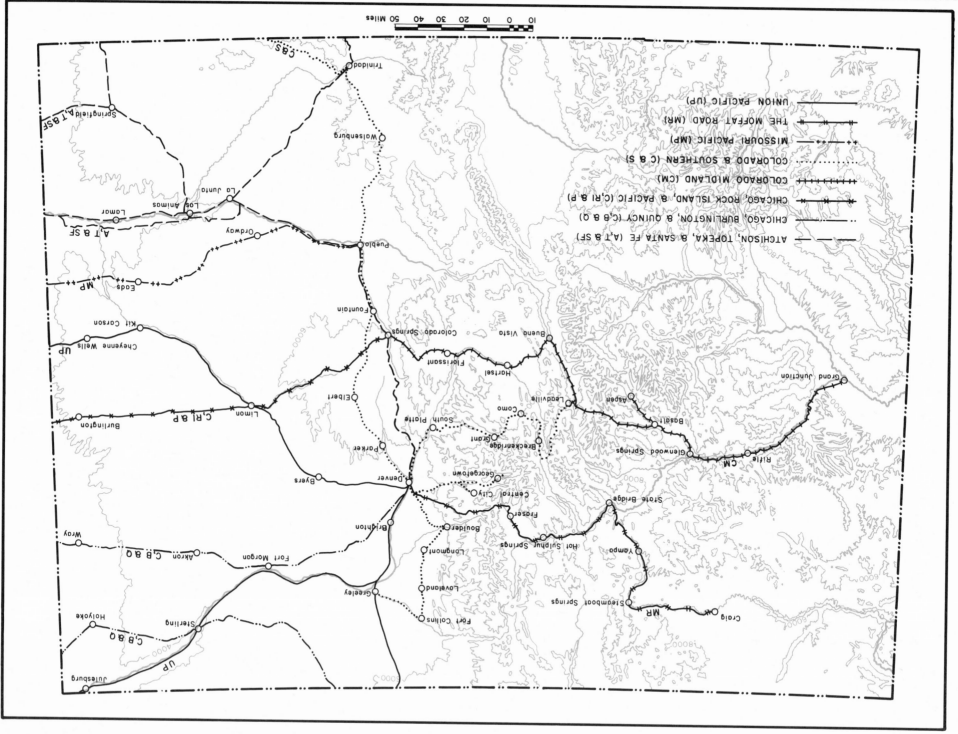

UNION PACIFIC (UP)

THE MOFFAT ROAD (MR)

MISSOURI PACIFIC (MP)

COLORADO & SOUTHERN (C & S)

COLORADO MIDLAND (CM)

CHICAGO, ROCK ISLAND, & PACIFIC (C,RI & P)

CHICAGO, BURLINGTON, & QUINCY (C,B & Q)

ATCHISON, TOPEKA, & SANTA FE (A,T & SF)

50 40 30 20 10 0 10 Miles

Approximately 175 different railroads laid track in Colorado. Many were small mining railroads or commuter trolleys. Numerous name changes, and the common practice of building branches and extensions under a name different from that of the parent rail firm, further explain why the state had so many railroads.

The Denver and Rio Grande (see preceding map), the largest rail network, was reorganized as the Denver and Rio Grande Western in 1921. The D & RGW remained an independent Denver-based outfit even after owner Philip Anschutz purchased the Southern Pacific in the 1980s. In the 1990s, to the dismay of Colorado rail fans, Anschutz began replacing the D & RGW logo with Southern Pacific livery. While "Colorado's Pet" is a favorite with rail fans, critics claimed D & RGW meant "Dangerous and Rapidly Growing Worse."

While the D & RGW survived, the Denver Pacific, Kansas Pacific, Colorado Central, and Denver, South Park and Pacific (all on the preceding map) became Union Pacific (UP) lines in the 1880s. The UP was chartered by Congress in 1862, shortly after Pres. Abraham Lincoln signed the Pacific Railway Act to help finance construction of a transcontinental railroad. Jay Gould, the robber baron who seized control of the UP in the 1870s, collected Colorado railroads built by other companies. The UP did construct one major Colorado line from Julesburg to La Salle in 1881, boosting the towns of Sterling and Fort Morgan in the process. Jay Gould and the UP were the principals behind the construction of Denver's Union Station in 1881.

The Chicago, Burlington, and Quincy (CB & Q), an 1855 consolidation of Illinois, Iowa, Missouri, and Nebraska railroads, built into Denver through Wray, Akron, and Fort Morgan in 1882. Five years later the CB & Q completed its second Colorado line, which ran from the Nebraska border through Holyoke and Sterling to Cheyenne, Wyoming. The CB & Q, the Great Northern, and the Northern Pacific merged in 1970 to form the Burlington Northern Railroad.

In 1898 the Colorado and Southern (C & S) was formed by consolidating some older lines, such as the old Colorado Central and the Denver, South Park and Pacific. Ultimately the C & S became a major Front Range railroad serving both southern and northern Colorado coalfields, as well as north-central farming centers. The C & S, a subsidiary of the CB & Q, officially merged with the parent road in 1908, although the C & S retained its own management and corporate identity until 1982.

The Atchison, Topeka and Santa Fe (AT & SF), founded in 1859, reached the Colorado border in 1873. Following the old Santa Fe Trail westward along the Arkansas River, this Kansas-based road created many towns, including Lamar, Las Animas, and La Junta (Spanish for "the junction"). At La Junta the main line cut southwest to Trinidad and Santa Fe, New Mexico, while a branch followed the Arkansas River to Pueblo and ultimately to Denver. The Santa Fe's efforts to tap Colorado's mining towns backfired when it lost the "Royal Gorge War" to the D & RG. It recouped by hauling cattle, grain, and tourists, and the company rolls on to this day as one of America's more-prosperous roads.

The Chicago, Rock Island and Pacific (CRI & P), chartered in 1852, built from the Colorado-Kansas border to Colorado Springs. Towns such as Burlington and Limon sprouted along the Rock Island tracks. When the CRI & P disintegrated in 1980, Kansas and Colorado farmers and local officials helped persuade the Cadillac and Lake City Railroad to maintain the stretch from Limon to Goodland, Kansas, during the wheat harvest. The Missouri Pacific (MP) started west from Saint Louis in 1851. Thirty-six years later it reached its western terminus, Pueblo, via Eads and Ordway.

Colorado Springs entrepreneurs founded the Colorado Midland (CM) in 1883. Via spectacular tunnels, trestles, and mountain climbing, the Midland became the first standard-gauge railroad to cross the Colorado Rockies. The CM, like most railroads, led a short and troubled life, expiring in 1922. A part of the line, the Midland Terminal between Colorado Springs and Cripple Creek was not abandoned until 1948.

The Denver and Salt Lake Railroad, formed by David H. Moffat in 1903 as the Denver, Northwestern, and Pacific, was popularly known as the Moffat Road. In 1904 the Denver and Salt Lake became the first railroad to conquer the continental divide directly west of Denver. Although the Moffat Road never got past Craig, Colorado, it did dig the 6.2-mile Moffat Tunnel under the continental divide (see Map 30). When completed in 1928, the Moffat Tunnel was the longest in the United States. It is now used by the D & RGW, which absorbed the Denver and Salt Lake in 1947.

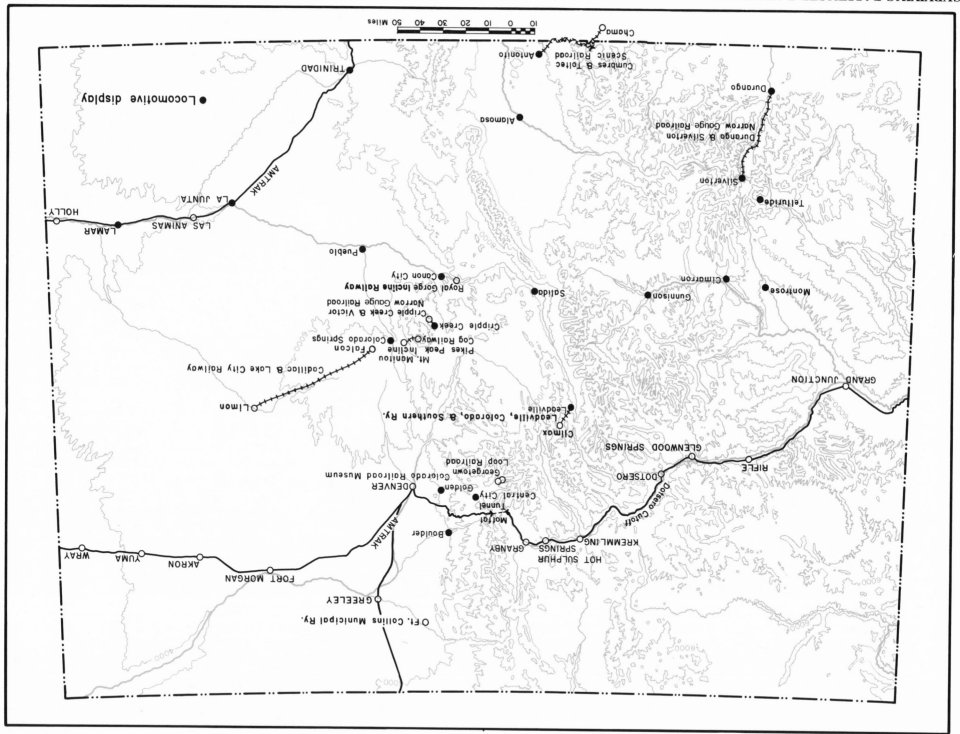

Cumbres & Toltec
Scenic Railroad

Chama

Antonito

Durango

Durango & Silverton
Narrow Gauge Railroad

Alamosa

Silverton

Telluride

TRINIDAD

● Locomotive display

AMTRAK

LA JUNTA

LAS ANIMAS

HOLLY

LAMAR

Pueblo

Canon City

Royal Gorge Incline Railway

Cripple Creek & Victor
Narrow Gauge Railroad

Cripple Creek

Salida

Cimarron

Montrose

Gunnison

Colorado Springs
Cog Railway

Pikes Peak Incline

Mt. Manitou
Falcon

Cadillac & Lake City Railway

Limon

Leadville, Colorado, & Southern Ry.

Leadville

Climax

GLENWOOD SPRINGS

GRAND JUNCTION

Georgetown
Loop Railroad

Colorado Railroad Museum

DENVER

Golden

Central City

Tunnel

Moffat
Tunnel

Boulder

DOTSERO

RIFLE

Dotsero Cutoff

AMTRAK

KREMMLING

HOT SULPHUR
SPRINGS

GRANBY

WRAY

YUMA

AKRON

FORT MORGAN

GREELEY

●Ft. Collins Municipal Ry.

10   0   10   20   30   40   50 Miles
50 Miles

Sharp-eyed tourists have little trouble tracking Colorado's ghost railroads. Their cuts and fills, tunnels and rockwork, haunt every corner of the state. Because rail grades never exceeded 4.5 percent (a rise of 4-1/2 feet along 100 feet of track), these gentle roadbeds make easy hiking, biking, and cross-country ski trails.

With most of the trains are gone, many towns have recycled their depots as homes, businesses, restaurants, and museums. Pueblo's Union Station is the most spectacular architectural survivor, having been subjected to a minimum of "improvements." Denver's Union Station has undergone numerous changes, but is still the grand centerpiece of the Lower Downtown Historic District. In the basement, O-gauge model-train buffs have entertained the public free of charge on the last Friday evening of every month for decades. Their huge subterranean model-train layout includes miniatures of many famous railroad landscapes.

The Intermountain Chapter of the National Railway Historical Society offers rail buffs various programs and special excursions from its office in Denver's Union Station. So do the Colorado Midland (Colorado Springs) and Rio Grande (Grand Junction) chapters and Denver's Rocky Mountain Railroad Club. A top stop is the Colorado Railroad Museum in Golden, with its rolling stock, excursions, railroadiana, research materials, and book and gift shop. As the map indicates, many communities proudly display locomotive reminders that railroads created or brought prosperity to many a Colorado community.

Passenger service continues on a few stretches of Colorado's once-extensive spiderweb of steel tracks, although only AMTRAK offers year-around service. Once dozens of Colorado railroads welcomed passengers, but only three survive under their original names: the Pike's Peak Cog Railway, the Royal Gorge Incline Railway, and the Denver and Rio Grande's Ski Train. The Ski Train has been operating on winter weekends since the Winter Park ski area opened in 1941.

Since its 1971 creation, AMTRAK has revived the old California Zephyr route—the only passenger service to cross the state. AMTRAK'S Southwest Chief follows the old Santa Fe Railroad route through the southeast quadrant of the state between Holly and Trinidad, on its way from Chicago to Los Angeles. In 1991, AMTRAK added Denver-to-Cheyenne service via Greeley.

Two of the most spectacular narrow-gauge passenger trains in the world operate in Colorado, using former Denver and Rio Grande Railroad tracks and rolling stock. America's highest and longest narrow gauge, the Cumbres and Toltec Scenic Railroad, climbs and winds for 63.4 miles between Chama, New Mexico, and Antonito, Colorado. The Durango and Silverton Narrow Gauge, a route in continuous operation since it opened in 1882, still uses coal and antique narrow-gauge equipment. A large rail yard, a roundhouse, and repair shops have been built in Durango to repair or fabricate all the parts of the feisty little antique trains.

In 1984, a century after the Georgetown Loop opened, the Colorado Historical Society restored the narrow-gauge line and its 300-foot steel trestle soaring 75 feet above Clear Creek. Once again, tourists are flocking to the famed Georgetown Loop, a National Engineering Landmark that uses three and a half miles of loops and curves to make the steep climb between Georgetown and Silver Plume. At Cripple Creek, once the world's richest gold camp, the 2-foot-gauge Cripple Creek and Victor Railway boards tourists at the old Colorado Midland Depot (now the Cripple Creek District Museum). Even shorter rides are possible at Central City and the Royal Gorge, which uses an incline railway.

Two urban street railways have been revived in recent years. The Fort Collins Municipal Railway reopened the West Mountain Avenue Line from City Park to College Avenue in 1985. Four years later, the Denver Rail Heritage Society began trolley service on exiting track between Confluence Park and Sheridan Boulevard aboard the Platte Valley Trolley.

The Leadville, Colorado, and Southern Railway inaugurated diesel-powered standard-gauge passenger service in 1987 for an excursion from Leadville's restored 1884 Denver, South Park, and Pacific Depot to the top of Fremont Pass. Another summer excursion train is the Cadillac and Lake City Railway, a revived standard-gauge stretch of the Chicago and Rock Island Line operating between Falcon, an eastern suburb of Colorado Springs, and Limon.

Recent rail revivals have encouraged dreamers and schemers to consider other possibilities, including a light rail network begun in Denver in 1993 that may ultimately reach Denver International Airport and other Front Range communities. Perhaps Coloradans and tourists may ride into the twenty-first century the same way so many rode into the twentieth century—on rails.

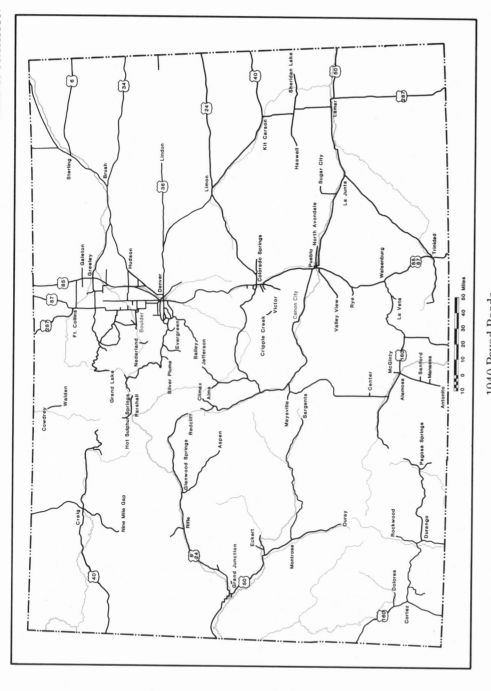

1940 Paved Roads

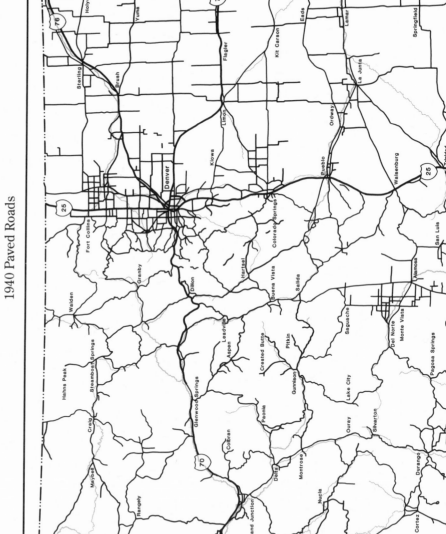

1980 Paved Roads

PAVED ROADS, 1940 AND 1980

31. PAVED ROADS, 1940 AND 1980

Colorado's isolation, rugged terrain, and long distances between settlements made transportation a primary concern. Road building became a major thrust as early as the 1860s, when private entrepreneurs started constructing toll roads.

The dirt-road network continued to grow until the 1900s, when bicyclists and automobilists began promoting paved roads. At first many felt that the wealthy who owned autos should build their own roads, as millionaire Spencer Penrose did. Penrose, who bought a new car each year, constructed a highway to the top of Pike's Peak as the ultimate challenge for motor cars. "Cement Bill" Williams began a paved road to the top of Lookout Mountain, but ran out of gas, leaving the project for the city of Denver to finish in 1913.

Meanwhile, motorists began pressuring the state to build and pave more roads. The Colorado Auto Club (1902) and the Colorado Chapter (1905) of the National Good Roads Association helped persuade the legislature to establish the Colorado Highway Commission in 1909. By the 1920s the Colorado Highway Department was spending $2.5 million a year on roads. The Federal Highway Act of 1916 provided a 50-50 match for "primary roads." These state and federal matching funds were used to construct the first paved road in 1918, a $73,939 concrete thoroughfare between Denver and Littleton.

Colorado highway construction accelerated with the use of convict labor beginning in 1905. Lime, gravel, and stone for road building could be obtained from the quarry conveniently located behind the state penitentiary at Canon City. Convicts built many of the first paved roads shown on the 1940 map, including the state highway built in 1919 from Pueblo to Leadville and the scenic highways in Big Thompson, Boulder, Colorado River, and St. Vrain canyons, and the Ute Pass Road connecting Colorado Springs with Leadville. From Canon City, convicts built a road to the penitentiary ranch at North Avondale, to the quarries near Valley View, and to the resort town of Rye. Prisoners also built the 1911 highway from Canon City to the Royal Gorge Suspension Bridge and Canon City's 1905 Skyline Drive. Colorado led the country in the use of convicts to build roads until the practice was abandoned in 1926. Prisoners then began making Colorado's license plates, as they still do.

Civic and commercial groups raised money to help build, pave, and promote highways such as the O.L.D. (Omaha, Lincoln, Denver), which became U.S. 6; the Victory Highway (U.S. 40); the Rainbow Trail (U.S. 50); and the Pike's Peak Ocean-to-Ocean Highway (U.S. 24). Thirty-one uniquely marked and named "auto trails" crisscrossed Colorado by 1924, when the federal government ordered that highways be systematically numbered with standardized signs.

In 1919, Colorado became one of the first four states to tax gasoline to help finance road construction. The penny-per-gallon tax was doubled in 1923 and then raised to three cents in 1927, four cents in 1929, and twenty cents a gallon by the 1990s.

As the 1940 map illustrates, federal highways were the first paved, border-to-border Colorado thoroughfares. State and local politics contributed to a somewhat haphazard paving of secondary roads. Stretches often were paved from one small town to another, as shown by the blacktop between Walden and Cowdrey and Cripple Creek and Victor. Thanks largely to federal funding of New Deal programs during the 1930s, Colorado paved roads increased from 500 miles in 1930 to 4,000 paved miles in 1940.

Roads over mountain passes were among the last to be paved. The state bought the Berthoud Pass toll road in 1931 and made U.S. 40 the first paved crossing of the continental divide. This was followed by the paving of U.S. 50 over Monarch Pass. Denver, which began paving city streets before 1900, undertook an ambitious program of constructing mountain touring roads, including the country's highest auto road to the summit of Mount Evans.

Colorado's first limited-access auto freeway was West Sixth Avenue, built during World War II from downtown Denver to the federal war-production plant near Golden. The Denver-Boulder Turnpike (1952) proved so popular that tolls were removed in 1967 after the turnpike paid for itself ahead of schedule. Although I-25, the north-south interstate highway, was completed in 1967, I-70 took much longer. Colorado's portion of this east-west freeway was delayed for five years (1968–73) during blasting and burrowing under the continental divide for the Eisenhower-Johnson Tunnel. It took another twenty years to complete I-70 through the Glenwood Canyon of the Colorado River. Not only the deep, narrow canyon, but also protests from environmentalists, delayed the Glenwood Canyon project, prodding engineers to design I-70 as an eye-pleasing complement to the landscape.

As the 1980 map shows, north-south roads in rural eastern Colorado still have many unpaved sections, while the Front Range between Colorado Springs and Fort Collins is heavily paved, and metro Denver is building its second belt-loop freeway on the outer edge of the metropolis. Paved roads remain sparse and crooked in the western, mountainous portion of the state. Rising objections from environmentalists have curtailed road building and even led to the abandonment of automobile roads in some areas. In Colorado's back country travelers tackle difficult passes, deep canyons, and other terrain as their ancestors did—on narrow dirt roads that often follow old railroad grades, wagon roads, and Indian trails.

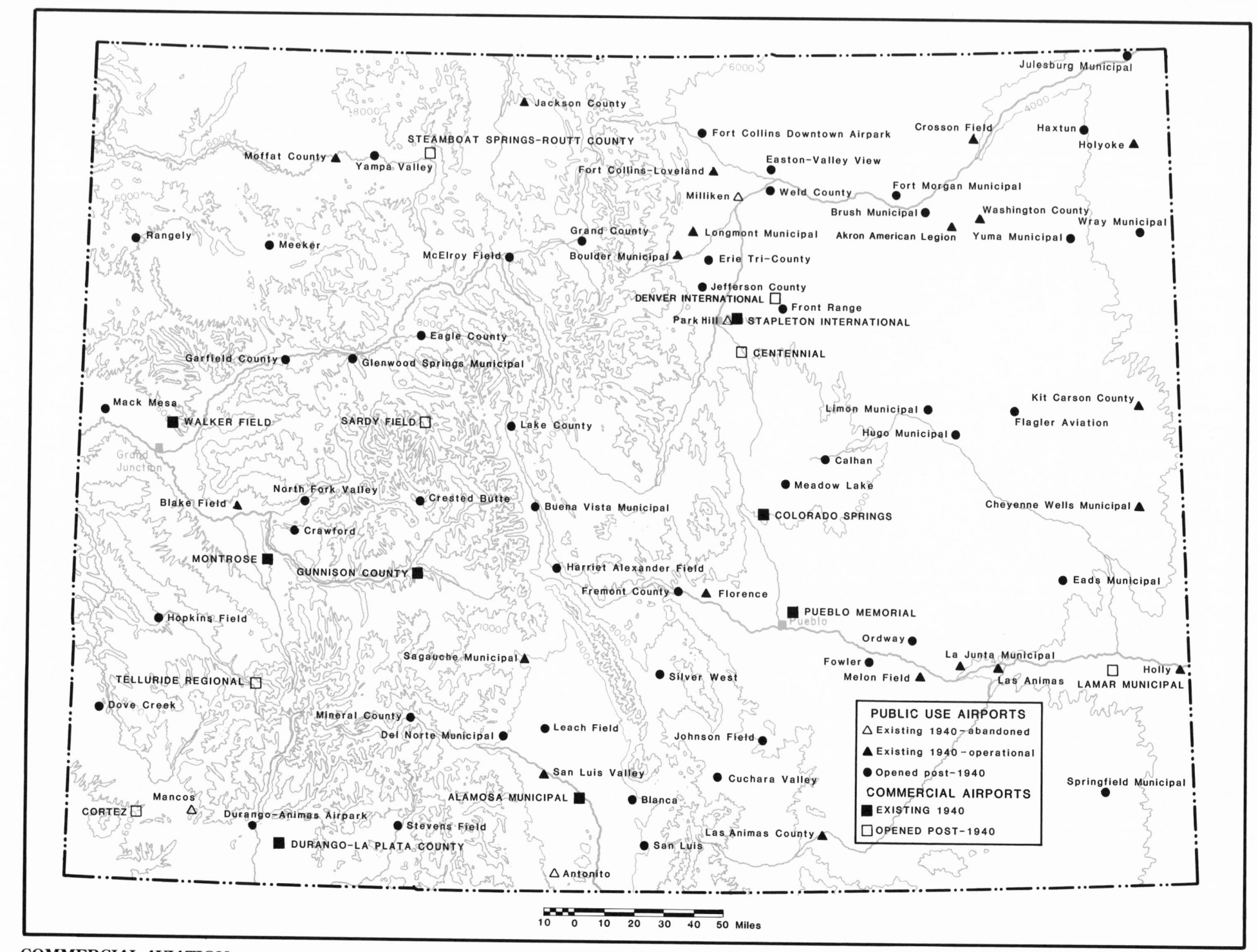

Julesburg Municipal

▲ Jackson County

● Fort Collins Downtown Airpark   Crosson Field ▲   Haxtun ●

STEAMBOAT SPRINGS-ROUTT COUNTY □

Moffat County ▲   Easton-Valley View   Holyoke ▲

● Yampa Valley   Fort Collins-Loveland ▲   Fort Morgan Municipal

Milliken △   ● Weld County

Washington County ▲   Wray Municipal

Rangely ●   Meeker ●   Grand County   ▲ Longmont Municipal   Brush Municipal ●   Akron American Legion ▲   Yuma Municipal ●

McElroy Field ●   Boulder Municipal ▲   ● Erie Tri-County

● Jefferson County

Eagle County ●   DENVER INTERNATIONAL □   ● Front Range

Park Hill △■ STAPLETON INTERNATIONAL

Garfield County ●   Glenwood Springs Municipal ●   □ CENTENNIAL

Mack Mesa ●   Limon Municipal ●   Kit Carson County ▲

■ WALKER FIELD   SARDY FIELD □   ● Lake County   Hugo Municipal ●   Flagler Aviation

Grand Junction   Calhan ●

Blake Field ▲   North Fork Valley ●   ● Crested Butte   Meadow Lake ●   Cheyenne Wells Municipal ▲

● Buena Vista Municipal

Crawford ●   ■ COLORADO SPRINGS

MONTROSE ■   Harriet Alexander Field ●   Eads Municipal ●

GUNNISON COUNTY ■   Fremont County ● ▲ Florence

Hopkins Field ●   ■ PUEBLO MEMORIAL

Ordway ●

Sagauche Municipal ▲   Fowler ●   La Junta Municipal ▲   □ Holly

TELLURIDE REGIONAL □   Silver West ●   Melon Field ▲   Las Animas ▲   LAMAR MUNICIPAL

Dove Creek ●

Mineral County ●   Leach Field ●   Johnson Field ●   Springfield Municipal ●

Mancos △   Del Norte Municipal ●   San Luis Valley ▲   Cuchara Valley ●

CORTEZ □   ● Blanca

Durango-Animas Airpark ●   Stevens Field ●   ALAMOSA MUNICIPAL ■   San Luis ●   Las Animas County ▲

■ DURANGO-LA PLATA COUNTY

△ Antonito

PUBLIC USE AIRPORTS
△ Existing 1940-abandoned
▲ Existing 1940-operational
● Opened post-1940
COMMERCIAL AIRPORTS
■ EXISTING 1940
□ OPENED POST-1940

10 0 10 20 30 40 50 Miles

COMMERCIAL AVIATION

Coloradans welcomed aviation as a fast, direct way to fly over the many geographical obstacles in the Highest State. Communities endeavored to construct airports just as they had once built depots to capture railroad service. As the map shows, a fairly even statewide distribution of airports made this the transportation network that has most successfully conquered tough terrain.

Initially, Colorado hosted "Birdmen" who experimented with balloon ascensions. In 1894 the Army Signal Corps built a balloon station at Fort Logan in southwest Denver, which housed the nation's entire air force—a single tethered hydrogen-filled balloon. Denver's Overland Park hosted the first flight in a "heavier-than-air machine" in 1910 when French aviator Louis Paulhan made six short flights to the cheers of thousands of spectators.

Flying fever led many towns and individuals to rig up primitive airfields. Denver's first "aerodrome" opened in 1910 in the Park Hill neighborhood, where various other short-lived private airports were also established. In 1921 the Curtis-Humphreys Airplane Company launched Colorado's first commercial passenger service from its Park Hill aerodrome to Cheyenne, Wyoming, Estes Park, and the Broadmoor Hotel in Colorado Springs. This pioneer firm abandoned the business after a 1921 fire destroyed its hangar and three planes. Denver had at least nine different private airports before Denver Municipal Airport opened in 1929 and consolidated most air activity.

Post-office air-mail contracts first made flying profitable and led to the establishment in 1926 of Colorado's first postal route from Denver to Pueblo's Heinshon Field. Aviationists in Pueblo launched an annual air show in the 1940s and opened the Pueblo Historical Aircraft Society Museum in 1978. In 1927, Colorado Springs welcomed the first air-mail service to Nichols Field. The Springs also boasted a second airport, that of the local Alexander Aircraft Company, maker of the Eaglerock, a popular early airplane.

By 1930, Colorado had twenty-seven airfields and landing strips, ranging from the American Legion field in Akron to the original Lowry Army Air Corps Field in Park Hill. Eleven were municipally owned, while six were private. Eventually, Denver, Fremont, Garfield, Grand, Jackson, Jefferson, Lake, Las Animas, Mineral, Moffat, Montezuma, Routt, and Weld counties constructed airports.

By 1940 the number of airplanes in Colorado had grown from 91 to 143, and four more airports had opened. Following World War II, Colorado Springs, Pueblo, and La Junta bought local army air bases, which they converted to municipal airports. By 1960, Colorado boasted more air service to small communities than any other state; twelve cities offered regularly scheduled public flights, and thirty-two others provided call-and-demand private aviation.

The air-age aspirations of small towns were shot down in the 1980s when the Federal Aviation Administration deregulated airlines, allowing carriers to abandon less-profitable rural routes. Although smaller commuter airlines picked up some of the towns, regularly scheduled passenger service was abandoned to Canon City, Craig, Delta, Glenwood Springs, Grand Lake, Greeley, Fort Collins, La Junta, Leadville, Salida, and Trinidad. Many small airports deteriorated, and some closed, while bigger cities such as Denver, Durango, and Grand Junction improved or built new airports. As the map shows, the airports in Aspen, Cortez, Arapahoe and Douglas counties (Centennial), Telluride, and Steamboat Springs have all been built since 1940.

Denver Municipal Airport was renamed in 1944 for its sponsor, Mayor Benjamin Franklin Stapleton. By the 1980s Stapleton International had become the world's fifth busiest airport and Denver began building a new airport, which opened by 1994. Denver International, with its 55-square-mile site, is the nation's largest airport in terms of area and boosts the air age aspirations of the Highest State.

Table 1. Airport growth, 1950–1980 *(total number of passengers)*

Airport	1950	1960	1980
Alamosa	1,085	3,058	9,264
Aspen (Sardy Field)			79,937
Colorado Springs	14,088	42,141	276,119
Cortez	841	2,941	10,227
Denver Stapleton	243,437	906,929	9,615,785
Durango Municipal Airport	2,625	6,902	47,122
Grand Junction Walker Field	6,100	23,250	154,675
Gunnison	1,083	1,247	19,589
Lamar		1,054	1,752
Montrose	1,576	2,502	4,694
Pueblo	9,984	18,992	24,756
Steamboat Springs			11,619

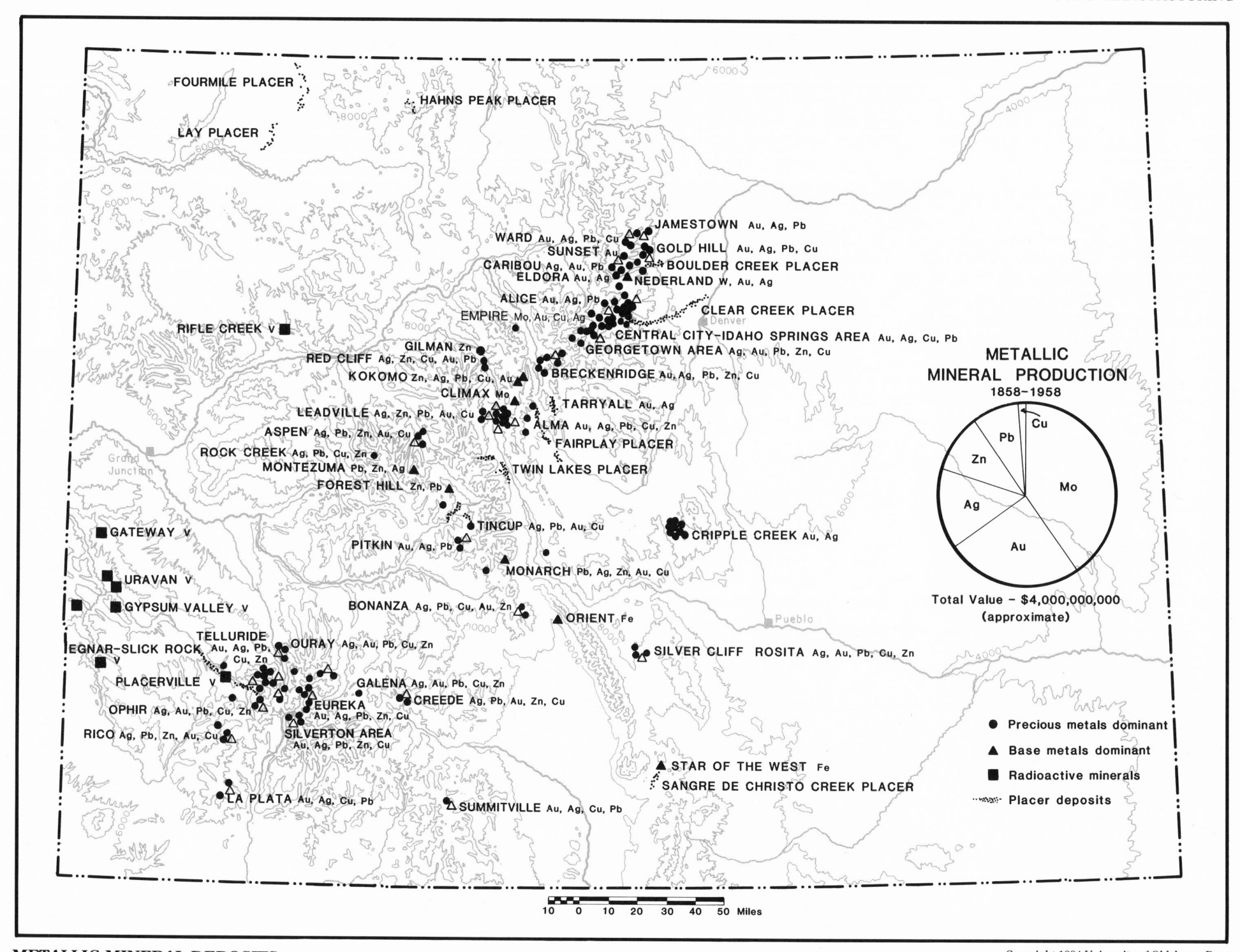

FOURMILE PLACER

HAHNS PEAK PLACER

LAY PLACER

JAMESTOWN Au, Ag, Pb
WARD Au, Ag, Pb, Cu
SUNSET Au GOLD HILL Au, Ag, Pb, Cu
CARIBOU Ag, Au, Pb BOULDER CREEK PLACER
ELDORA Au, Ag NEDERLAND W, Au, Ag
ALICE Au, Ag, Pb CLEAR CREEK PLACER
RIFLE CREEK v EMPIRE Mo, Au, Cu, Ag CENTRAL CITY-IDAHO SPRINGS AREA Au, Ag, Cu, Pb
GILMAN Zn GEORGETOWN AREA Ag, Au, Pb, Zn, Cu
RED CLIFF Ag, Zn, Cu, Au, Pb BRECKENRIDGE Au, Ag, Pb, Zn, Cu
KOKOMO Zn, Ag, Pb, Cu, Au
CLIMAX Mo
LEADVILLE Ag, Zn, Pb, Au, Cu TARRYALL Au, Ag
ASPEN Ag, Pb, Zn, Au, Cu ALMA Au, Ag, Pb, Cu, Zn
ROCK CREEK Ag, Pb, Cu, Zn FAIRPLAY PLACER
MONTEZUMA Pb, Zn, Ag
FOREST HILL Zn, Pb TWIN LAKES PLACER

GATEWAY v TINCUP Ag, Pb, Au, Cu CRIPPLE CREEK Au, Ag
PITKIN Au, Ag, Pb
URAVAN v
MONARCH Pb, Ag, Zn, Au, Cu
GYPSUM VALLEY v
BONANZA Ag, Pb, Cu, Au, Zn ORIENT Fe

TELLURIDE Au, Ag, Pb, Cu, Zn OURAY Ag, Au, Pb, Cu, Zn SILVER CLIFF ROSITA Ag, Au, Pb, Cu, Zn
EGNAR-SLICK ROCK v
PLACERVILLE v GALENA Ag, Au, Pb, Cu, Zn
OPHIR Ag, Au, Pb, Cu, Zn EUREKA Au, Ag, Pb, Zn, Cu CREEDE Ag, Pb, Au, Zn, Cu
RICO Ag, Pb, Zn, Au, Cu SILVERTON AREA Au, Ag, Pb, Zn, Cu

STAR OF THE WEST Fe
SANGRE DE CHRISTO CREEK PLACER
LA PLATA Au, Ag, Cu, Pb SUMMITVILLE Au, Ag, Cu, Pb

Grand Junction

Denver

Pueblo

METALLIC MINERAL PRODUCTION
1858–1958

Cu
Pb
Zn
Mo
Ag
Au

Total Value – $4,000,000,000
(approximate)

● Precious metals dominant
▲ Base metals dominant
■ Radioactive minerals
⋯ Placer deposits

Scale: 10 0 10 20 30 40 50 Miles

METALLIC MINERAL DEPOSITS

33. METALLIC MINERAL DEPOSITS

Gold discoveries in 1858–59 started a massive mineral hunt that put Colorado first among the states in total production of silver (Ag), molybdenum (Mo), and vanadium (V); second in gold (Au); third in tungsten (W); fourth in lead (Pb); sixth in zinc (Zn); and eight in copper (Cu). Various other metallic minerals, including iron (Fe), tungsten (W), and uranium (U), have swelled Colorado's total production to more than $4 billion.

As the map indicates, metallic mineral deposits are found in a band stretching northeast to southwest across the state from Boulder County to the San Juans. Within this mineral belt, mining districts occur as irregular clusters in certain mountain areas dominated by igneous rock.

Placer (surface) gold first lured prospectors to upper South Platte River tributaries such as Boulder, Cherry, and Clear creeks. Argonauts also panned the upper Arkansas River and its rich tributary, California Gulch. Side streams of the upper Colorado River, such as the Animas, Blue, Roaring Fork, San Miguel, and Snake rivers, likewise experienced mineral rushes.

As placer mining played out, Coloradans concentrated on lode (underground) mining, which transformed Central City, Leadville, Breckenridge, Ouray, Telluride, and Cripple Creek into multimillion-dollar jackpots. Colorado is second only to California in total gold production. Among the 505 major U.S. gold districts, 46 are in Colorado. Cripple Creek ranks second nationally, Central City, eleventh; Telluride, fourteenth; and Leadville, sixteenth.

Early silver discoveries at Georgetown and Caribou were followed by much richer finds in Leadville, Aspen, and the San Juan Mountains. The white metal became the most important industry in "the Silver State" until the Silver Panic of 1893. Colorado has seven of the twenty-five principal silver districts in the United States. Among the nation's silver producers, Leadville ranks fifth; Aspen, ninth; Red Cliff, eleventh; Creede, fourteenth; Telluride, fifteenth; Georgetown–Silver Plume, twenty-fourth; and Idaho Springs, twenty-fifth.

Molybdenum, rather than gold or silver, became Colorado's biggest metallic-mineral payoff. Low-grade ore from the Climax Mine, which opened north of Leadville in 1917, provided eighty percent of the world supply for decades. Another huge mine, the Urad near Empire, became a big producer during World War II. Molybdenum, used principally to strengthen steel, became a crucial component for automobiles and armaments. By 1958 the cumulative value of molybdenum production, as shown on the map pie chart, surpassed that of all other metallic minerals. The inevitable crash came during the 1980s when a glut on the world market arrested Colorado's moly boom.

Lead has long been mined with silver in Breckenridge and other areas, but large-scale production of lead-bearing ores, which often contain silver and gold, began, as the name indicates, in Leadville. Along with other Lake County mining centers, Leadville has yielded a third of Colorado's total lead production of more than $340 million. San Miguel, San Juan, Pitkin, and Eagle counties have also been major sources of lead, which is used for shot, as an alloy, and in plumbing and construction supplies, gasoline, and batteries, as well as other industrial capacities.

Zinc ranks fourth among Colorado metals. Once despised as a nuisance that hampered the smelting of silver, zinc has become important as a rust retardant in steel, as an alloy of copper in brass, and for die casting. Zinc emerged as a million-dollar-a-year industry by 1900 with major mines in Lake and Eagle counties, most notably the Eagle Mine in Gilman, the state's dominant zinc mine until it closed in 1981.

Copper, like zinc and lead, has been produced primarily as a by-product of precious metal mining in San Miguel, San Juan, Ouray, and Lake counties. This useful and ornamental metal is Colorado's seventh most important, with production ranking tenth nationally.

Gold and silver miners once cursed "that damn black iron," which proved to be tungsten. During World War I, however, military use of tungsten caused the price per pound to skyrocket from $0.45 in 1914 to $4.16 in 1918. During the wartime boom Caribou and Nederland in Boulder County produced 75 percent of the nation's supply.

The first discovery of pitchblende in the United States was at the Wood mine of Central City in 1871. Pitchblende contains both radium and uranium, two radioactive metals whose importance mushroomed during the 1950s. Most of the deposits, as well as associated vanadium, were in the Uravan mineral belt stretching from Gateway to Egnar near the Utah border.

Colorado is second only to California in mineral variety and total production. In addition to the metals mentioned above, Colorado's treasure chest contains manganese, bismuth, cobalt, nickel, arsenic, antimony, and cadmium. By the 1980s sand and gravel had become the most valuable mined resources, surpassing even gold, molybdenum, and silver production. Metallic minerals, which gave rise to the state of Colorado and were the primary resource until about 1910, have been eclipsed in recent decades by nonmetallic riches of the earth.

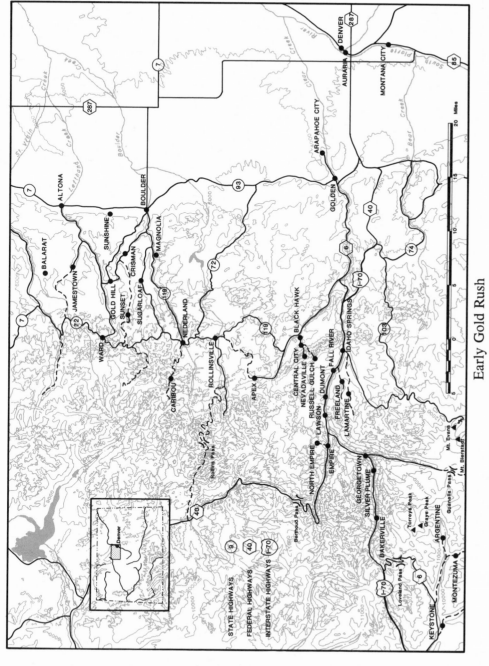

Early Gold Rush

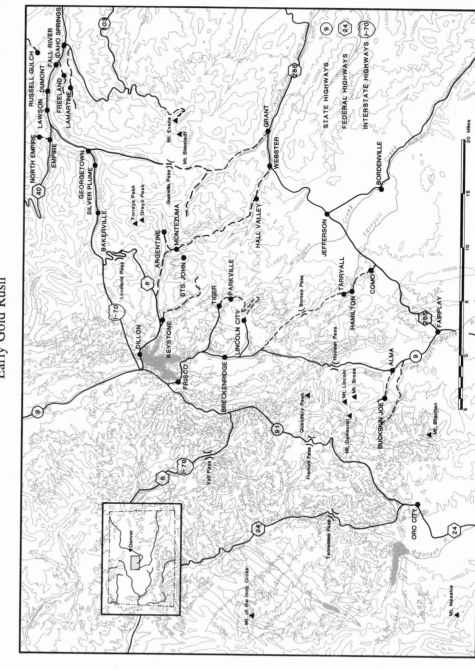

Later Gold Rush

GOLD RUSH, 1858–1870s

William Green Russell's party of veteran Georgia and California gold miners first found gold in the summer of 1858 in the South Platte River near Cherry Creek. By fall Montana City, Auraria, and Denver City had popped up on the present site of metropolitan Denver. By the next spring an estimated one hundred thousand fortune seekers were headed for the diggings.

Americans welcomed the golden rumors drifting out of the Rockies. The 1849 California gold rush had left the country highly susceptible to what Mark Twain called the "Californian sudden-riches disease." The panic of 1857 and the approaching Civil War also inspired many to leave "the States" for the land of gold. "Wheelbarrow" McGraw went west telling his friends they could find him camped beside Cherry Creek, in which he parked his wheelbarrow, expecting it to be gold-plated by the auriferous waters. "Wheelbarrow" McGraw and thousands of others were disappointed in Denver, where Russell's $200 discovery proved to be the only significant find. Thousands of "Go-Backs" damned the "Pike's Peak Hoax" and hightailed it home. Persistent prospectors headed up the Front Range canyons and found gold in Clear Creek in 1859. By summer ten thousand people flooded Gregory Gulch. In that golden ditch, Central City emerged as the hub, surrounded by mines, mining camps, and the robust towns of Black Hawk, Nevadaville, and Russell Gulch.

This pattern of a central city surrounded by smaller mining camps became a common one. So did the miners' form of self-government established in Central City in 1860. During the next two decades more than one hundred mining districts sprang up in Colorado. Miners wrote their own district constitutions and laws, elected officials, and created miners courts to protect the claims of working miners. They standardized placer and lode mining claims. After staking a claim a miner had to record it with the mining-district officials. Then the claim taker had to make certain improvements and pay taxes to retain the claim.

Hastily organized miners courts settled contested claims, disallowing appeals and enforcing punishments rapidly. Claim jumpers were whipped or banished, while murderers were turned over to "Judge Lynch." One thief in the Central City district was lashed and banished after being shaved on "the right side of his head and also the left side of his whiskers and mustache." Such fast, simple, and effective frontier government was replaced in 1861 by conventional law and order.

Central City called itself "the richest square mile on earth" and was at least the richest in Colorado until the Leadville boom of the 1880s. Central City and its neighboring camps became the population center of the territory before many fortune seekers moved to the south fork of Clear Creek, hoping to strike it rich at Idaho Springs, Lamartine, Freeland, Fall River, Empire, Lawson, Dumont, Georgetown, Silver Plume, or Bakerville.

Clear Creek bonanzas inspired prospectors to test other waters. From Boulder, founded by gold seekers in 1858, parties pushed up Boulder Creek and its tributaries. Gold camps arose at Balarat, Gold Hill, Jamestown, Magnolia, Nederland, Sunset, Ward, and elsewhere.

Argonauts also found gold in 1859 in the headwaters of the South Platte River. After gold grubbers staked out all possible claims at Tarryall, latecomers nicknamed it Graball. They founded another town nearby, Fairplay, where everyone would have a chance at a working claim. Fairplay prospered, as did the other Park County mining towns of Alma, Bordenville, Buckskin Joe, Como, Grant, Hall Valley, Hamilton, Jefferson, and Webster.

From South Park some prospectors used "snowshoes" (early-day wooden skis) to cross the continental divide to the Blue River diggings. Breckenridge, Lincoln City, and Frisco on the Blue River; Tiger and Parkville on the Swan River; and Dillon, Keystone, Montezuma, Saints John, and Argentine in the Snake River Valley sprang up in Summit County. Breckenridge produced some of the purest gold as well as Colorado's largest pure nugget, the fourteen-pound "Tom's Baby" now on exhibit at the Denver Museum of Natural History.

Another major gold producer of the early 1860s was Oro City on the headwaters of the Arkansas. There Abe Lee found the yellow metal in California Gulch, which he predicted would rival the wealth found by forty-niners in the Golden State. After a brief boom, which produced several million dollars in gold, Oro City nearly became a ghost town before reemerging in the 1870s after the discovery of silver in nearby Leadville.

Between 1859 and 1864 the gold rush glittered. Then surface gold played out, leaving miners with lode mines and hard-to-process gold ores. Not until 1869 did Nathaniel P. Hill, a chemistry professor, open the Blackhawk Smelter. Here he used the Swansea smelting process successfully to extract gold from complex ores, and handsome profits from a risky business. Although Central City, Cripple Creek, and a few other towns continued to mine gold for decades, most of the gold camps lasted only a few years. After the pay dirt played out, these communities switched to silver or some other source of livelihood, or took their last gasp.

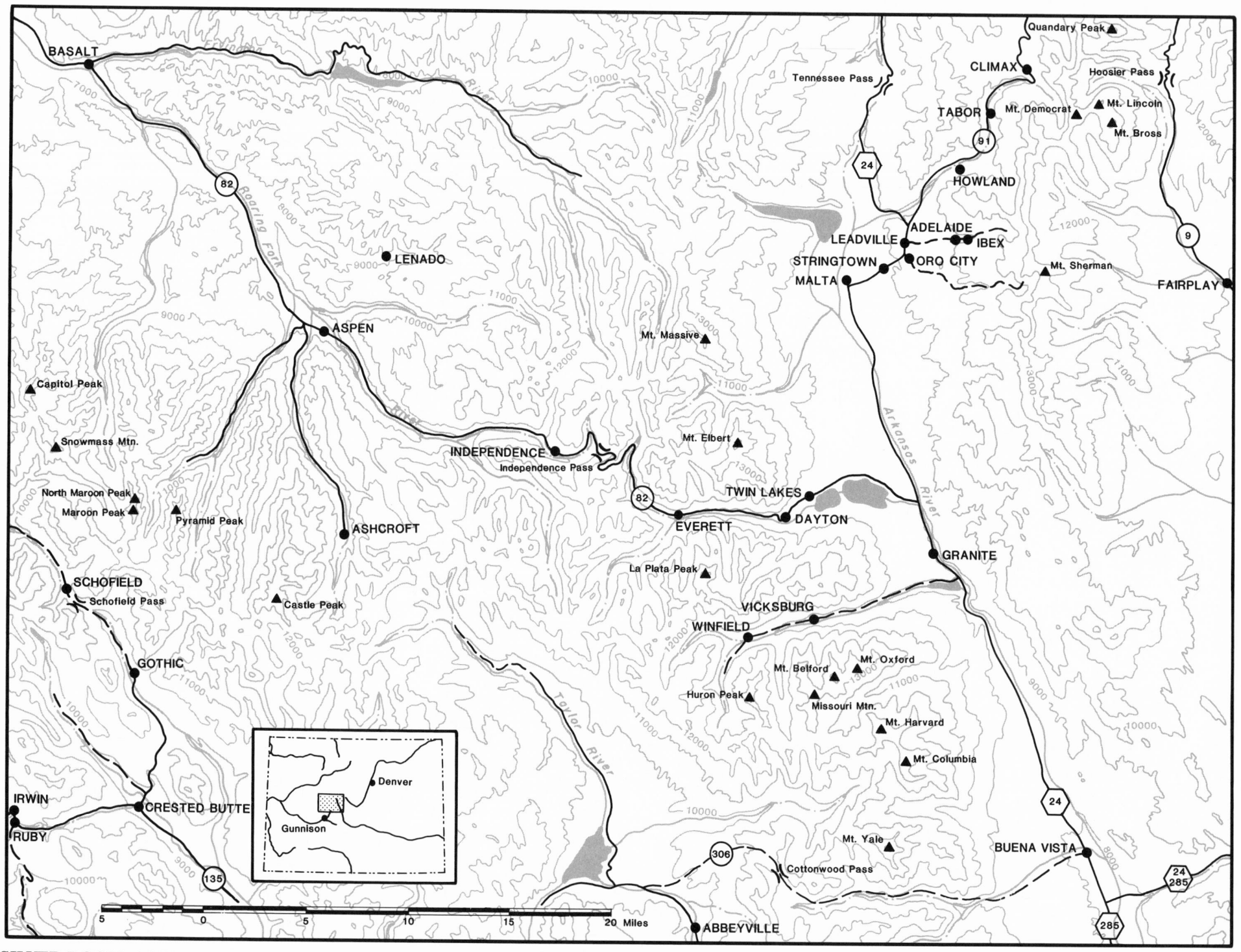

SILVER BOOM, 1870s–1893

35. SILVER BOOM, 1870s–1893

Gold gave Colorado its start, but by the 1880s silver shone brighter. The price of gold, set by the federal government in 1792, was $20.76 per ounce, while silver was pegged at one-sixteenth of the price of gold, or about $1.40 an ounce.

In Colorado silver was first mined profitably from the Belmont Lode near Georgetown in 1864 and at Caribou in 1869 (see Map 34). Silver's bonanza days began late in the 1870s in the Leadville district, which ultimately yielded one-third of the Silver State's production. Gold miners at Oro City in the 1860s had damned the black sands clogging their pans and sluices. Then in the mid-1870s they found that the black sand assayed as high-grade silver ore, a discovery that triggered Colorado's second great mineral rush.

The "Magic City" of Leadville sprang up overnight in 1878. In 1880 this two-mile-high city had more saloons (106) than Denver and almost as many people. Million-dollar mines crowded California, Stray Horse, and Evans gulches on the east side of town.

By 1890, Leadville shared the argentiferous headwaters of the Arkansas River with a dozen lesser mining towns.

Leadville, "the Mother of Millionaires," enriched characters such as the Guggenheims, Molly and J. J. Brown, Charles Boettcher, and Horace and Augusta Tabor. The mad rush to Leadville spilled into neighboring Pitkin, Gunnison, and Chaffee counties. A stray burro supposedly led prospectors to what became Vicksburg and Winfield in 1881.

Silver seekers swarmed up Twin Lake Creek, where the old gold town and early Lake County seat of Dayton was eclipsed by nearby Twin Lakes (1879) and Everett (1881). Prospectors pushed up Twin Lake Creek and over Independence Pass to strike silver on July 4, 1880, at a place they named Independence.

Bigger bonanzas were unearthed in the Roaring Fork River Valley, where 1879 discoveries led town promoters to establish Ute City, Roaring Fork City, and Ute Springs. Consolidated as Aspen in 1880, those settlements emerged as a city of 5,108 by 1890. Aspen rivaled even Leadville in silver production, and boasted the largest nugget in the world, a 1,870-pound chunk that was ninety-three percent silver, from the Smuggler Mine. Finds on nearby Castle Creek gave birth to Ashcroft (1880), while Lenado (1881) served mines on Woody Creek.

Clear Creek and Park counties, settings for 1860s gold rushes, also emerged as rich silver producers in the 1870s and 1880s. Events of 1893, however, turned the silver boom to bust. The U.S. government had demonetized silver in 1873, shifting from a bimetallic to a gold standard. To placate silver supporters, Washington continued to subsidize silver mining by vigorous purchase programs, including the Sherman Silver Purchase Act of 1890. In 1893, when the Sherman Act was repealed, the price of silver sank to less than sixty cents an ounce. It would not return to a dollar an ounce until the 1960s. Many of the silver miners, who had unearthed over $300 million by 1893, turned to other pursuits, while many of the silver towns turned to ghosts.

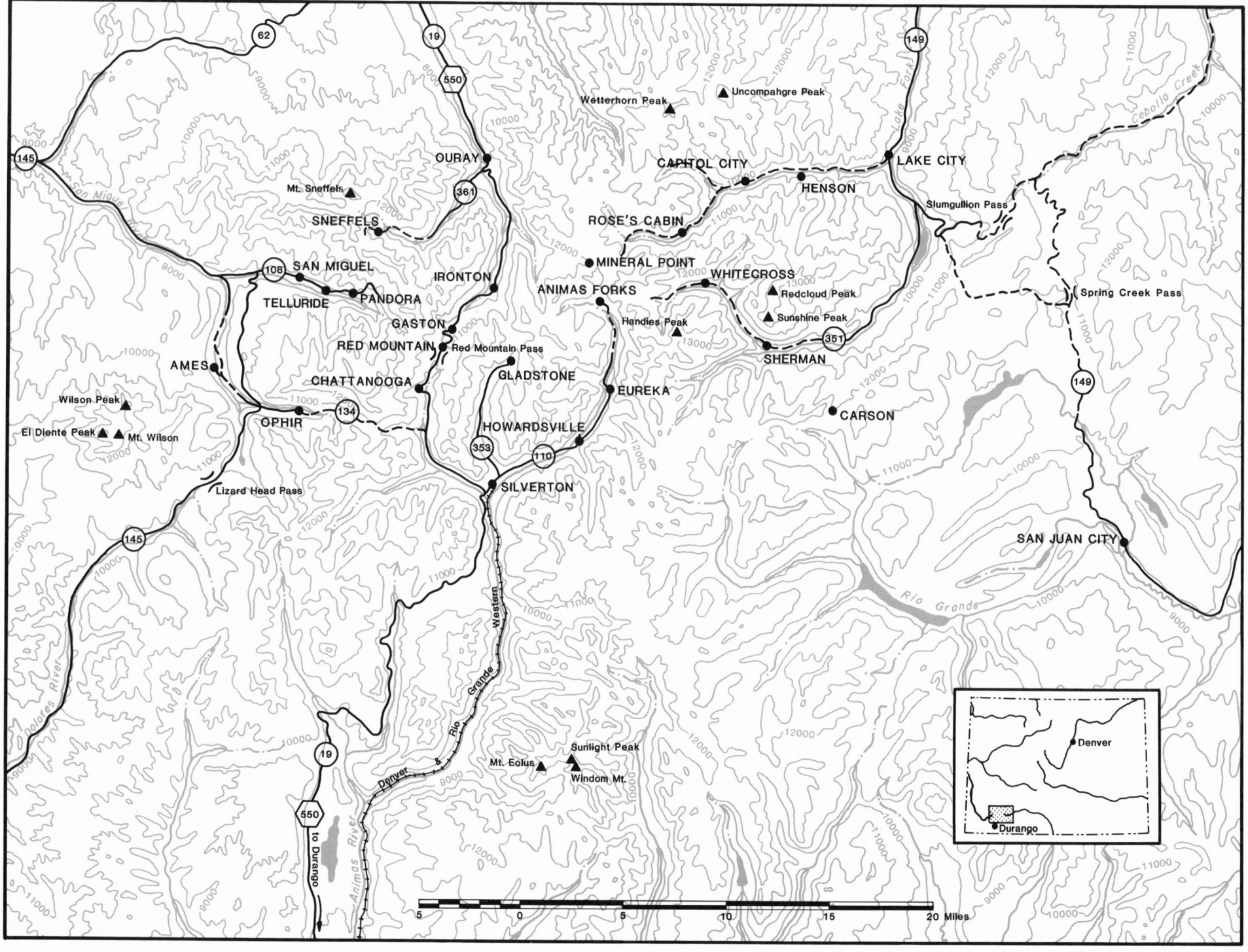

THE SAN JUANS

36. THE SAN JUANS

The soaring, snow-capped summits of the San Juan Mountains, rich in ore and lore, are visible from one hundred miles away. Here Alfred Packer, Colorado's celebrated cannibal, feasted on five fellow gold seekers. Slightly more civilized prospectors founded a hundred gold and silver towns, most of which are now skeletons also.

Spanish explorers had found gold and silver in the San Juan Mountains of southwestern Colorado, but the 1859 gold rush led to the first serious mining effort. Hundreds of gold hunters trekked through the uncharted mountains to the headwaters of the Animas River. Bitterly disappointed, these argonauts denounced the 1860s false start as the "San Juan Humbug."

Other early prospectors followed the Rio Grande west from Del Norte (1873), the gateway for foot, horse, mule, wagon, and stage traffic into the San Juans. Not until Nicholas Creede struck silver in a side gorge of the upper Rio Grande in 1889 did Creede and several smaller Mineral County towns emerge during Colorado's last major silver rush.

After the Utes ceded the San Juans in 1873, miners reexamined the upper Animas River regions, finding gold near Howardsville (1874) and "silver by the ton" at Silverton (1875). Soon the headwaters of the Animas bustled with mining centers such as Animas Forks (1875), Gladstone (1878), Mineral Point (1875), and Eureka (1875), where the Sunnyside Mine has been a major Colorado producer for over one hundred years.

Two prospectors from the Silverton area found rich silver veins at what became Ouray (1875). By 1880 Ouray had a population of 864, making it the largest town in the San Juans. Telluride and Silverton later caught up with Ouray, and all three towns peaked between 1900 and 1910 with populations approaching 2,500, while Lake City and Creede never reached the 1,000 mark. Ouray thrived because of long-lived, multimillion-dollar gold mines such as the Camp Bird near Sneffels (1895) and the Idarado near Red Mountain (1883).

Golden gravel on the headwaters of the San Miguel River gave birth to Telluride (1880), a center for rich gold mines such as the Liberty Bell, the Smuggler-Union, and the Tomboy. To power the Gold King mine, Lucien L. Nunn installed an electrical generator using alternating current at Ames in 1891, a first in the history of electric power.

Lake City on the Lake Fork of the Gunnison River popped up during the 1875 silver rush to the Lake San Cristobal region. Henson, Capitol City, and Rose's Cabin sprouted as mining camps on Henson Creek, which also served as a route to the richer mines of Ouray, San Juan, and San Miguel counties. Lake City and two dozen other Hinsdale County mining camps enjoyed brief booms. Carson (1889), a precarious silver camp perched on the continental divide, gave up the ghost early, as did Sherman and Whitecross. By 1920, Lake City was the sole survivor—the only community with a post office in Hinsdale County.

The "Silvery San Juans" survived the Silver Crash of 1893 by concentrating on other minerals, especially gold. Aerial trams carried ore from mountainside mines to huge mills located along the tracks of the Rio Grande Southern, the Silverton, the Silverton Northern, and the Silverton, Gladstone, and Northerly—four tiny narrow-gauge lines that tackled vertical mountainsides where even the D & RG feared to lay track.

Durango (1880), founded by the D & RG as a rail hub, emerged as the smelter city and trade center of the San Juans. By developing agriculture, coal mining, education (Fort Lewis College), and tourism, Durango thrived. It has remained the urban center for southwestern Colorado.

By 1920 the mines had played out, with a few notable exceptions such as the Camp Bird, the Idarado, and the Sunnyside. Mineral and San Juan, like Hinsdale, became one-town counties, haunted by the possibility of becoming ghost counties. Today San Juaners survive mainly by mining the tourists now rushing into these remote and breathtakingly beautiful highlands.

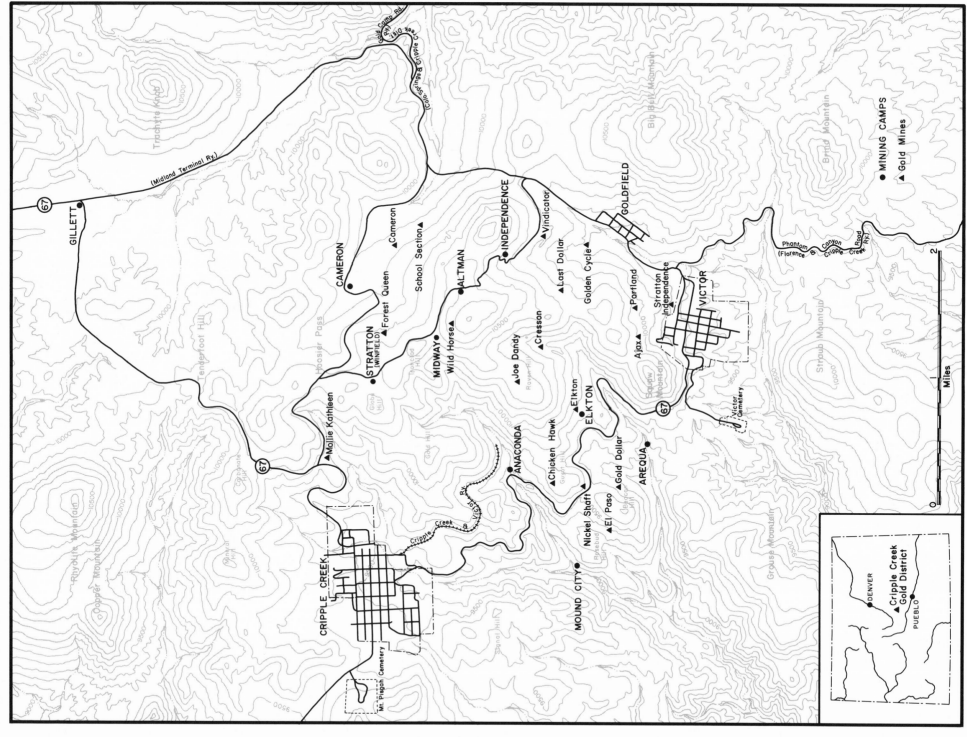

CRIPPLE CREEK GOLD

MINING CAMPS
Gold Mines

GILLETT

CAMERON
▲Cameron
School Section▲
▲Forest Queen
STRATTON
(WINFIELD)
MIDWAY
Wild Horse▲
ALTMAN
INDEPENDENCE
▲Vindicator
▲Last Dollar
Golden Cycle▲
GOLDFIELD
▲Joe Dandy
▲Cresson
Ajax▲ ▲Portland
Stratton
Independence
VICTOR
Victor
Cemetery
▲Mollie Kathleen
ANACONDA
▲Chicken Hawk
ELKTON
▲Elkton
Nickel Shaft▲
▲El Paso
▲Gold Dollar
AREQUA
MOUND CITY
CRIPPLE CREEK
Mt. Pisgah Cemetery

Trachyte Knob
Big Bull Mountain
Bmd Mountain
Straub Mountain
Grouse Mountain
Squaw Mountain
Rhyolite Mountain
Copper Mountain
Tenderfoot Hill
Hoosier Pass
Cognate Hill
Mineral Hill
Signal Hill
Globe Hill
Gold Hill
Bull Hill
Guyot Hill
Raven Hill
Beacon Hill
Rosebud Hill

(Midland Terminal Ry.)
Gold Camp Rd.
Phantom Canyon
(Florence & Cripple Creek Road Ry.)
Cripple Creek
Victor Ry.
67

0 1 2
Miles

DENVER
Cripple Creek
Gold District
PUEBLO

37. CRIPPLE CREEK GOLD

The last and richest Colorado gold district lay on the 9,500-foot western flank of Pikes Peak. Ironically, prospectors took thirty years to discover the bowl of gold hidden beside the mountain that gave the Pikes Peak gold rush its name. Even Ferdinand V. Hayden, the famed surveyor and geologist, who reported that Cripple Creek drained an ancient volcanic crater, never realized that it was veined with one of the world's greatest gold deposits.

Not until 1890 did "Crazy Bob" Womack, a poor and only occasionally sober cowboy, find an outcropping of color. Womack had come to Colorado from Kentucky at the age of seventeen, hoping to make his fortune in the Clear Creek mines around Idaho Springs. Busted, Womack took a job tending cattle on a ranch along Cripple Creek, a rocky stream notorious for tripping animals and men. While herding cows, Womack also hunted gold. He took promising ore samples to an assay office in Colorado Springs and spent the proceeds at the nearest saloon. Few believed his furry-tongued tales of Cripple Creek gold.

When Womack located the El Paso lode in Poverty Gulch with ores assaying at $250 a ton, his shack and the cattle ranch were overrun by gold seekers. Part of the ranch was platted as the city of Cripple Creek in 1891. During the next decade thousands of people and three railroads rushed in, and two dozen million-dollar mines were located. Ten post-office towns soon sprang up in the Cripple Creek District, a 25-square-mile region whose population peaked at around 30,000 in the early 1900s. Gross gold production also peaked in 1900 at $18 million, making Cripple Creek "the World's Greatest Gold Camp." Not until the 1920s did Witwatersrand, South Africa; Porcupine and Kirkland Lake, in Ontario, Canada; and the Homestake Mine, in Lead, South Dakota, all surpass Cripple Creek in total gold production.

Cripple Creek blossomed as an instant city complete with streetcars, suburbs, and a stock exchange. Even two devastating 1896 fires did not stop growth of this golden city, whose population peaked in 1900 at 10,147. Miners' homes climbed the hills in every direction. Grand hotels and splendiferous saloons lined Bennett Avenue, the main street, while an opera house, elegant brothels, and gilded gambling halls crowded Myers Avenue.

Of the Cripple Creek millionaires, the most unforgettable was Winfield Scott Stratton. Once a poor carpenter, Stratton ultimately sold his Independence Mine to British interests for $11 million, the highest price ever paid for a Colorado mine. Stratton, an eccentric bachelor, fancied women, whiskey, and philanthropy. He supposedly bought a bicycle for every laundry girl in Colorado Springs, gave $5,000 to poor "Crazy Bob" Womack, cleared title to the Matchless Mine for the impoverished Baby Doe Tabor, and,

upon his death in 1902, left $6 million to establish the Myron Stratton Home for aged indigents in Colorado Springs. In the Cripple Creek District the towns of Stratton (1900) and Independence (1899) were named for him and for his legendary gold mine.

Victor (1894), the second largest city in the Cripple Creek District, prided itself on being "the City of Mines and Miners." Victor, like Cripple Creek, was at the center of the 1894 and 1903–1904 labor wars. Those conflicts, the rapid extraction of easily recovered gold, and the frequent flooding of the mines brought Cripple Creek's golden days to an end by the 1920s. Despite occasional revivals and the introduction of new processes such as cyanide leaching to reprocess old mine dumps, population and production declined steadily.

Today the Cripple Creek driving loop shown on the map is a favorite of ghost-town buffs. In Cripple Creek burros roam unpaved streets as unofficial garbage collectors. Two Victorian hotels survive—the Palace and the Imperial—and the latter produces a famed summer melodrama. The old Teller County Hospital has been rehabilitated as the roomy Hospitality House, and the old high school also has been recycled as hotel rooms. The Midland Terminal Depot has been converted to the Cripple Creek District Museum. Cripple Creek also offers underground tours of the Mollie Kathleen Mine. Colorado's only brothel-museum, the Homestead, is the sole survivor of the Myers Avenue red-light district. Victor, a city mostly of abandoned buildings, is a spectral reminder that the Pike's Peak gold rush was ultimately a bust.

Of the towns on this map, all but Cripple Creek and Victor are among the three hundred Colorado mining camps that are ghost towns today. Silver mining never recovered from the crash of 1893, and gold production revived only slightly after 1933, when the U.S. government set the price at $34 an ounce. When Pres. Gerald R. Ford removed federal restrictions on the private ownership of gold and allowed the price to float in 1975, it shot up to $875 an ounce. Some gold mines reopened, but many closed again when the price fell to $300 to $400 an ounce in the 1980s. Between 1858 and 1958, Colorado produced gold valued at $914,717,009—about three percent of the world's total gold supply. Over half of Colorado's gold came from Cripple Creek, which still boasts that it was "the World's Greatest Gold Camp."

Since limited-stakes gambling began in Cripple Creek in 1991, the town has seen a new boom and the rejuvenation of many historic structures to house casinos jammed with black jack and poker tables and slot machines. Today's real-estate and construction boom echoes the original rush when fortune seekers first bet on a golden gamble called Cripple Creek.

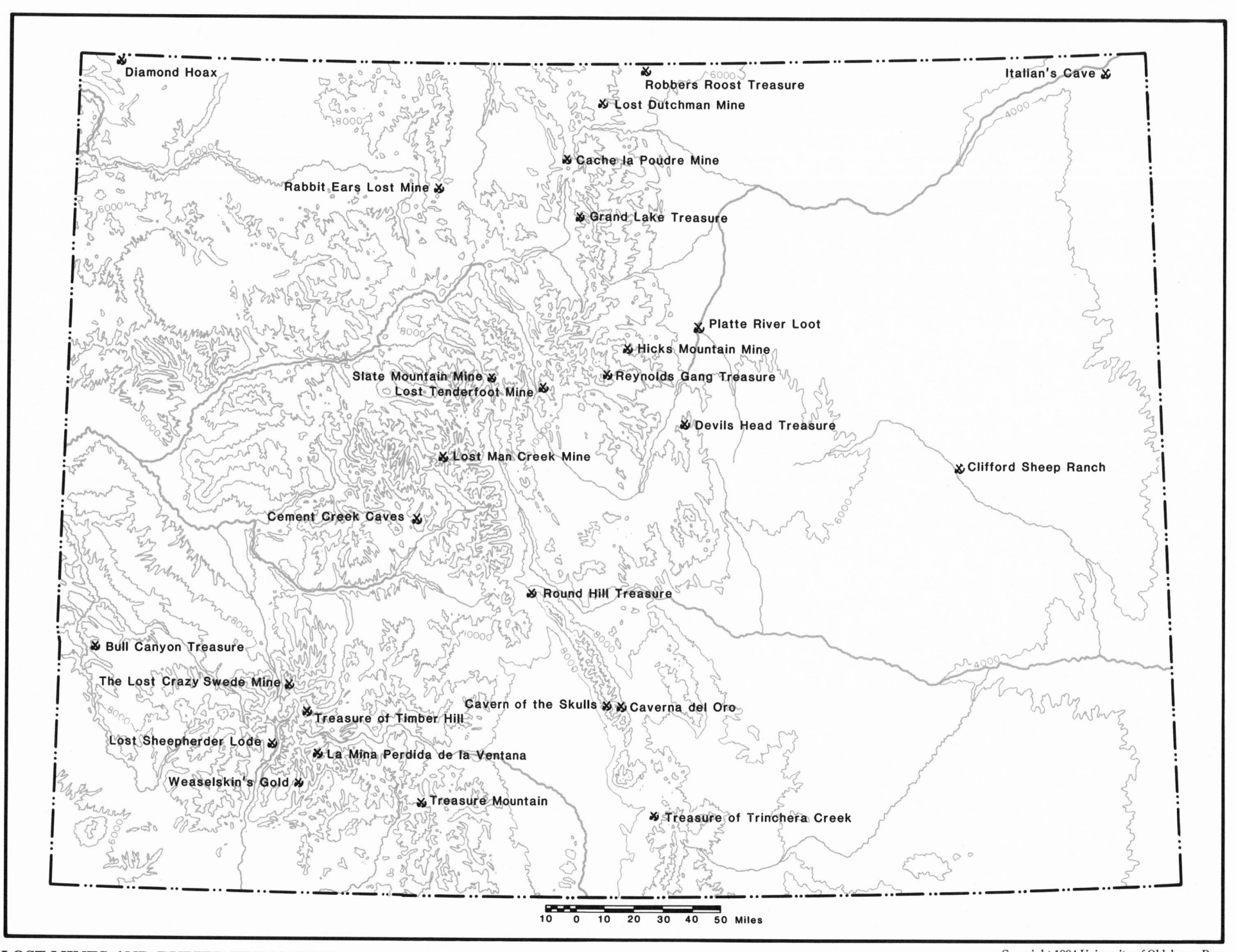

Diamond Hoax

Robbers Roost Treasure

Italian's Cave

Lost Dutchman Mine

Cache la Poudre Mine

Rabbit Ears Lost Mine

Grand Lake Treasure

Platte River Loot

Hicks Mountain Mine

Slate Mountain Mine

Reynolds Gang Treasure

Lost Tenderfoot Mine

Devils Head Treasure

Lost Man Creek Mine

Clifford Sheep Ranch

Cement Creek Caves

Round Hill Treasure

Bull Canyon Treasure

The Lost Crazy Swede Mine

Cavern of the Skulls   Caverna del Oro

Treasure of Timber Hill

Lost Sheepherder Lode

La Mina Perdida de la Ventana

Weaselskin's Gold

Treasure Mountain

Treasure of Trinchera Creek

10 0 10 20 30 40 50 Miles

LOST MINES AND BURIED TREASURES

38. LOST MINES AND BURIED TREASURES

Thousands of gold and silver mines dot Colorado, which abounds with tales of lost mines and buried loot. Treasure seekers should keep in mind Mark Twain's definition of a mine as a hole in the ground owned by a liar. Yet these tales persist, and occasionally a lucky treasure hunter stumbles upon a lost bonanza, inspiring interest and new searches.

Probably the best known of Colorado's mythical lost fortunes are those of the Reynolds Gang, the Devils Head Treasure, the Spanish stash on Treasure Mountain, and the Caverna del Oro. Of more than one hundred Colorado lost-mine and buried-treasure legends, the following are among the most persistent:

Italian's Cave. Uberto Gabello, a former miner, enlarged the natural cavern five miles south of Julesburg for his stash.

Clifford Sheep Ranch Treasure. A triangle of gravestones marks the buried bonanza in the ghost town of Clifford, once known as Mirage.

Robbers Roost Treasure. Bandits preying on Overland Trail traffic used this nearly impregnable natural fortress at the end of a rocky path.

Lost Dutchman Mine. A Dutchman and an Irishman found this fabulous gold lode, but both went to their graves without revealing the location.

Cache la Poudre Lost Mine. Near the headwaters of the river named for hidden (but recovered) gunpowder lies a lost lode reputedly marked with the bones of a dead ox.

Grand Lake Treasure. A Dutch oven full of gold buried here in the 1850s should have been found by now.

Rabbit Ears Lost Mine. This lost digging near Rabbit Ears Pass has been rediscovered without the accompanying sacks of gold ore.

Diamond Hoax. Fortunes were lost on this corporate scam exposed by the famous geologist Clarence King.

Platte River Loot. Hypnotists and spiritualists failed to find this supposed Denver bonanza, later unearthed by a storm.

Hicks Mountain Mine. An eastern tenderfoot discovered—and lost—this lode near Mount Evans one day in 1895.

Reynolds Gang Treasure. John Reynolds and eight Rebels raided gold-carrying stages to help finance the Confederate cause, reputedly hiding some of the bullion in Handcart Gulch.

Devils Head Treasure. Double-eagle gold pieces amounting to $60,000 were stolen from a government train car and hidden somewhere in this rocky formation.

Slate Mountain Mine. One of Colorado's earliest mines still hides its treasures.

Lost Tenderfoot Mine. Tenderfeet who find rich gold deposits and then forget the location are probably the richest source of lost-treasure legends.

Lost Man Creek Mine. A prospector who showed up in Leadville with rich gold ore later was killed by an Independence Pass avalanche. His discovery, never relocated, was along the Roaring Fork tributary named for him.

Cement Creek Caves. These are actually grottoes where stolen loot was found in 1883.

Round Hill Treasure. Successful miners pursued by Utes left a donkey skin full of gold buried here.

Cavern of the Skulls. At the head of Deadman Creek, above Deadman Cow Camp, in what some call Deadman Cave, prospectors found human skeletons and gold.

Caverna del Oro. This often-explored cave once sheltered Spaniards, who marked its entrance with a Maltese cross.

Treasure of Trinchera Creek. A Fort Garland paymaster, pursued by Utes, threw a yet-to-be-found strongbox of gold into the creek.

Treasure Mountain. About 1790 a large, but unconfirmed, French expedition reputedly buried a fortune in gold here.

Weaselskin's Gold. Weaselskin, a Ute with little use for gold, found pay dirt that awaits rediscovery on Vallecito Creek.

La Mina Perdida de la Ventana. This is said to be one of the richest of the lost Spanish mines.

Treasure of Timber Hill. Two bandits of the 1880s buried here four bars of bullion that have yet to be unearthed.

Lost Crazy Swede Mine. In 1906 a Swede discovered this rich gold mine only to lose it and his mind.

Lost Sheepherder Lode. Sasario, a Mexican sheepherder, found this still-untapped bonanza in the Upper Lime Creek Basin.

Bull Canyon Treasure. Hermit Harry Huff was murdered after burying his still-undiscovered fortune in these parts.

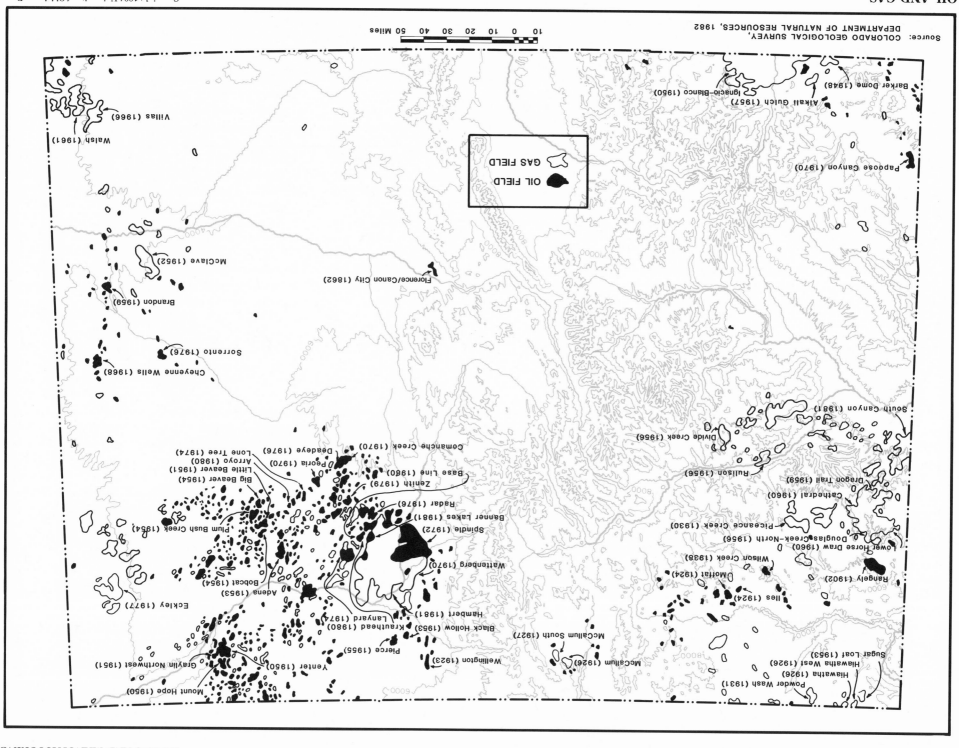

Source: COLORADO GEOLOGICAL SURVEY,
DEPARTMENT OF NATURAL RESOURCES, 1982

39. OIL AND GAS

Oil has been around for eons, but until recently people did not have much use for the slimy black stuff. Native Americans sometimes skimmed it from surface pools for face paint; Spaniards used it for waterproofing and for lubricating axle wheels; Yankee pioneers burned it in lamps and used it against dandruff.

Colorado, the second state to produce oil commercially, has been among the top ten producers nationally. Commercial use began when Alexander M. Cassidy developed an "oil spring" near Florence in 1862, three years after the first U.S. oil well was dug at Titusville, Pennsylvania. To exploit the Florence Field, Cassidy formed a firm that evolved into the Continental Oil Company, or CONOCO. Headquartered in Denver until the 1930s, CONOCO inadvertently erected the first Colorado gas station in 1909 when two large hot-water boilers were put on the warehouse platform and filled with gas to fuel autos.

Oil became important for more than illumination and lubrication after the automobile age dawned in 1900. Big oil corporations converged on Colorado after the 1901 discovery of rich fields near Boulder and Rangely. By the 1920s oil wells had become more profitable than gold and silver mining combined. Discovery and development accelerated during the 1920s after openings of the Wellington Field near Fort Collins and the Moffat Field south of Craig. In 1925 yearly crude-oil production exceeded one million barrels for the first time. Production soared after World War II, climbing from 1.7 million barrels in 1940 to a record 58 million barrels in 1956. Another boom in oil drilling, production, and refining came after the 1973 Arab oil embargo pushed gas prices over a dollar a gallon.

The 1970s spurt of domestic oil drilling and production pumped up many subsidiary businesses ranging from law firms to wildcat drillers like Marvin Davis and Philip Anschutz, two Denver oil billionaires. Denver began to dream of eclipsing Houston as America's oil hub. Oil refineries thrived in Commerce City, a Denver suburb, and in Florence. Big oil firms either were headquartered in Denver or maintained offices there, fueling an eruption of high-rise office towers downtown.

During the 1970s mammoth oil-shale extraction and refining operations were launched in Garfield and Rio Blanco counties around Rulison. Colorado supposedly contains enough oil shale to satisfy all of America's energy needs. Oil shale had been discovered and successfully processed in the early 1900s—after Mike Callahan's memorable housewarming. Everyone gathered in Mike's newly finished cabin, the story goes, only to flee when his oil-shale fireplace burst into flames. "The rock that burns" attracted a good deal of attention, but it proved very expensive to squeeze a few drops of oil from a ton of shale.

After the 1973 energy crisis, EXXON, the world's largest corporation, with several partners, began a $5 billion program to wring oil out of western-Colorado shale. Boom turned to bust on Black Sunday, May 22, 1982, when EXXON abruptly abandoned the project.

EXXON's exit climaxed a regional bust triggered by the drop of crude-oil prices from $42 per barrel in 1979 to $9 in 1983 after Middle Eastern oil exporters flooded the world market. The oil crash exacerbated a statewide recession in the mid-1980s, showing that Colorado's extractive industries remain vulnerable to fluctuations in international resource markets.

Oil's sister resource, natural gas, usually lies trapped in rock formations above oil deposits. Although gas had been found in the Florence Field and elsewhere in Colorado, the Public Service Company of Colorado did not start providing natural gas to customers until 1928. Natural gas was cleaner, cheaper, and more efficient than either coal or manufactured gas. Partly due to the popularity of natural gas for heating homes and businesses, the coal industry gradually was replaced as Colorado's major extractive industry by oil and gas. By 1950 major Eastern Slope cities, and Craig, Durango, Grand Junction, and Rangely on the Western Slope, had gas for heating and cooking. By the 1990s gas pipelines reached most parts of Colorado.

Oil and natural-gas fields, as the maps shows, are concentrated on the corners and edges of Colorado, not in the gold- and silver-laced central mountains. Rangely has been far and away the richest oil field, producing over half of the state's black gold. Wattenberg-Spindle, near Longmont, has been the richest natural-gas field, followed by Ignacio-Blanco in southwestern Colorado. Florence, the pioneer field, is waning, although it still ranks among the state's top ten for all-time oil production, along with Wilson Creek, Adena, Spindle, Plum Bush Creek, Iles, Little Beaver, Graylin Northwest, and Big Beaver. Oil production tapered off after the mid 1980s, but natural-gas production has been steadier.

Despite ups and downs since the original 1920s boom, it seems safe to say that, as long as America remains addicted to gasoline-powered engines and natural-gas energy, oil and gas will remain Colorado's most-lucrative natural resources.

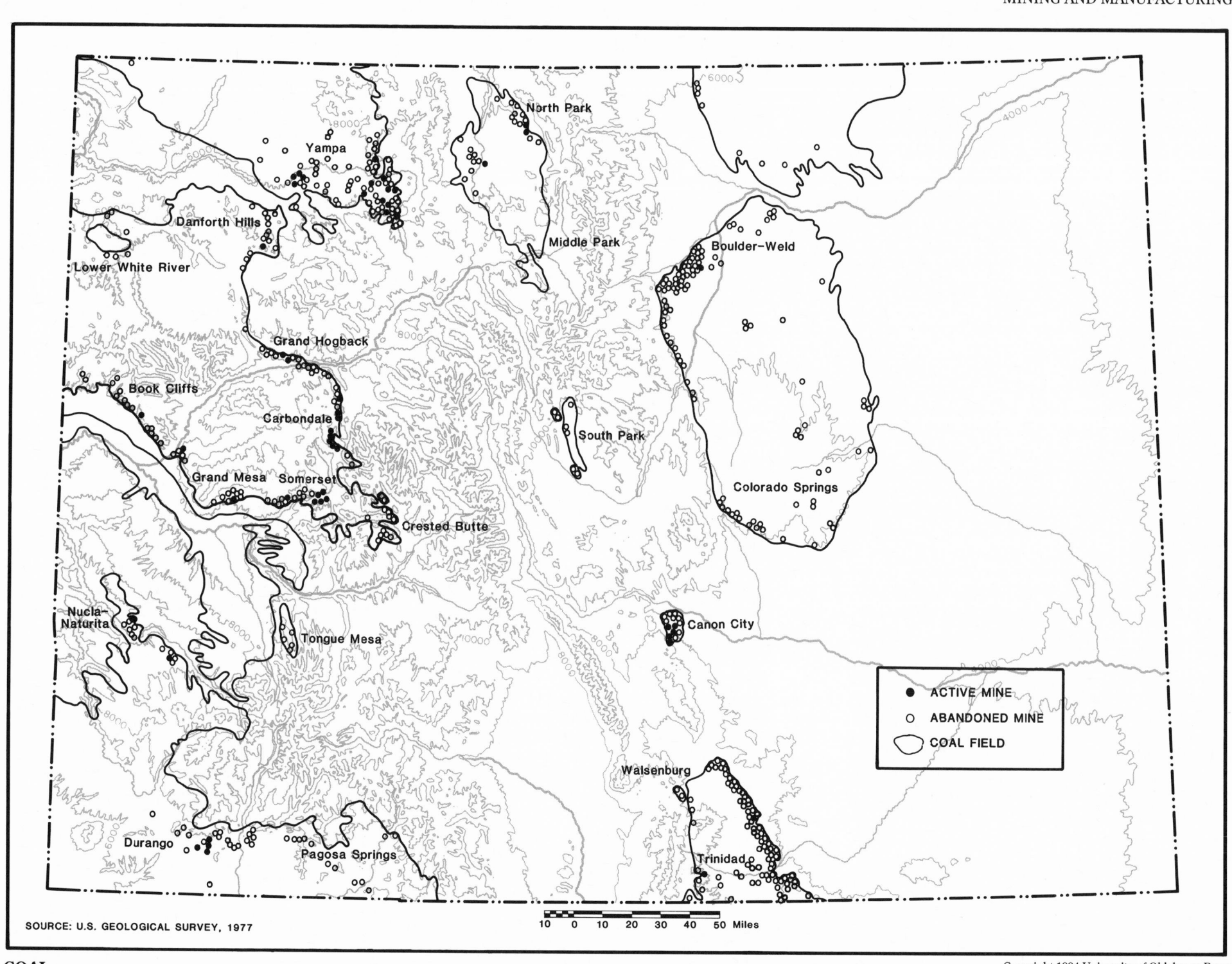

North Park

Yampa

Danforth Hills

Lower White River

Middle Park

Boulder–Weld

Grand Hogback

Book Cliffs

Carbondale

South Park

Grand Mesa   Somerset

Colorado Springs

Crested Butte

Nucla–Naturita

Canon City

Tongue Mesa

ACTIVE MINE

ABANDONED MINE

COAL FIELD

Walsenburg

Durango

Pagosa Springs

Trinidad

SOURCE: U.S. GEOLOGICAL SURVEY, 1977

10   0   10   20   30   40   50 Miles

40. COAL

Like oil and gas, coal is a fossil fuel created from decomposing vegetable and animal matter. Its discovery is a reminder of an ancient past when dinosaurs and other now-extinct creatures roamed a swampy, lushly vegetated Colorado.

Less than 2 percent of Colorado's vast coal reserves are anthracite, which is found only in Gunnison and Routt counties. Approximately 89 percent are bituminous, and 10 percent are subbituminous. Gold seekers first found coal along Clear Creek in 1859, and prospectors have frequently stumbled across it since then. One indication of the mineral's abundance is that Colorado has forty-five different streams named Coal Creek.

In the nineteenth century coal mining was concentrated around Boulder and Trinidad, in the "northern" and "southern" coalfields. Today those fields are largely played out; production has shifted to huge open-pit mines in northwestern Colorado. Coal also has been heavily mined around Oak Creek; in the Book Cliffs northeast of Grand Junction, Crested Butte, Somerset, and Nucla; and around Durango. Smaller fields include North Park, Middle Park, South Park, Canon City, and Tongue Mesa. Of approximately fifty coal-mining towns, the handful that have survived have done so by switching to other pursuits. These include Crested Butte, Erie, Lafayette, Louisville, and Redstone.

Railroad builders examining maps of the vast, treeless Great Plains looked for coal to fuel steam locomotives. They began an intensive search for coal and built rail lines to any significant deposits they found. By carrying and burning coal, trains helped transform Colorado production from 13,500 tons in 1870 to 1,229,593 tons in 1883. Coal mining also provided coke for the giant smelters and steel mills that opened between the 1880s and the early 1900s. Besides fueling trains and factories, coal heated most Colorado homes and businesses. Acrid coal smoke, coal ash, clinkers, and the constant need for more coal, were part of nearly everyone's life until the introduction in 1928 of cheaper, cleaner, more-efficient natural-gas heating. Slowly, natural gas and electricity replaced coal for heating and cooking in most homes.

Coal mining revived during World War II, but slumped during the 1950s and 1960s. Conversion of railroads to diesel fuel and the 1969 federal Environmental Protection Act did not help the coal industry. The industry was bolstered by the energy crisis of the early 1970s, which increased the demand for coal to fuel electrical power plants. Colorado coal production climbed to its all-time high of 19.3 million tons in 1981. With the 1980s recession, production fell to 14 million tons, but by 1990 it had bounced back to 17 million tons. Coal companies, which have long enjoyed political clout in Colorado, ensured their comeback by persuading the legislature to slash the state severance tax on coal by 40 percent in 1988 and to give state tax credits to coal buyers. By the 1990s more than sixty coal mines, including northwestern Colorado giants such as the ColoWyo and Trapper pit mines, were providing coal primarily for power plants.

Coal's effect on the quality of life is mixed. It darkens not only the skies but many lives. Coal mines and company towns were notorious for wretched working and living conditions. Protests against such conditions resulted in violent labor-management confrontations at Ludlow, Serene, and elsewhere (see Map 55). The state's *Reports of the Inspector of Coal Mines* tell some tragic tales. In 1900 one of twenty-seven mine fatalities was John Vigil, a 21-year-old working at the Toltec Mine in southern Colorado. He was killed instantly by a cave-in at 2:00 A.M. on July 18. Investigators found, in a typical company account, that "a few minutes previous to the accident, foreman Kyle directed the deceased to 'brush' a piece of the roof that was supported by three props put up by the day men. . . . It is to be regretted that a young and inexperienced Mexican was employed to do such work. . . . The death of aforesaid J. Vigil is due to his own negligence and we attach no blame to the company whatever."

Coal mining remained the most deadly—and the most lucrative—underground occupation in Colorado for years. Even after the labor wars and the alleged industry reforms of the early 1900s, seventy workers lost their lives in Colorado coal mines in 1920. Not until the 1930s did more effective governmental regulation and acceptance of union representatives begin to make mines safer.

For a century Colorado has been among the top five states in coal production and in untapped coal reserves. Coalfields varying from two to sixty feet thick underlie many areas of the state. Although surpassed in recent years by the total combined value of oil and gas production, coal remains Colorado's second most-valuable mineral.

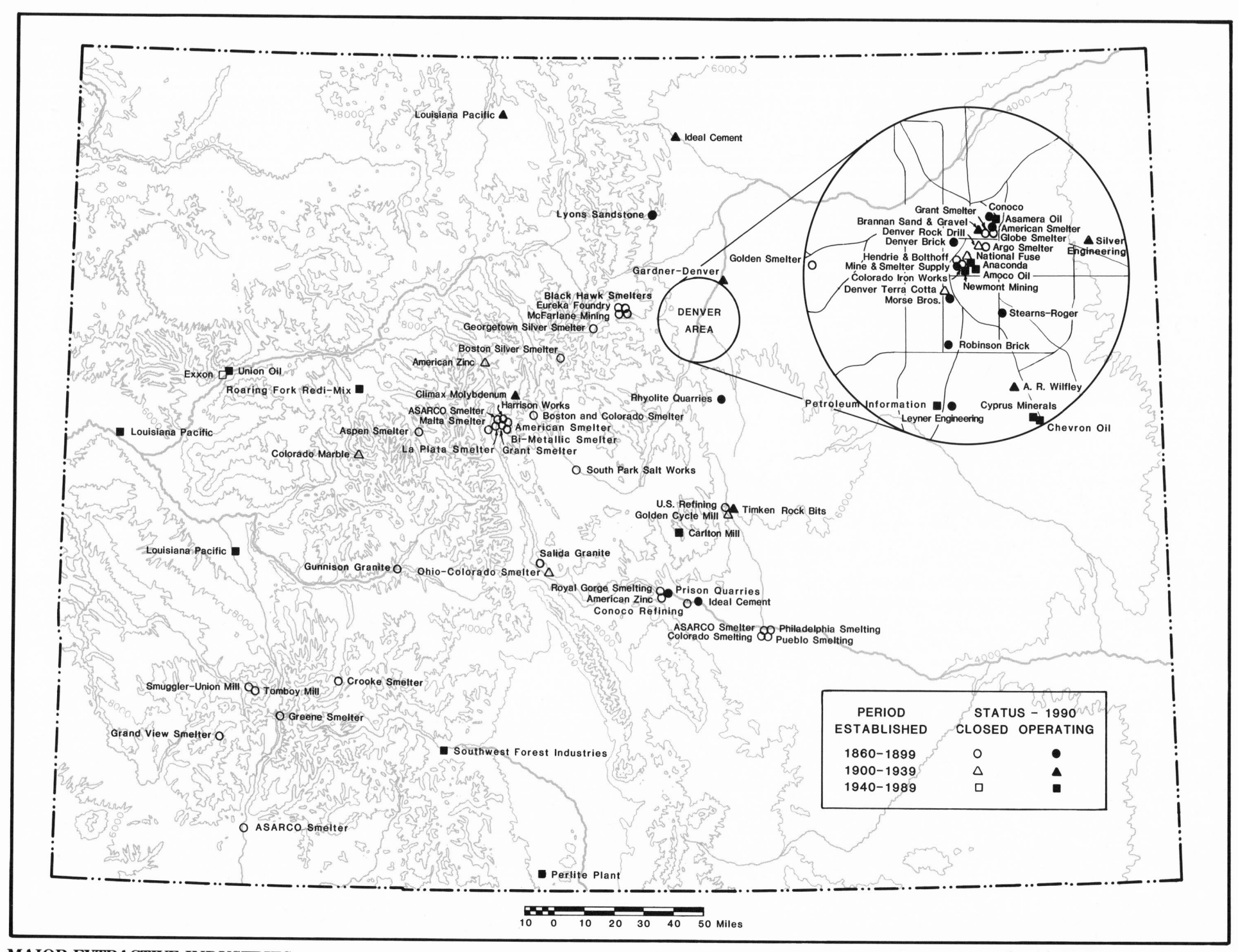

Louisiana Pacific ▲

▲ Ideal Cement

Lyons Sandstone ●

Golden Smelter ○

Gardner-Denver ▲

DENVER
AREA

Black Hawk Smelters
Eureka Foundry ○○
McFarlane Mining
Georgetown Silver Smelter ○

Boston Silver Smelter ○

American Zinc △

Exxon □ □ Union Oil
Roaring Fork Redi-Mix ■

Climax Molybdenum ▲
Harrison Works
ASARCO Smelter ● Boston and Colorado Smelter
Malta Smelter ○ ● American Smelter
Aspen Smelter ○ Bi-Metallic Smelter
La Plata Smelter Grant Smelter

Rhyolite Quarries ●

Louisiana Pacific ■

Colorado Marble △

○ South Park Salt Works

U.S. Refining ○△ ▲ Timken Rock Bits
Golden Cycle Mill △
■ Carlton Mill

Louisiana Pacific ■

Salida Granite
Gunnison Granite ○ Ohio-Colorado Smelter △

Royal Gorge Smelting
American Zinc ○ ● ● Prison Quarries
Conoco Refining ● Ideal Cement

ASARCO Smelter ○○ Philadelphia Smelting
Colorado Smelting ○○ Pueblo Smelting

Smuggler-Union Mill ○○ Tomboy Mill ○ Crooke Smelter

○ Greene Smelter

Grand View Smelter ○

■ Southwest Forest Industries

○ ASARCO Smelter

■ Perlite Plant

Denver Area inset:
Grant Smelter ● Conoco
Brannan Sand & Gravel ▲ ● Asamera Oil
Denver Rock Drill ▲ ▲ American Smelter
Denver Brick ● △○ Globe Smelter ▲ Silver
△ Argo Smelter Engineering
Hendrie & Bolthoff △ ▲ National Fuse
Mine & Smelter Supply ■■ Anaconda
Colorado Iron Works ● Ampco Oil
Denver Terra Cotta △ Newmont Mining
Morse Bros. ●
● Stearns-Roger

● Robinson Brick

▲ A. R. Wilfley

Petroleum Information ■ ● Cyprus Minerals
Leyner Engineering ● Chevron Oil

PERIOD ESTABLISHED	STATUS – 1990	
	CLOSED	OPERATING
1860–1899	○	●
1900–1939	△	▲
1940–1989	□	■

10 0 10 20 30 40 50 Miles

MAJOR EXTRACTIVE INDUSTRIES

41. MAJOR EXTRACTIVE INDUSTRIES

Dazzling profits from precious metals jump-started Colorado's economy, but ore processing and the manufacturing of mining machinery kept it going. Indeed, some of the engineering and manufacturing firms that grew up with the early mining industry thrive to this day.

At first stamp mills crushed gold and silver ores, which were then smelted in furnaces to extract gold, silver, and other valuable minerals. The first highly efficient smelter, Nathaniel P. Hill's Boston and Colorado Smelter at Black Hawk, used the Swansea Wales smelting process. Soon a dozen other smelters sprang up in Black Hawk, the state's first major ore-processing center.

Of more than two hundred Colorado smelters, many were small, short-lived operations such as the Boston and Colorado at Alma, the Aspen Mining and Smelting Company, Georgetown's Silver Smelter, the Golden Smelter, the Crooke Smelter at Lake City, the Malta Smelting and Mining Company, the Grand View Smelter in Rico, the Boston Smelter at Saints John, and Silverton's Greene Smelter. Many small local operations closed after 1880 with the rise of larger, more-efficient smelting operations that were developed first at Black Hawk, then at Leadville, whose skies at one time were darkened by smoke from forty-four plants. Other large smelters belched forth at Canon City, Durango, Pueblo, Salida, and Colorado City. Hill moved his smelter from Black Hawk to Denver in 1878, and the Mile High City had become the smelter capital by 1900. Today Denver is the last city in Colorado with an operating smelter—the American Smelting and Refining Company (ASARCO) cadmium plant. ASARCO, formed in 1899 as a consolidation of various Colorado smelters, became an international colossus, operating a Leadville plant until 1962 and the Globeville plant to this day.

Although mining and smelting have dwindled, many associated engineering and manufacturing firms have survived. Central City's Eureka Foundry (1861) and McFarlane Mining Machinery Company (1871) were two of the pioneers. Eureka evolved into Hendrie and Bolthoff, which moved to Denver and claimed to be "the World's Largest Manufacturer of Mining Machinery." Other substantial Denver-area firms provided drills, ore buckets and cars, dynamite, ore concentrators, and engineering expertise. Several of these survive, such as Anaconda Minerals, Cyprus Minerals, Morse Brothers, Newmont Mining, and Stearns-Roger. The George Leyner Engineering Works at Littleton, which invented and made compressed-air safety drills, merged with the international conglomerate Ingersoll-Rand in 1920. Cripple Creek's Carlton Mill is the only major gold mill still in operation, although extensive ruins survive near Telluride at the Smuggler-Union and Tomboy.

As precious metals lost their luster in the 1900s, other riches of the earth became economically more important. The richest mine in Colorado, Climax Molybdenum atop Fremont Pass, is a titanic mining and milling operation sprawling over miles of diggings, holding ponds, and tailings. Climax claimed to be the largest underground mine in the world before closing in the 1980s. The American Zinc Company's mine in Gilman and its smelter in Canon City reflect another once-mighty twentieth-century industry now shut down.

Mineral riches financed a building boom that capitalized on local stones, particularly granite, limestone, marble, and sandstone. Many notable structures were dressed in red sandstone from various Colorado quarries. Colorado Yule marble, from Marble; travertine, from Beulah and Salida; rhyolite, from

Castle Rock; and granite, from Gunnison, Salida, and Silver Plume, were also popular building stones. Limestone has been quarried at various places, including the Fryingpan River, Manitou Springs, the upper Arkansas River, and Canon City, where state penitentiary labor was used to produce both building and paving material. Other economically important nonmetallic riches of the earth are fluorspar, feldspar, mica, gypsum, volcanic scoria, perlite, pumicite, peat moss, and gemstones.

Brick, long a basic Colorado building material, was used for sidewalks and streets as well as structures. Numerous brickyards were scattered around the state wherever firebrick and pottery-clay deposits were found. Two of the oldest and largest firms are Denver Brick and Robinson Brick and Tile, but nearly every city once boasted a local brickyard.

Lumber, the other key building material, emerged as a mainstay of the Colorado economy. Two Denver-based giants, the Halleck and Howard and the McPhee and McGinnity companies, dominated the state's lumber production. Both are gone now, and logging, once important in many mountain counties, is a fading industry. Southwest Forest Industries in South Fork is one of the few survivors. Another is the Louisiana Pacific Company, which has been reducing Colorado aspen groves to matchsticks, waferboard, and other wood products at its plants in Fruita, Olathe, and Kremmling.

After 1900 concrete revolutionized the construction industry. One of the giant cement makers of the West was Colorado's Ideal Cement Company, which erected plants at La Porte near Fort Collins and at Portland, near Canon City. Large Redimix concrete plants, such as the one at Carbondale, gobbled up sand and gravel, which have become two of the most-lucrative extractive resources.

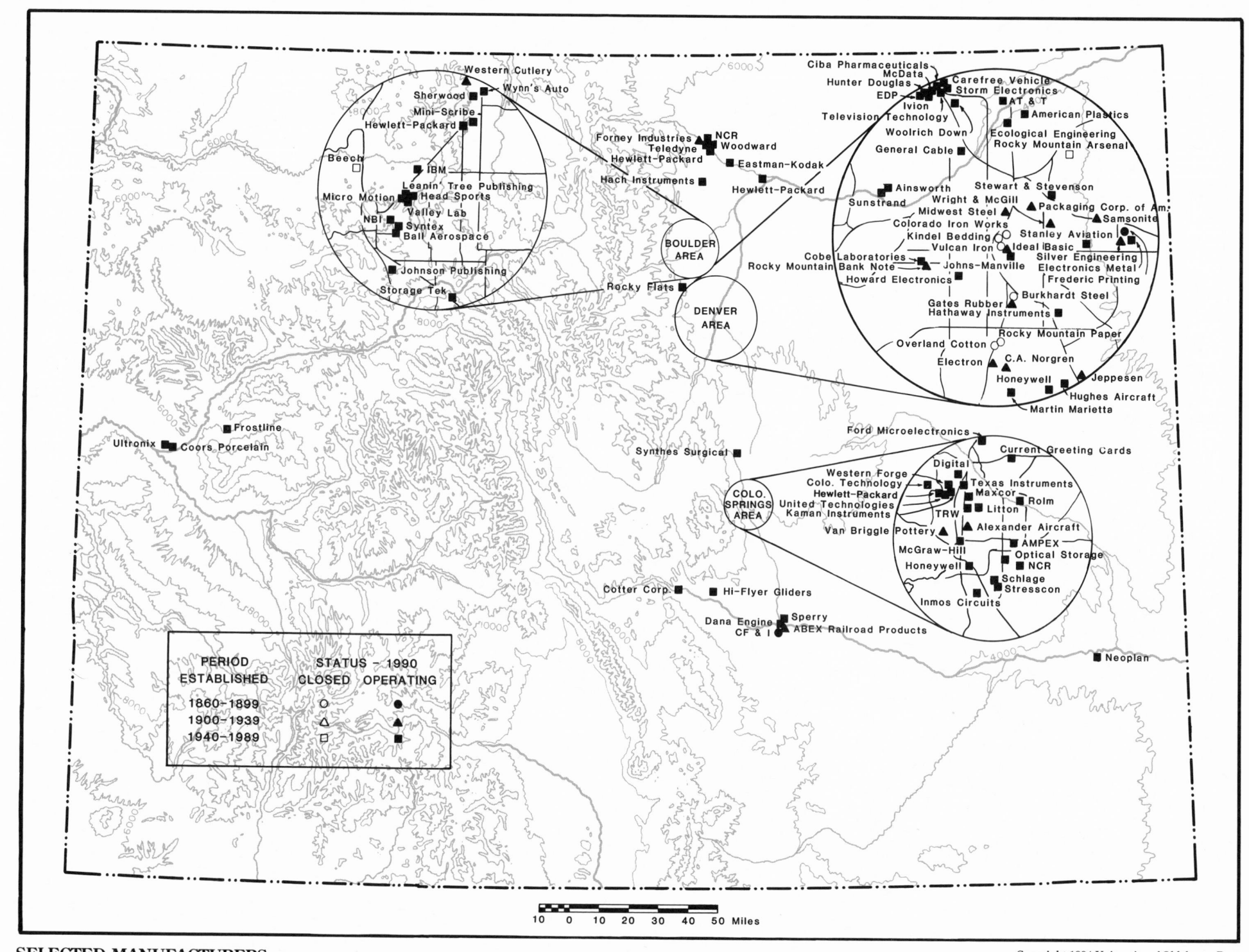

Western Cutlery
Sherwood
Wynn's Auto
Mini-Scribe
Hewlett-Packard
Beech
IBM
Leanin' Tree Publishing
Head Sports
Micro Motion
Valley Lab
NBI
Syntex
Ball Aerospace
Johnson Publishing
Storage Tek

Forney Industries
Teledyne
Hewlett-Packard
NCR
Woodward
Eastman-Kodak
Hach Instruments
Hewlett-Packard

Ciba Pharmaceuticals
McData
Hunter Douglas
EDP
Ivion
Television Technology
Woolrich Down
General Cable

Carefree Vehicle
Storm Electronics
AT & T
American Plastics
Ecological Engineering
Rocky Mountain Arsenal

Ainsworth
Sunstrand
Wright & McGill
Midwest Steel
Colorado Iron Works
Kindel Bedding
Vulcan Iron
Cobe Laboratories
Rocky Mountain Bank Note
Howard Electronics

Stewart & Stevenson
Packaging Corp. of Am.
Samsonite
Stanley Aviation
Ideal Basic
Silver Engineering
Electronics Metal
Johns-Manville
Frederic Printing

Gates Rubber
Hathaway Instruments
Burkhardt Steel
Rocky Mountain Paper
Overland Cotton
Electron
C.A. Norgren
Honeywell
Jeppesen
Hughes Aircraft
Martin Marietta

BOULDER AREA
DENVER AREA
Rocky Flats

Frostline
Ultronix
Coors Porcelain
Synthes Surgical

Ford Microelectronics
Current Greeting Cards
Western Forge
Colo. Technology
Hewlett-Packard
United Technologies
Kaman Instruments
Van Briggle Pottery
Digital
Texas Instruments
Maxcor
Rolm
TRW
Litton
Alexander Aircraft
AMPEX
Optical Storage
NCR
McGraw-Hill
Honeywell
Schlage
Stresscon
Inmos Circuits

COLO. SPRINGS AREA

Cotter Corp.
Hi-Flyer Gliders
Dana Engine
CF & I
Sperry
ABEX Railroad Products
Neoplan

PERIOD ESTABLISHED | STATUS - 1990 CLOSED OPERATING
1860-1899 ○ ●
1900-1939 △ ▲
1940-1989 □ ■

10 0 10 20 30 40 50 Miles

SELECTED MANUFACTURERS

From the start, Colorado encouraged domestic industry, hoping to manufacture goods for the state and its Rocky Mountain hinterland. In the early years Coloradans paid exorbitant freight on products hauled in from Chicago, St. Louis, Kansas City, and other manufacturing centers. Indeed, the freight charges sometimes exceeded the cost of the products.

To overcome this expensive isolation, Coloradans promoted home-state industries, an early "Always Buy Colorado" campaign. While not an industrial giant like New York, Illinois, Pennsylvania, Massachusetts, or California, Colorado did produce a wide variety of goods, sometimes for national as well as a regional markets.

While the agricultural and extractive industries treated in Maps 22 and 41 have been dispersed throughout the state, other major industries are concentrated in five Front Range cities: Denver, Boulder, Fort Collins, Colorado Springs, and Pueblo. Manufacturing began with the iron and steel business, often in connection with mining equipment. Colorado Iron Works, Marshall's, and the Blackhawk Foundry first made mining, milling, and smelting machinery in Denver. Denver's industrial might grew with Burkhardt Steel (1889), Eaton Metal Products (1919), Midwest Steel (ca. 1900), Stearns-Roger (1883), Thompson Pipe and Steel (1878), and Vulcan Steel (1894). The colossus, the Colorado Fuel and Iron Company of Pueblo, reigned as the state's leading employer and the West's largest producer of coal and steel from the 1890s until its decline began in the 1960s.

While many of the metal makers have disappeared, Denver and its suburbs have emerged as a center for high-tech industries ranging from medical supplies (Ciba, Cobe, Synthes Surgical) to aerospace (Ball Aerospace, Jeppesen, Hughes Aviation, and Martin Marietta). At Martin Marietta, which opened a $27 million aerospace plant in south-metro Denver in 1956, 13,500 employees were making rockets and spacecraft in 1991 for military and civilian uses. That year Hewlett-Packard employed 8,250 at its plants in Colorado Springs, Fort Collins, and Loveland. Since the 1980s telecommunications, especially cable television, has become one of the fastest-growing industries in metro Denver.

Long-time Denver-area industries include Gates Rubber, Samsonite Luggage, Hathaway Instruments, Ainsworth Instruments, C. A. Norgren, Frederic Printing, and Wright and McGill Fishing Tackle. The Gates Company has been manufacturing rubber, battery, and fiber products since 1911. Sales climbed over $1.2 billion in 1990, when Gates had plants or affiliates in Canada, Mexico, South America, Europe, Asia, and Africa. Samsonite Luggage, founded by the Shwayder family in 1910, likewise has become a Denver-based international operation.

Textiles, a major industry in the early 1900s, declined following the failure of the Overland Cotton works and Kindel Bedding. George J. Kindel found that railroads charged him three times more to ship his mattresses to the West Coast than his East Coast competitors paid. "Freight Rates" Kindel spent a term in the U.S. House of Representatives protesting discriminatory freight rates, which he claimed retarded the development of Colorado manufacturing by favoring eastern firms.

Outside Denver, manufacturing is important in several other Front Range cities. Colorado Springs harbors many new firms as well as two old-timers—Van Briggle Pottery and Western Forge. The University of Colorado and federal scientific and technical agencies at Boulder have boosted that town as a high-tech hub with major plants of IBM, Hewlett-Packard, and Storage Tek, a Colorado company that during the 1980s claimed to be America's tenth largest computer firm. Boulder is also a publishing center, with the University Press of Colorado; Johnson, Pruett; and Leanin' Tree among the oldest and best-known houses. Note the cluster of industries in Broomfield, on the northwest edge of the Denver area enlargement, a remarkable recent development in a village formerly known for raising broom corn.

A few other major industries are scattered around the state, including Neoplan, a German bus maker in Lamar, and Frostline, a sleeping-bag-kit maker in Mesa, Colorado. Colorado's sports and recreation-minded citizenry have encouraged local sporting-goods firms such as Hi-Flyer Gliders of Penrose, Carefree Vehicle accessories of Broomfield, Head Sports of Boulder, and Gart Brothers of Denver.

Although individual industries tend to come and go, they have been consistently concentrated in the Front Range cities. After the first nineteenth-century industrial boom led to overspecialization in mining and metals, Colorado business has developed a healthy diversity. No single industry has dominated during the twentieth century, although the computer-age businesses, which have created a "Silicon Valley" between Fort Collins and Colorado Springs, represent a new and potentially vulnerable specialization. Ups and downs in computer-related commerce led to the near-collapse of Storage Tek during the 1980s, when the firm declared bankruptcy and laid off thousands of Coloradans.

High birth and death rates have always characterized Colorado industry. The gambling, boom-and-bust spirit of the original mineral rushes survives, prompting frequent start-ups—and frequent failures—of many small new industries each year.

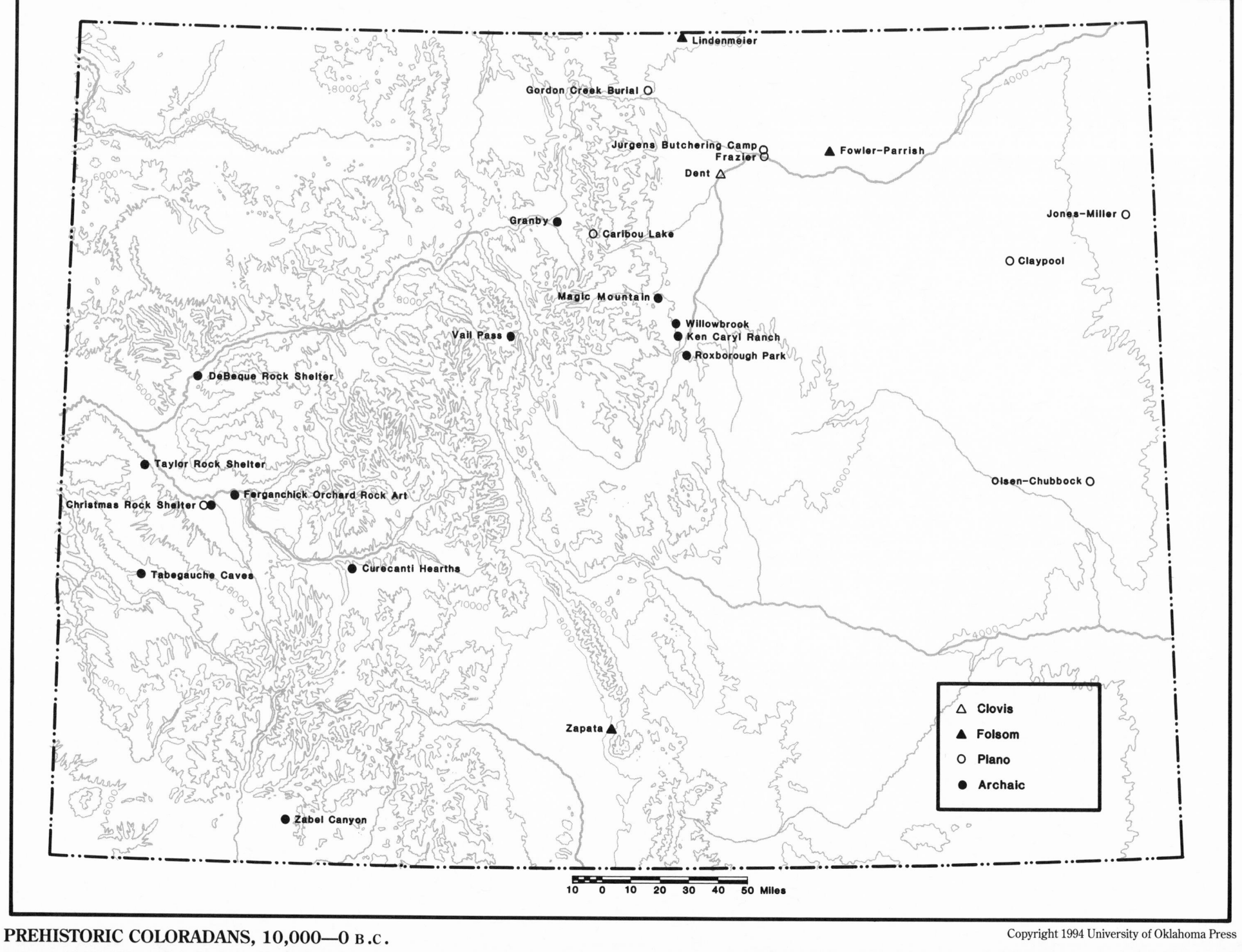

▲ Lindenmeier

Gordon Creek Burial ○

Jurgens Butchering Camp ○
Frazier ○
Dent △

▲ Fowler-Parrish

Granby ●
○ Caribou Lake

Jones-Miller ○

○ Claypool

Magic Mountain ●

Willowbrook ●
Ken Caryl Ranch ●
Roxborough Park ●

Vail Pass ●

DeBeque Rock Shelter ●

Taylor Rock Shelter ●

Olsen-Chubbock ○

Christmas Rock Shelter ○● Ferganchick Orchard Rock Art ●

Tabeguache Caves ●

Curecanti Hearths ●

Zabel Canyon ●

Zapata ▲

△ Clovis
▲ Folsom
○ Plano
● Archaic

10 0 10 20 30 40 50 Miles

PREHISTORIC COLORADANS, 10,000—0 B.C.

Copyright 1994 University of Oklahoma Press

43. PREHISTORIC COLORADANS, 10,000—0 B.C.

Precisely who the first Coloradans were will probably always be a mystery. Most scholars agree that they were Asiatic peoples whose ancestors immigrated to North America via the Bering Straits between twelve thousand and forty thousand years ago. After crossing into Alaska in various expeditions made over thousands of years, these Asian Americans moved southward, peopling North and South America.

They were dark-eyed people with straight black hair who probably came in search of game or to escape the hostile climate. Archaeologists have found some relics, making it possible to speculate on the nature of these prehistoric civilizations. The oldest known Colorado Indian cultures are the Clovis (ca. 10,500–9,000 B.C.), Folsom (ca. 9,000–8,000 B.C.), Plano (ca. 8,000–5,500 B.C.), and Archaic (5,500 B.C.–0).

George McJunkin, an African American cowboy, made a key discovery during the 1920s while working on a ranch just south of the Colorado border near Folsom, New Mexico. The prehistoric bison McJunkin unearthed prompted an investigation by Jesse D. Figgins, director of the Denver Museum of Natural History. Figgins found a stone projectile point embedded between bison ribs, evidence that Folsom People hunted in the area eleven thousand years ago.

Subsequent discoveries suggest that human beings have hunted in Colorado since at least 10,000 B.C. Rev. Conrad Bilgery, S. J., and some of his Regis College students made a major discovery at Dent, Colorado, in 1932. Assisted by Figgins, Father Bilgery found projectile points amid bones of woolly mammoths. They concluded that the fluted points were the 10,000-year-old craftsmanship of Clovis Man, named after Clovis, New Mexico, where similar points were first found.

The Lindenmeier Ranch, Colorado's most-important Folsom site, was a camp and kill site, unearthed in 1924. There various archaeological teams have found stone scrapers, knives, and projectile points as well as bone needles, beads, and engraved bones, which possibly served as a gambling device. Among other Colorado Folsom sites are Fowler-Parrish in the northeast and several discoveries on and around the Zapata Ranch on the south side of the Great Sand Dunes National Monument.

More-recent prehistoric sites, called Plano after discoveries on the plains of Texas, are more numerous than the Folsom or Clovis finds. Evidence from Plano bison kills reveals large-scale hunting where coordinated groups trapped and slaughtered entire herds. Robert Jones, Jr., discovered one of the earliest Plano sites on his ranch near Wray, where spear-

points amid the bones of about three hundred bison suggest that human hunters trapped and slaughtered the animals around 8,000 B.C. Another important Plano site is Frazier, where Frank Frazier found projectile points amid bones along the South Platte River in 1965. These were excavated by the grand dame of Colorado anthropologists, Marie Wormington. Subsequently Plano artifacts were found at Caribou Lake, Christmas, Claypool, Gordon Creek, Jurgens, and Olsen-Chubbuck.

By 5,000 B.C., Ice Age creatures such as the *Bison antiquus* and woolly mammoth were extinct. Archaic-era Indians turned to hunting smaller game and gathering wild fruits, seeds, and plants, which they ground up with handstones (manos) and grinding slabs (metates). Archaic Indians also fished with bone hooks and net sinkers; they hunted with spear throwers and projectile points. Some of the more-important Archaic sites include Christmas Rock Shelter, Curecanti Hearths, DeBeque Rock Shelter, Granby, Tabeguache Caves, Taylor Rock Shelter, and Vail Pass.

Like a single piece in a huge jigsaw puzzle, each new discovery adds a bit to a picture of prehistoric Coloradans that will never be completed. Yet each new piece leads to more exploration, scientific excavation, interpretations, and reinterpretations.

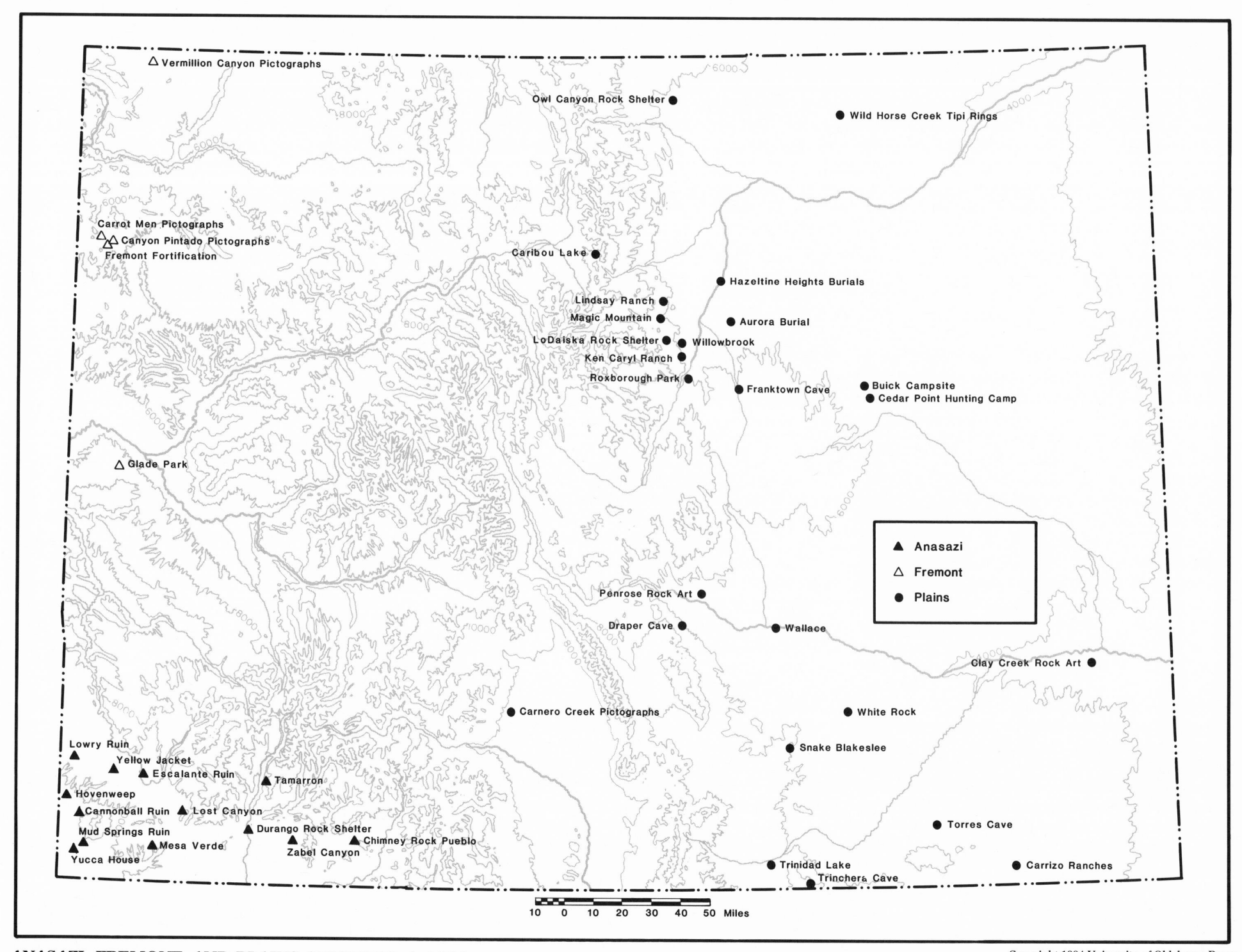

△ Vermillion Canyon Pictographs

● Owl Canyon Rock Shelter

● Wild Horse Creek Tipi Rings

Carrot Men Pictographs
△△ Canyon Pintado Pictographs
Fremont Fortification

● Caribou Lake

● Hazeltine Heights Burials

● Lindsay Ranch

● Magic Mountain

● Aurora Burial

LoDaiska Rock Shelter ● ● Willowbrook

Ken Caryl Ranch ●

Roxborough Park ●

● Franktown Cave

● Buick Campsite
● Cedar Point Hunting Camp

△ Glade Park

● Penrose Rock Art

● Draper Cave

● Wallace

Clay Creek Rock Art ●

● Carnero Creek Pictographs

● White Rock

Lowry Ruin
▲

Yellow Jacket
▲ ▲ Escalante Ruin

▲ Tamarron

▲ Hovenweep

▲ Cannonball Ruin ▲ Lost Canyon

Mud Springs Ruin
▲ ▲ Mesa Verde

▲ Durango Rock Shelter

Zabel Canyon

▲ Chimney Rock Pueblo

● Snake Blakeslee

● Torres Cave

● Trinidad Lake
● Trinchera Cave

● Carrizo Ranches

Yucca House

▲ Anasazi
△ Fremont
● Plains

10 0 10 20 30 40 50 Miles

ANASAZI, FREMONT, AND PLAINS CULTURES, 1–1300 A.D.

44. ANASAZI, FREMONT, AND PLAINS CULTURES, 1–1300 A.D.

Native Americans in Colorado built some of the most remarkable structures in North America between around A.D. 1 and 1300. Mesa Verde's fabulous cliff dwellings, now part of a national park, were the first U.S. site to be designated a World Heritage Site by the United Nations. Mesa Verde, however, contains only a fraction of Colorado's cliff dwellings, pit houses, pictographs, and rock shelters.

The Anasazi (Navajo for "ancient ones") flourished in southwestern Colorado. These agrarians built urban centers that sometimes housed several hundred people. They cultivated corn, beans, squash, cotton, and other crops, besides hunting and gathering food. They created yucca baskets and woven textiles, as well as clay figurines, pipes, pots, and utensils. For community housing, they built pit houses, and then cliff dwellings.

The Anasazi left remarkable stone and clay architecture, rock art, and dams behind when the great drought between 1275 and 1300 apparently forced them to migrate to Arizona and New Mexico. Their descendants still occupy pueblos in the Rio Grande Valley. At the zenith of Anasazi culture in Colorado, from around 1000 to 1275 A.D., the Mesa Verde region contained more residents that it does today, a tribute to the skillful agriculture and peaceful, cooperative culture of the Anasazi.

The Fremont Culture is named for the Fremont River of central Utah, where many ruins have been found since the 1890s. These semiagricultural Great Basin people advanced into northwestern Colorado. They lived in masonry pit houses and produced clay pottery and rock art, which may be seen at Canyon Pintado, Vermilion Canyon, Carrot Men Cliff, and other Colorado sites. Many distinctive shallow, round Fremont pit houses have been excavated in Dinosaur National Monument (Map 50). Apparently Fremont people depended more on a migratory, hunting life-style than did the Anasazi, but corncobs and corn tassels and kernels have been discovered in Fremont sites in northwestern Colorado along Douglas Creek and the Colorado River. Fremont culture emerged around 400 A.D. and seems to have disappeared around 1200 A.D. From a more sedentary corn-growing existence, they had shifted to the foraging and hunting tradition of the Utes, who may be Fremont-culture descendants.

Prehistoric Plains Indians practiced some agriculture, unlike most of the historic, horseback Plains Indians. Known Prehistoric Plains sites include caves, rock shelters, pit houses, and earth lodges. Burial sites, sometimes with multiple corpses and grave offerings, have been found in Aurora and at Hazeltine Heights, now a Denver subdivision. Recovered artifacts include pots, paddles, scrapers, drills, manos, metates, and various stone, bone, and shell ornaments. Such relics suggest that Prehistoric Plains Indians borrowed from Native American cultures of the central and eastern United States rather than from the Fremont or Anasazi cultures. They apparently intermingled in southeastern Colorado, where the distinctive Anasazi rectangular masonry and pottery have been found with Plains Indian artifacts.

Some prehistoric peoples left the plains for the mountains to hunt game at such sites as Caribou Lake, close to the continental divide. At other mountainous sites these early Coloradans left stone walls, pits, and cairns. But like modern Coloradans, most Prehistoric Plains Indians sought out water sources, settling in and around today's Front Range cities. In the Denver area prehistoric Indians, like the Archaic cultures before them, once occupied part of what is now Aurora, and three up-scale suburban subdivisions, Ken Caryl, Roxborough Park, and Willowbrook.

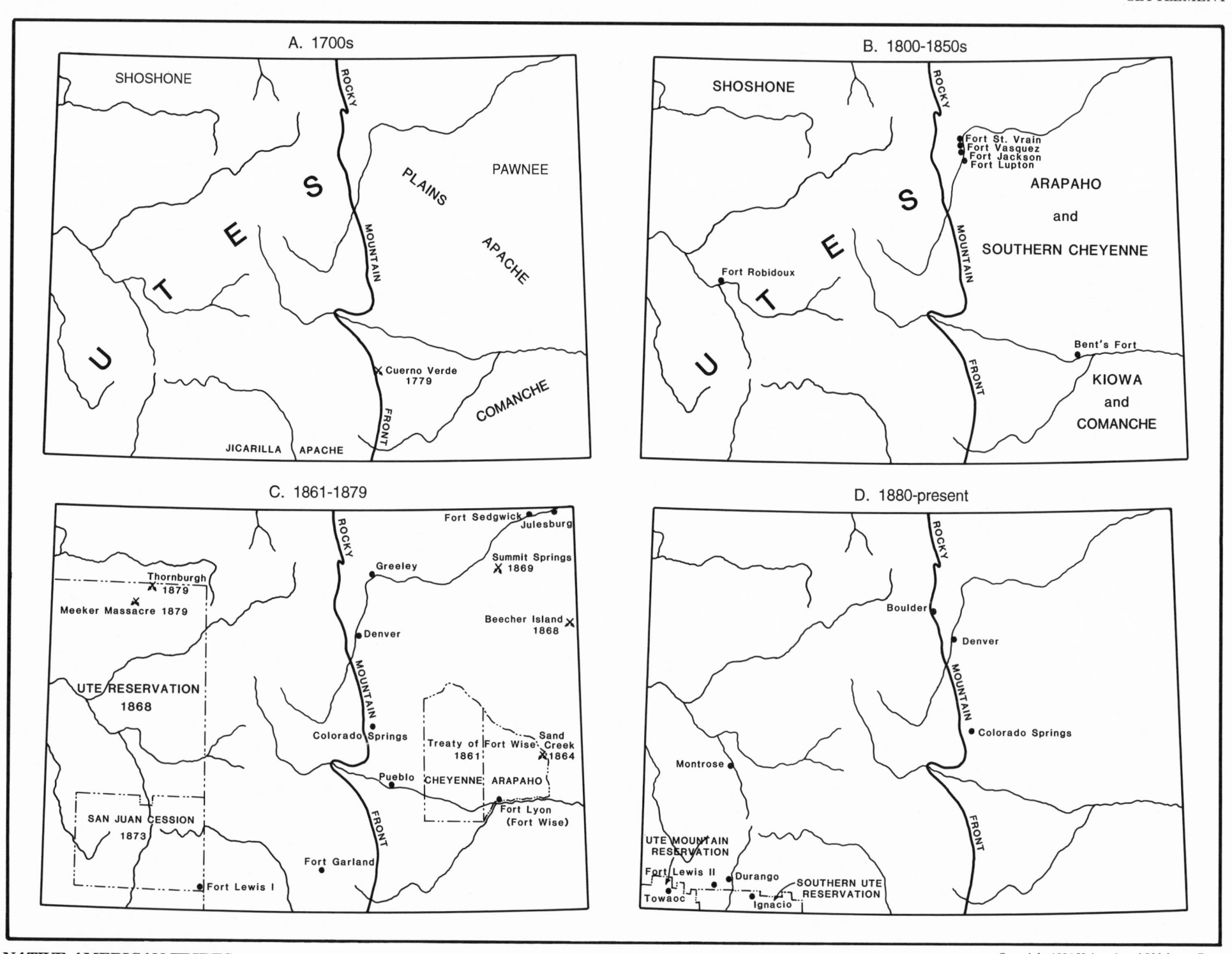

A. 1700s

SHOSHONE

ROCKY

UTES

PLAINS

PAWNEE

APACHE

MOUNTAIN

X Cuerno Verde
1779

FRONT

COMANCHE

JICARILLA APACHE

B. 1800-1850s

SHOSHONE

ROCKY

UTES

Fort St. Vrain
Fort Vasquez
Fort Jackson
Fort Lupton

ARAPAHO

and

SOUTHERN CHEYENNE

Fort Robidoux

MOUNTAIN

Bent's Fort

FRONT

KIOWA
and
COMANCHE

C. 1861-1879

Fort Sedgwick

ROCKY

Julesburg

Summit Springs
X 1869

Thornburgh
X 1879

Greeley

Meeker Massacre 1879

Denver

Beecher Island X
1868

MOUNTAIN

UTE RESERVATION
1868

Colorado Springs

Treaty of Fort Wise
1861

Sand
Creek
X 1864

Pueblo

CHEYENNE ARAPAHO

SAN JUAN CESSION
1873

FRONT

Fort Lyon
(Fort Wise)

Fort Garland

Fort Lewis I

D. 1880-present

ROCKY

Boulder

Denver

MOUNTAIN

Colorado Springs

Montrose

FRONT

UTE MOUNTAIN
RESERVATION

Fort Lewis II

Durango

SOUTHERN UTE
RESERVATION

Towaoc

Ignacio

NATIVE AMERICAN TRIBES

45. NATIVE AMERICAN TRIBES

During the 1700s the eastern plains sustained various tribes, most notably the Apache, the Pawnee, and the Comanche. All of the tribes fought with the Spanish, whose horses they took. The Spanish retaliated in 1779 against the Apache when New Mexico governor Juan Bautista de Anza and his troops defeated a band and killed their leader Cuerno Verde (Green Horn), for whom a southern Colorado community, creek, and mountain are named.

Before becoming horseback hunters, the Apache had farmed in the Arkansas River Valley, raising corn, squash, beans, melons, and sunflowers. After acquiring horses, they became fierce hunters and moved south and west. As Euro-American settlement pushed eastern tribes west, the Apache, the Comanche, and the Pawnee were shoved out of Colorado and were replaced by the Arapaho and the Cheyenne. These two allied tribes moved into Colorado during the early 1800s. The Kiowa frequented the southeastern corner, and the Shoshone the northwestern corner of the state.

Initially the Arapaho and the Cheyenne were friendly to whites. Both tribes traded with the whites at Forts Jackson, Lupton, St. Vrain, and Vasquez as well as Bent's Fort, where William bent married a Cheyenne, Owl Woman. As the whites' numbers increased, some of the Indians considered moving east, reckoning that it must be empty after the mass migration of palefaces. Native Americans did not understand the sticks and stones, the fences, and blazed trees that the newcomers used to claim land. Nor did they understand why whites could slaughter their buffalo when they were punished for hunting the white men's cattle.

After the Minnesota Sioux uprising of 1862, warfare swept across the Great Plains. Colorado, where gold seekers poured in and sought to dispossess Native Americans, did not escape the conflict. Plains Indians had agreed to the 1851 Treaty of Fort Laramie, which promised the land between the Platte and Arkansas rivers to the Arapaho and Southern Cheyenne. Ten years later those two tribes, or their alleged representatives, agreed to the Treaty of Fort Wise, which gave them the much-smaller reservations shown on the 1861–1879 map.

Many Native Americans did not sign the treaties and resisted white advances. Nor did the whites keep the promises that they made in the flawed Fort Laramie and Fort Wise treaties. Increasingly hostile incidents culminated in the 1864 Sand Creek Massacre, where more than one hundred Arapaho and Cheyenne—mostly children, women, and old men—were slaughtered. This bloody attack on peaceful Indians led to further conflict. Native Americans raided and burned Julesburg in 1865, but were defeated at Beecher Island and Summit Springs, the last Colorado battles for the Plains Indians. The Southern Cheyenne and Arapaho were removed to reservations in Oklahoma and Wyoming.

Central and western Colorado had been the homeland of the Utes for hundreds, if not thousands, of years. The Utes differ from the Plains tribes in that they belong to the Shoshonean linguistic family centered in Utah and the Great Basin. They may be the descendants of such prehistoric cultures as the Fremont people who occupied Colorado ten thousand years ago. Physically, the Utes are shorter, darker, and stockier than Plains Indians. Sometimes they are called the Black Indians, as opposed to the Buffalo Indians of the plains. The Utes divided into seven bands. The Weminuche, Capote, and Mouache bands, long-time southwestern Coloradans, now live on the Southern Ute and Mountain Ute reservations, while the Uintah, Uncompahgre, Grand River, and Yampa bands of northwest Colorado are concentrated on the Uintah Reservation in northeastern Utah.

As a mountain tribe, the Utes used deer, elk, and rabbit skins to make shirts, leggings, dresses, and blankets. After they acquired the horse, they became buffalo hunters and built tipis out of buffalo hides. The Utes are noted for the fine beadwork that often adorns their leather clothing. For their villages they fancied protected mountain valleys and hot springs—a source of physical and spiritual renewal.

Utes, often represented by Chief Ouray, negotiated various treaties with the whites. As the 1861–1879 map shows, the tribe gave up the Central Rockies and San Luis Valley, agreeing to move onto a western-Colorado reservation established in 1868. Five years later they ceded the San Juan region to gold-seeking whites.

Resisting white efforts to make them farmers, Utes slaughtered Nathan Meeker, the White River Ute Indian agent, and his male associates. They also ambushed Maj. Thomas Tipton Thornburgh, who was coming to Meeker's rescue, killing the major and thirteen of his troops. After that episode Euro-Americans demanded that the Utes go. The Ute removal of 1881 left the tribe with only the two reservations in the southwest corner of Colorado.

On the Southern Ute Reservation today's visitors are welcomed to a cultural center, museum, casino, and trading center at Ignacio. The Mountain Utes have created a tribal park, where they operate a casino, a bingo hall, and a craft shop. They also serve as guides for visitors desiring to inspect Anasazi ruins and Ute sites on their reservation.

In Denver the art, artifacts, and culture of once-despised "savages" are showcased in exhibits at the Colorado Historical Society, the Denver Art Museum, and the Denver Museum of Natural History. The Colorado Historical Society maintains a museum in Montrose that focuses on the Ute Indians. Far from being a vanished race viewable only in a museum, Native Americans are a growing, evolving group of Coloradans. Several thousand reside on the two Ute reservations and more than five thousand live in metro Denver. One Coloradan of Native American ancestry, Ben Nighthorse Campbell, in 1993 became the first Indian to sit in the U.S. Senate.

45. NATIVE AMERICAN TRIBES

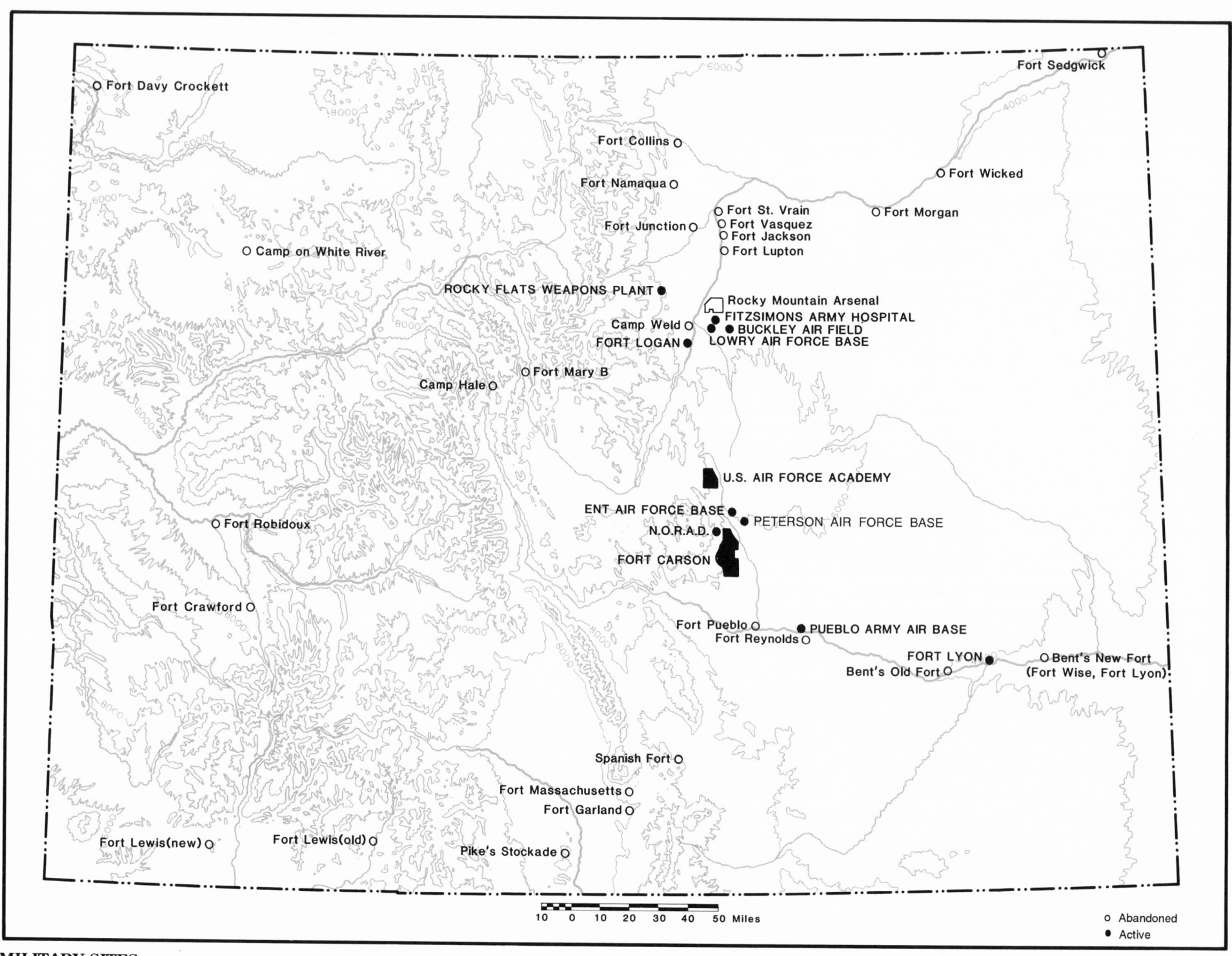

O Fort Davy Crockett

O Fort Sedgwick

Fort Collins O

O Fort Wicked

Fort Namaqua O

O Fort St. Vrain
O Fort Vasquez   O Fort Morgan
Fort Junction O   O Fort Jackson
O Fort Lupton

O Camp on White River

ROCKY FLATS WEAPONS PLANT ●

Rocky Mountain Arsenal
FITZSIMONS ARMY HOSPITAL
Camp Weld O   ● BUCKLEY AIR FIELD
FORT LOGAN ●   LOWRY AIR FORCE BASE

O Fort Mary B

Camp Hale O

U.S. AIR FORCE ACADEMY

ENT AIR FORCE BASE ●
                      PETERSON AIR FORCE BASE
O Fort Robidoux   N.O.R.A.D. ●

FORT CARSON

Fort Crawford O

Fort Pueblo O   ● PUEBLO ARMY AIR BASE
Fort Reynolds O

FORT LYON ●   O Bent's New Fort
Bent's Old Fort O   (Fort Wise, Fort Lyon)

Spanish Fort O

Fort Massachusetts O
Fort Garland O

Fort Lewis(new) O   Fort Lewis(old) O
Pike's Stockade O

10 0 10 20 30 40 50 Miles

O Abandoned
● Active

MILITARY SITES

As a disputed land claimed by various European, North American, and Indian nations, Colorado did not lack a military presence. Once those disputes were settled, the United States established bases to maintain control and to train soldiers for foreign wars. The military continues to be a major factor in Colorado's economy, pumping billions each year into salaries, facilities, contracts, and purchases.

When Lt. Zebulon Pike and his command explored the boundary of the Louisiana Purchase, they strayed into Spanish territory. Pike's cottonwood stockade in the San Luis Valley was the first U.S. military post in Colorado, although it did not stop the Spanish from capturing Pike in 1807. In order to prevent further Yankee invasions, Gov. Facundo Melgares of New Mexico ordered construction of a military post five miles east of Sangre de Cristo Pass, on Oak Creek above the town of Badito. When Jacob Fowler camped nearby in 1822, the fort was already in ruins. After the Treaty of Guadalupe Hidalgo ended the Mexican War, the United States constructed Fort Massachusetts (1852), which was replaced five years later by Fort Garland.

Paramilitary posts included Bent's Old and Bent's New Fort, Fort Mary B (Breckenridge), Fort Namaqua (Loveland), and Fort Wicked. More arose during the Civil War when Fort Sedgwick, Fort Morgan, Fort Collins, Fort Junction, and Camp Weld were established along the Platte River to ward off Native Americans and their alleged Confederate allies. While most of these installations were small and short-lived, Fort Lyon (which opened in 1860 as Fort Wise) was relocated in 1867 and is now a veterans hospital.

The army began constructing Fort Stevens on the Huerfano River near the Spanish Peaks in 1866, only to abandon it a few months later to build Fort Reynolds instead. Built overlooking the Arkansas River eighteen miles east of Pueblo, Fort Reynolds was completed in 1867 and abandoned in 1872.

Neither Confederates nor Indians proved to be a sustained threat to Colorado, but communities hungry for military payrolls continued to lobby for military installations. One of the few actual Indian uprisings, the Meeker Massacre, led to the establishment of the White River Cantonment, part of which is preserved in Meeker as a museum. Camp Crawford, established in 1880 as a cantonment on the Uncompahgre River, was another base established to help usher the Utes out of Colorado. Fort Lewis, initially established at Pagosa Springs in 1878, moved in 1880 to what became the town of Durango. The second Fort Lewis became an Indian school, which has evolved into Fort Lewis College.

Although short-lived, the Indian wars helped promote a long-term standing military. During the 1880s it was army policy to close small posts in favor of larger consolidated bases. This led to the establishment of Fort Logan in 1887 on a site on the southwest outskirts of Denver with railroads to dispatch troops quickly to wherever they might be needed. Although Fort Logan troops sporadically put down labor wars and civil disturbances, the garrison was fairly quiet until the Spanish American War. Then it had to be augmented by a temporary Camp Adams, which was set up in Denver's City Park to help mobilize troops. Fort Logan also bustled during World War I, when it was Colorado's only major military post.

After World War I, Aurora gained a gigantic veterans health complex, Fitzsimons Army Hospital, while Denver's old Agnes Phipps Memorial Tuberculosis Sanatorium was recycled in 1937 as Lowry Army Air Base. The outbreak of World War II led to establishment of Buckley Air Field in what is now Aurora, and Camp Carson and Ent and Petersen air fields in Colorado Springs. Army air bases were established at Colorado Springs, Pueblo, and La Junta. In 1947 the Air Force became an independent branch of the military, and army air bases become Air Force bases. At Camp Hale, near Leadville, the army trained ski troops of the Tenth Mountain Division. Many prisoners of war were sent to Colorado locations, and Japanese-American civilians were forced into Amache, a concentration camp near Granada. With over eight thousand men, women, and children, Amache became the eighth largest city in Colorado before it closed after the war.

After World War II the huge Denver Ordnance Plant became the even-larger Denver Federal Center. Denver's role as a munitions maker has been perpetuated by the Rocky Mountain Arsenal (1942) and the Rocky Flats Weapons Plant (1953). Serious toxic-waste problems reoccurring at both sites have led to repeated protests and the closure of the arsenal and scaling down of operations at Rocky Flats. The army air bases at Colorado Springs, La Junta, and Pueblo were purchased by those towns and converted into municipal airports.

Colorado Springs remains a military town, with Fort Carson and Peterson Air Force Base still active and reenforced by the Air Force Academy (1958) and the North American Air Defense Command (1966). The latter is a huge, subterranean, allegedly Armageddon-proof nuclear-war headquarters under Cheyenne Mountain.

Although most of the early-day military posts are now gone, settlements that sprang up around them often turned into permanent cities and towns such as Fort Collins and Fort Morgan. Some forts, including Pike's Stockade and Fort Garland, have been reconstructed by the Colorado Historical Society for visitors to inspect.

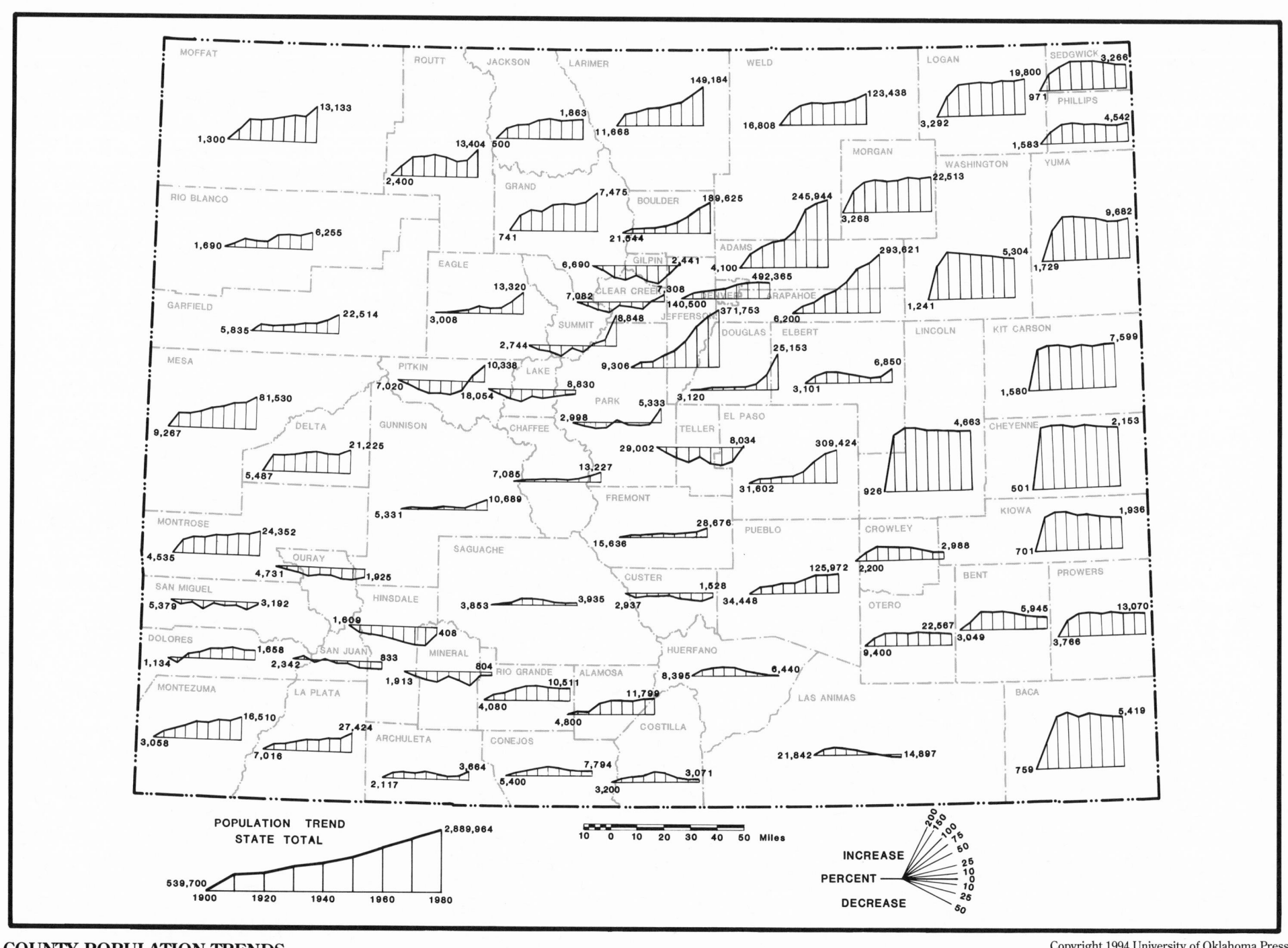

POPULATION TREND
STATE TOTAL

2,889,964

539,700

1900 1920 1940 1960 1980

10 0 10 20 30 40 50 Miles

INCREASE

200
150
100
75
50
25
10
0
10
25
50

PERCENT

DECREASE

COUNTY POPULATION TRENDS

47. COUNTY POPULATION TRENDS

Booms and busts have washed large populations in and out of Colorado's sixty-three counties. Between 1860 and 1900, Colorado's population skyrocketed from 34,277 to 539,700. Five general trends characterized county growth between 1900 and 1980: an early boom and long stagnation on the eastern plains; soaring growth in most Front Range urban and suburban counties; decline in mountain mining counties, sometimes reversed in recent decades by ski and tourist-industry success; slow growth peaking between 1940 and 1950 and then decline in south-central Colorado; and slow growth in the western tier of counties.

The eastern plains prospered during the first two decades of the 1900s when crop prices were high. Wetter years, irrigation projects, newly plowed soils, World War I food shortages, and mechanization also contributed to the blossoming of the high-plains region. When crop and livestock prices fell more than fifty percent during the 1920s, the plains prosperity wilted. Between 1920 and 1930 the price of a bushel of wheat fell from $1.05 to $0.60; corn fell from $0.79 cents a bushel to $0.32. This market collapse was compounded by the dust storms and the Great Depression of the 1930s. Population decline continues on the high plains: between 1980 and 1990, losses were recorded in such counties as Sedgwick (17.6%), Logan (11.3%), Cheyenne (11.3%), Kiowa (12.7%), Bent (15.1%), and Baca (15.9%).

In south-central Colorado the upper Arkansas and Rio Grande valleys generally have lost residents since 1900. Las Animas and Huerfano have been shrinking in population following the collapse of their once-mighty coal-mining industry. As crop and livestock centers, Conejos and Costilla counties peaked in population during the 1940s and 1950s when wartime demand revived agricultural prices. Alamosa, as the commercial hub of the San Luis Valley, has been growing, reaching a 1990 peak of 13,617, a 15.4 percent increase over 1980.

Shrinking populations characterize many mining counties in central and southwestern Colorado. Gilpin County, home of the first great gold rush, was Colorado's population center during the 1860s. Since 1900, Gilpin has faded along with its gold mining, although the establishment of legalized gambling in the 1990s may reverse this trend. Other mining counties have successfully switched to an economy based on tourism and recreation. The most successful have been Pitkin (Aspen), San Miguel (Telluride), and Summit (Breckenridge). Pitkin County, with its glitzy ski areas, summer arts programs, and deluxe accommodations, reached its all-time population high in 1990 with 12,661 residents. Summit County, a fading mining center until Interstate 70 tunneled into it under the continental divide, soared to a 1990 population of 12,881. In contrast, San Miguel County counted only 3,653 residents in 1990, although it had boasted more than 5,000 early in the century. Without major ski areas or other major tourist attractions, Fremont, Hinsdale, Lake, Mineral, Ouray, Park, San Juan, and Teller counties continue to lose people. San Juan (1990 pop. 745), Hinsdale (467), and Mineral (558) have become one-town counties.

Colorado's most spectacular growth since 1900 has turned the once-rural counties ringing Denver into the most populous: Jefferson County is second in population; Arapahoe, fourth; Adams, fifth; and Boulder, sixth. By the year 2000, Jefferson County will probably overtake Denver County, which has been losing population since its 1970 zenith of 514,678. The third most-populous county, El Paso (Colorado Springs), has eclipsed once-larger Pueblo, displaying a 28.3 percent growth rate during the 1980s, a boom fueled by its many military installations and contractors. Douglas County, situated on the suburban fringe of both Denver and Colorado Springs, grew during the 1980s by 140.5 percent. In the second fastest-growing county, Eagle, the lavish new resorts of Beaver Creek, Arrowhead, and Cordillera have sprung up between the boomtown of Vail and Eagle.

On the western edge of Colorado, slow, steady growth has characterized Moffat, Rio Blanco, Garfield, Mesa, Montrose, Dolores, and Montezuma counties. Moffat coal, Rio Blanco oil, and Mesa and Garfield oil shale have paid off, as well as uranium and vanadium in Montrose, Dolores, and Montezuma counties. Although the oil-shale bust of 1982 temporarily devastated Garfield and Mesa counties, they showed net population gains for the 1980s of 33.1 percent and 14.2 percent respectively.

The unrelenting loss of population on the eastern plains and in some mountain counties since 1920 has been most drastic in Pueblo, Lake, and Teller counties. In 1900, Pueblo was the second most-populous county; Teller, the fourth; and Lake, the seventh. Ninety years later Pueblo was ninth, while Lake and Teller had shrunk drastically, becoming two of the state's least-populous counties. Tremendous growth in the Front Range counties of Larimer, Weld, Boulder, Adams, Arapahoe, Jefferson, Douglas, and El Paso gave those counties two-thirds of Colorado's 1990 population of 3,272,460.

While county figures have fluctuated wildly, growth statewide has been steadily climbing. Although Colorado lost people during the mid-1860s, mid-1890s, and mid-1980s due to, respectively, gold, silver, and oil busts, the state has never sustained a net population loss over the course of a decade.

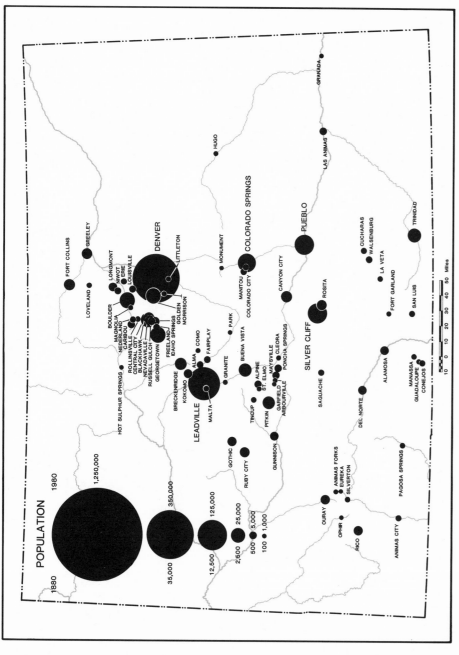

POPULATION

1880   1980

1,250,000

350,000

125,000

35,000

25,000

12,500

5,000

2,500

1,000

500

100

1880 Urban Population

FORT COLLINS
GREELEY
HOT SULPHUR SPRINGS
LOVELAND
LONGMONT
NIWOT
ERIE
LOUISVILLE
BOULDER
MAGNOLIA
NEDERLAND
CARIBOU
ROLLINSVILLE
CENTRAL CITY
BLACKHAWK
NEVADAVILLE
RUSSELL GULCH
GEORGETOWN
FREELAND
IDAHO SPRINGS
DENVER
LITTLETON
MONUMENT
HUGO
COLORADO SPRINGS
MANITOU
COLORADO CITY
CANYON CITY
PUEBLO
LAS ANIMAS
CUCHARAS
WALSENBURG
LA VETA
ROSITA
SILVER CLIFF
GOLDEN
MORRISON
PARK
ALMA
COMO
FAIRPLAY
GRANITE
BUENA VISTA
ALPINE
ST. ELMO
MAYSVILLE
CLEORA
PONCHA SPRINGS
GARFIELD
ARBOURVILLE
BRECKENRIDGE
KOKOMO
LEADVILLE
MALTA
GOTHIC
RUBY CITY
GUNNISON
TINCUP
PITKIN
OURAY
OPHIR
RICO
ANIMAS FORKS
EUREKA
SILVERTON
ANIMAS CITY
PAGOSA SPRINGS
DEL NORTE
SAGUACHE
ALAMOSA
FORT GARLAND
SAN LUIS
MANASSA
GUADALOUPE
CONEJOS
GRANADA
TRINIDAD

50 40 30 20 10 0   50 Miles
10 0 10 20 30 40 50 Miles

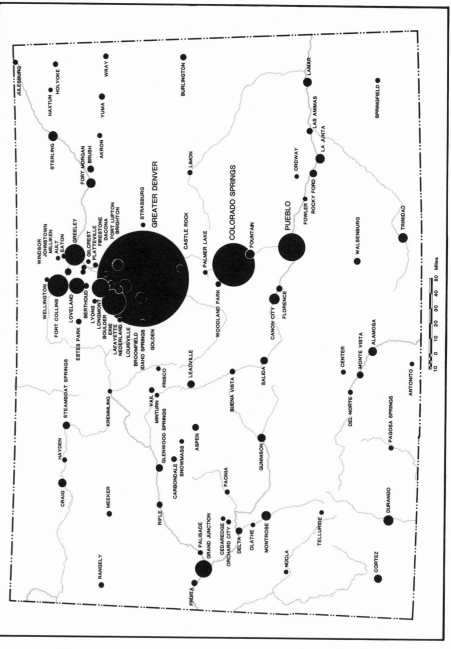

1980 Urban Population

JULESBURG
HAXTUN
HOLYOKE
STERLING
FORT MORGAN
BRUSH
AKRON
YUMA
WRAY
BURLINGTON
LIMON
WINDSOR
JOHNSTOWN
MILLIKEN
AULT
EATON
GREELEY
GILCREST
PLATTEVILLE
FIRESTONE
DACONA
FORT LUPTON
BRIGHTON
STRASBURG
GREATER DENVER
CASTLE ROCK
PALMER LAKE
WELLINGTON
FORT COLLINS
LOVELAND
BERTHOUD
LYONS
LONGMONT
ERIE
BOULDER
LAFAYETTE
NEDERLAND
LOUISVILLE
BROOMFIELD
GOLDEN
IDAHO SPRINGS
ESTES PARK
WOODLAND PARK
COLORADO SPRINGS
FOUNTAIN
PUEBLO
ORDWAY
FOWLER
ROCKY FORD
LA JUNTA
LAMAR
LAS ANIMAS
SPRINGFIELD
WALSENBURG
TRINIDAD
CRAIG
HAYDEN
STEAMBOAT SPRINGS
MEEKER
KREMMLING
VAIL
MINTURN
GLENWOOD SPRINGS
FRISCO
LEADVILLE
ASPEN
SNOWMASS
CARBONDALE
RIFLE
BUENA VISTA
SALIDA
GUNNISON
CANON CITY
FLORENCE
RANGELY
FRUITA
GRAND JUNCTION
PALISADE
CEDAREDGE
ORCHARD CITY
PAONIA
DELTA
OLATHE
MONTROSE
NUCLA
TELLURIDE
DURANGO
CORTEZ
DEL NORTE
CENTER
MONTE VISTA
ALAMOSA
PAGOSA SPRINGS
ANTONITO

10 0 10 20 30 40 50 Miles

URBAN POPULATION GROWTH

Colorado is celebrated for its wide open spaces—its sweeping prairies, soaring peaks, and spacious plateaus—yet most Coloradans live in urban areas. The 1950 federal census, the first to distinguish between urban towns (populations over 2,500) and rural communities, reported that 62.7 percent of the population was urban. Backtracking, the 1950 census reported that the state was 48.3 percent urban in 1900. By 1980, 80.6 percent of Coloradans lived in urban areas.

Urbanization began with the gold rush, as the highly specialized business of mining required concentrated support centers to provide nourishment, goods, and services, as well as labor and ore-processing facilities. In almost every decade from the 1860s to the 1920s a new mining center rose to spectacular but brief prominence as the state's fastest-growing community. During the 1860s Central City glittered with gold, briefly reigning as the most-populous city in Colorado. In 1880 two-year-old Leadville proved to be Colorado's second largest city. In the 1890s Cripple Creek boomed as one of the world's greatest gold producers, ranking as the fifth largest Colorado city in 1900, with nearby Victor the eighth largest. A decade later the coal town of Trinidad emerged as Colorado's fourth largest urban center.

All of the mining boomtowns have shriveled since the 1920s, but two former smelting centers, Pueblo and Durango, remain the urban hubs for southeast and southwest Colorado. Pueblo, once the mighty Pittsburgh of the West, has been declining in recent decades with the demise of the Colorado Fuel and Iron Company. Durango has shifted to other industries, notably tourism, and sustained steadier growth.

Mineral riches flowed most profusely to Denver and Colorado Springs. Colorado Springs first boomed with the Cripple Creek gold rush, then burgeoned after World War II as a hub of military facilities and contracts. Metro Denver, which contains slightly over half of the state's population, has grown on its suburban periphery while actually losing population in the core county (see Map 49). As the chart below shows, the suburbs are growing much more rapidly than Denver itself. Aurora, Boulder, Lakewood, Arvada, and Westminster ranked among the state's ten largest cities in 1990.

On the Western Slope, Grand Junction has remained the regional metropolis since 1900, trailed by Durango. Despite a profitable ski business, the former mining towns of Aspen, Breckenridge, Crested Butte, and Telluride have not yet recovered the populations they boasted during their bonanza days.

In northeastern Colorado, the leading agricultural centers have been Fort Collins, Greeley, and Sterling. While Fort Collins and Greeley have enjoyed Front Range prosperity, Sterling has stagnated in terms of population, like the South Platte Valley agricultural area for which it is a barometer. The same stagnation has characterized La Junta and Lamar on the southeastern plains. These agricultural hubs of the Arkansas Valley have suffered as improved transportation brought their hinterlands within the commercial sphere of Front Range cities, where many rural people drive to do their shopping.

Between 1880 and 1980 the pattern has been toward fewer, larger urban areas, with metro Denver and Colorado Springs swallowing many surrounding communities. The burgeoning population concentrated along the Front Range suggests that the map for 2080 might be blackened by a solid urban-suburban sprawl from Fort Collins to Pueblo.

Table 2. Population of urban centers, 1880–1990

City	1880	1900	1940	1990
Alamosa	802	1,141	5,613	7,579
Arvada	0	735	1,482	89,235
Aspen	0	3,303	777	5,049
Aurora	0	202	3,437	222,103
Boulder	3,069	6,150	12,958	83,312
Brighton	0	366	4,029	14,203
Canon City	1,501	3,775	6,690	12,687
Central City	2,629	3,114	706	335
Colorado Springs	4,226	21,085	36,789	281,140
Cripple Creek	0	10,147	2,358	584
Denver	35,629	106,713	322,412	467,610
Durango	235	3,317	5,887	12,430
Fort Collins	1,356	3,053	12,251	87,758
Golden	2,730	2,152	3,175	13,116
Grand Junction	0	3,503	12,479	29,034
Greeley	1,297	3,023	15,905	60,536
La Junta	0	2,513	7,640	7,637
Lakewood	0	462	1,701	126,481
Lamar	0	987	4,445	8,343
Leadville	14,820	12,455	4,774	2,629
Pueblo	3,217	28,157	52,162	98,640
Sterling	0	998	7,411	10,362
Trinidad	2,226	5,345	13,223	8,580
Westminster	0	115	534	74,625

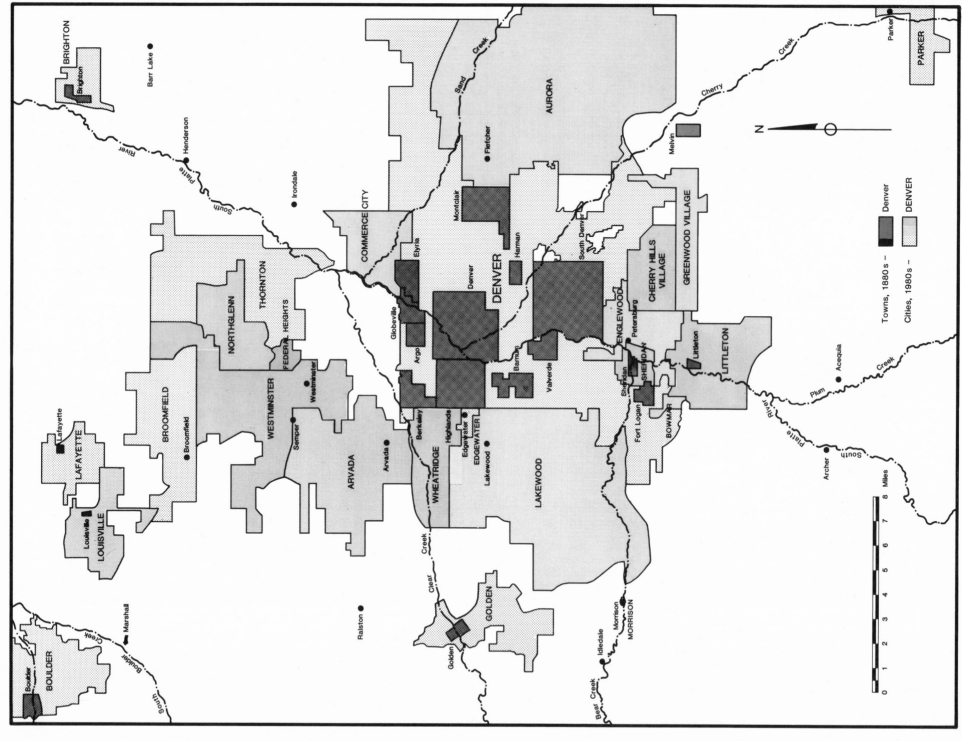

DENVER AND SUBURBS

During the past century many small communities have become part of the mushrooming Mile High Metropolis. This map shows how small 1880s towns have evolved into parts of Denver or its suburbs.

North Denver suburbs include the industrial towns of Argo (1878) and Globeville (1889), which grew up around the giant Argo and Globe smelters, and Elyria (1881), a town noted for its truck farms and dairies. Four miles east of Denver, Baron Walter von Richthofen, a German adventurer, developed Montclair (1885) as a pioneer residential suburb. Halfway between Montclair and Denver, Edwin Harman platted a town on his homestead and began selling lots in Harman (1882).

South Denver (1874) emerged as the largest of Denver's streetcar suburbs, bounded by the South Platte River and Colorado Boulevard, between Alameda and Yale avenues. On the southwest, the towns of Sheridan (1887) and Fort Logan (1889) sprang up around an army base. West Denver contained Valverde (1882) and Barnum (1887), the latter being named for its promoter, circus magnate Phineas T. Barnum. He boasted that Barnum's salubrious climate would rescue health seekers from the edge of the grave. Highlands (1875) and Berkeley (1892) likewise boasted of their fine climate and elevated sites.

Those ten separate, incorporated towns were annexed to Denver by 1902 when the City and County of Denver was carved out of Arapahoe County. Littleton replaced Denver as the seat of the new, reduced Arapahoe County. Richard Little had founded the town and its major industry, the Rough and Ready Mill, in the late 1860s. Despite steady growth, Littleton's population has been surpassed in recent years by Aurora.

Aurora traces its origins to Fletcher (1891). Town founder Donald K. Fletcher failed during the Panic of 1893 and left Colorado, leaving folks in Fletcher strapped with bonded indebtedness for his waterworks scheme. They renamed the town Aurora, but it remained a sleepy country hamlet until after World War II. Then its population zoomed from 3,437 in 1940 to 222,103 in 1990. Aurora in the 1970s and 1980s conducted aggressive annexation campaigns that have made it Denver's chief rival. Denver's annexation powers were severely limited in 1974 by a suburb-sponsored amendment to the state constitution. Aurora is now the third largest city in Colorado. Englewood, another large Arapahoe County town, is

now locked in by other suburbs, including the affluent suburban enclaves of Cherry Hills Village (1945), Greenwood Village (1950), and Bow Mar (1958).

Jefferson County, on the west side of Denver, includes Lakewood, the fourth largest city in Colorado. Platted in the spring of 1889 by William Loveland, Lakewood grew with the development of the huge Federal Center office complex after World War II. Arvada (1871) has become Jefferson County's second largest city and the sixth largest city in Colorado. This old farm town has become a suburban pacesetter with its large, active arts and humanities center, as well as an active historical society, museum, and downtown historic district. Just south of Arvada lies Wheat Ridge (1913), where former grainfields have resprouted as subdivisions. Golden, Jefferson County's oldest town and seat, dates to 1859, when prospector Tom Golden built his log cabin beside Clear Creek near North and South Table mountains. Golden rivaled Denver during the 1860s, when it served as the territorial capitol, a rail hub, and a mining and smelting center. Since those bonanza days, Golden's growth has slowed, being sustained primarily by Colorado's largest single industrial plant, the Adolph Coors Brewery.

Brighton, the county seat of Adams County, remains a rural community along the banks of the South Platte. Begun in 1870 as the railroad town of Hughes, it has grown into a town of 14,203. Commerce City, as its name suggests, has emerged as an industrial center. Westminster (1890) and the newer cities of Federal Heights (1940), Thornton (1956), and Northglenn (1964) are basically bedroom suburbs.

The only Colorado community to effectively control growth has been Boulder. Formed in 1859, Boulder has insulated itself against metropolitan sprawl with a ring of mountain parks and green space. While Boulder limited its population to around 80,000, neighboring Boulder County towns boomed with 1990 populations of 24,638 in Broomfield, 14,548 in Lafayette, 51,555 in Longmont, and 12,361 in Louisville.

In 1990 almost three-fourths of the metro Denver population of 1,622,980 lived outside the core City and County of Denver. Politically, the five-county metropolitan area is fragmented into seventy-five towns and a maze of fire, park, sanitation, school, and water districts. The only two notable efforts at cooperation are the Regional Transportation District and the Metropolitan Wastewater Reclamation District.

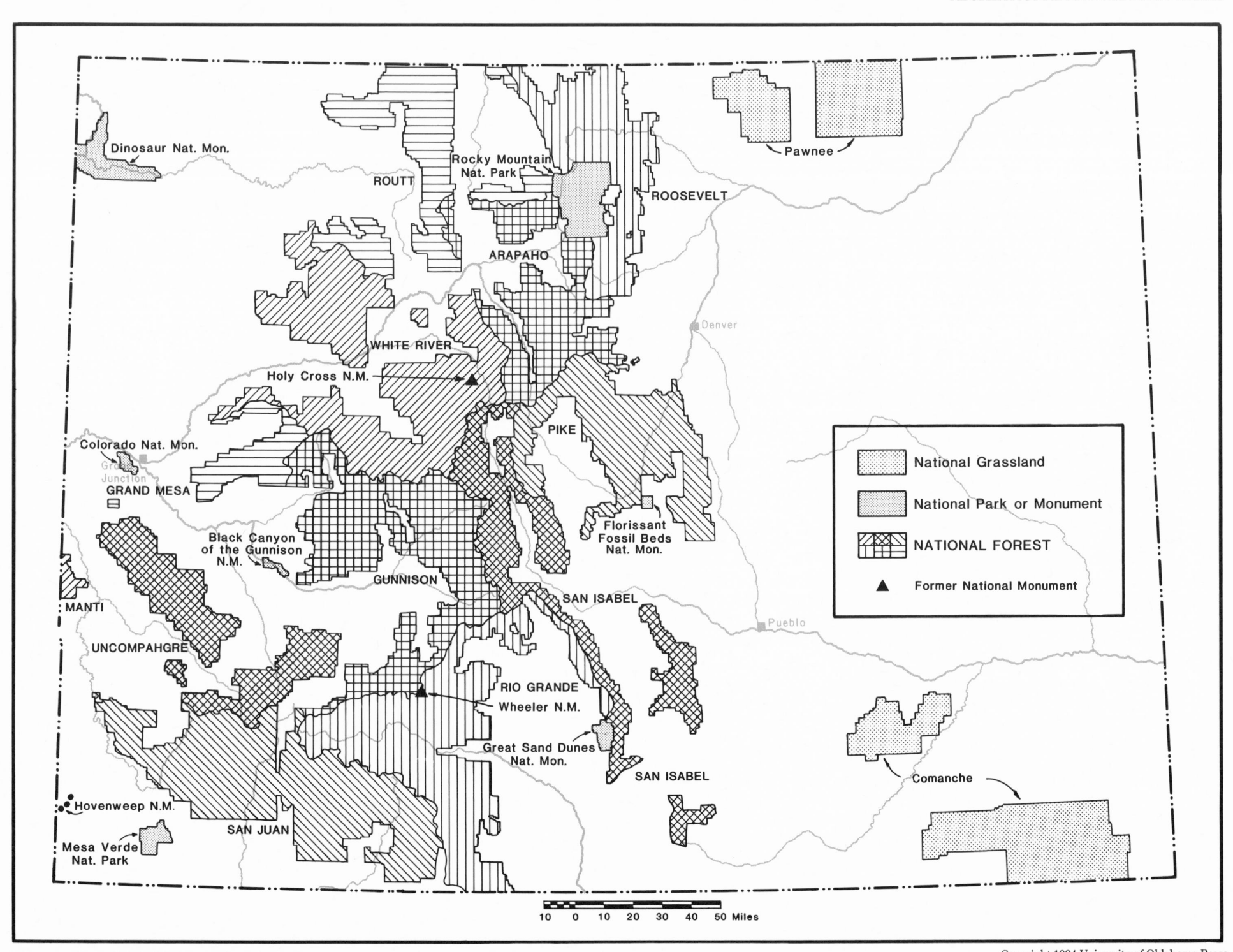

Dinosaur Nat. Mon.

ROUTT

Rocky Mountain
Nat. Park

ROOSEVELT

Pawnee

ARAPAHO

Denver

WHITE RIVER

Holy Cross N.M.

PIKE

Colorado Nat. Mon.

Grand
Junction

GRAND MESA

Black Canyon
of the Gunnison
N.M.

Florissant
Fossil Beds
Nat. Mon.

GUNNISON

MANTI

SAN ISABEL

Pueblo

UNCOMPAHGRE

RIO GRANDE

Wheeler N.M.

Hovenweep N.M.

Great Sand Dunes
Nat. Mon.

SAN ISABEL

Comanche

SAN JUAN

Mesa Verde
Nat. Park

| National Grassland |
| National Park or Monument |
| NATIONAL FOREST |
| ▲ Former National Monument |

10 0 10 20 30 40 50 Miles

NATIONAL FORESTS, GRASSLANDS, MONUMENTS, AND PARKS

50. NATIONAL FORESTS, GRASSLANDS, MONUMENTS, AND PARKS

During America's first 125 years, the U.S. government sold land cheaply or gave it away to promote settlement and exploitation of natural resources. By 1900, Americans began to realize that the supply of land and resources was not endless. This recognition gave birth to a conservation crusade to save some natural areas for future generations as national forests, grasslands, monuments, and parks.

The first flowering of this new policy was the 1891 Forest Reserve Act approved by Congress and Pres. Benjamin Harrison. Initially administered by the Department of the Interior, the Forest Service was transferred to the Department of Agriculture in 1905. The first forest reserve was Yellowstone, followed by the White River National Forest in Colorado. These 1891 designations were meant to curtail the exploitation of public lands by loggers, miners, ranchers, and developers.

Despite howls from some users of public lands, President Harrison in 1892 designated additional reserves, including what are now the Grand Mesa and Pike national forests. Pres. Theodore Roosevelt set aside San Isabel in 1902 and, in 1905, established Gunnison, Holy Cross, Routt, San Juan, and Uncompahgre national forests, adding Arapaho in 1907. Mounting opposition to forest reserves led to the 1907 Denver Public Lands Convention, which helped persuade Congress to prohibit presidential proclamations creating any more reserves in Colorado, Oregon, Washington, Idaho, Montana, or Wyoming.

Congress did not authorize another Colorado national forest until 1932, when it worked with Pres. Herbert Hoover to set aside Roosevelt National Forest. After various name changes, consolidations, and boundary changes, Colorado now has eleven national forests, which constitute about one-fifth of the state's terrain. Two national grasslands, Comanche and Pawnee, were created during the Dust Bowl era as attempts to reclaim overgrazed and overfarmed land and allow natural vegetation to reestablish itself.

The 15 million Colorado acres managed by the National Forest Service are put to multiple uses. Forests protect watersheds, shadowing snow so that it melts gradually over a period of many weeks. They also keep rain from running off too rapidly, preventing erosion and floods. National forests remain our major source of timber through government sales and supervision of the harvest and reforestation. Approximately one-third of the state's cattle and sheep graze on leased national-forest sites where federal authorities help keep the peace between cowboys and sheepmen. National forests also serve as wildlife preserves and recreational havens, with hunting and fishing seasons to harvest wildlife. To accommodate fishermen, streams are stocked with millions of fingerling trout each year. Nearly all of Colorado's thirty-three ski areas are on leased national-forest land.

Commercial uses of national forests led wilderness advocates to crusade for national parks and monuments where conservation would be more stringent. The National Park Service, an agency of the U.S. Interior Department, was created in 1916. Although initially designated for their spectacular scenery, parks came to include historical and cultural attractions. Colorado's first national park, Mesa Verde, was created in 1906 to preserve ancient Native American cliff dwellings from further plunder. The Federal Antiquities Act of 1906 made it a punishable offense to loot archaeological sites on federal land. Mesa Verde remains unique; it is the only major national park dedicated to preserving and interpreting a prehistoric people. Rocky Mountain National Park opened in 1915 after naturalist Enos Mills and the Colorado Mountain Club convinced Coloradans that it would be both an aesthetic and an economic boon.

Whereas both Congress and the president must approve a national park, the president can unilaterally designate a National Monument. Black Canyon of the Gunnison (1933), Colorado (1911), Dinosaur (1915), Florissant Fossil Beds (1969), Great Sand Dunes (1932), and Hovenweep (1923) survive, but Wheeler, established in 1908 as Colorado's first national monument, and Holy Cross were reclassified during the 1940s, when jurisdiction switched from the Park Service to the Forest Service.

As this map shows, much of Colorado is a playground, making tourism a major industry. It is the principal source of income in central and western Colorado, where federal lands are concentrated. Not shown on this map are the extensive remnants of the public domain controlled by the Bureau of Land Management—more than 8 million acres. After Pres. Franklin Roosevelt closed public land sales in 1936, the Bureau of Land Management was established to conserve and manage federal lands, unlike the old Federal Land Office, whose mission was to sell or give them away. Uncle Sam remains the state's largest landholder with jurisdiction over approximately 36 percent of Colorado.

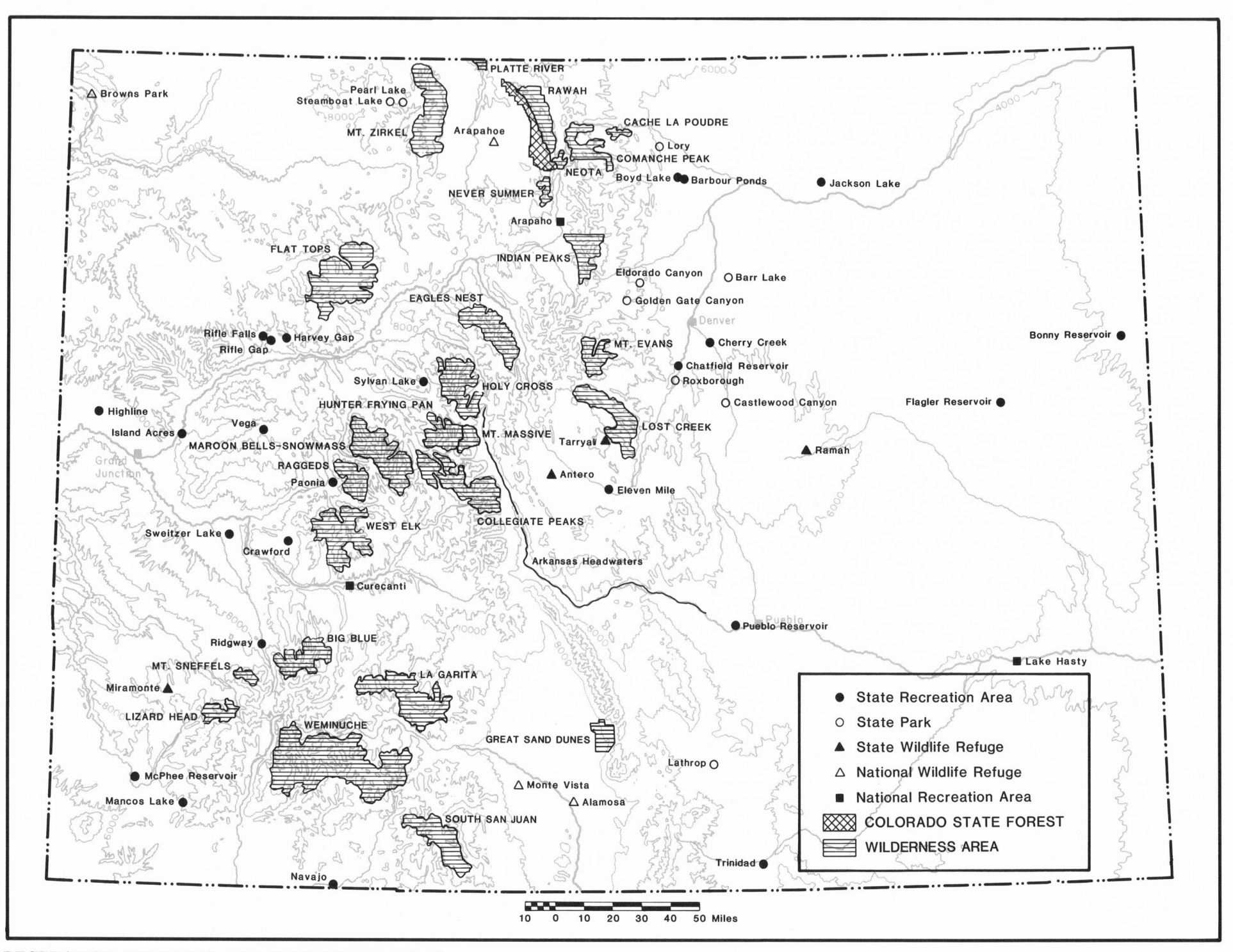

Browns Park △
Pearl Lake
Steamboat Lake ○ ○
PLATTE RIVER
RAWAH
CACHE LA POUDRE
MT. ZIRKEL
Arapahoe △
Lory ○
COMANCHE PEAK
NEOTA
Boyd Lake ● ● Barbour Ponds
Jackson Lake ●
NEVER SUMMER
Arapaho ■
FLAT TOPS
INDIAN PEAKS
Eldorado Canyon ○
Barr Lake ○
EAGLES NEST
Golden Gate Canyon ○
Denver
Rifle Falls ●
Harvey Gap
MT. EVANS
Cherry Creek ●
Bonny Reservoir ●
Rifle Gap
Chatfield Reservoir ●
Sylvan Lake ●
HOLY CROSS
Roxborough ○
HUNTER FRYING PAN
Castlewood Canyon ○
Flagler Reservoir ●
Highline ●
MT. MASSIVE
LOST CREEK
Island Acres ●
Vega ●
Tarryal ▲
MAROON BELLS-SNOWMASS
Ramah ▲
RAGGEDS
Grand Junction
Antero ▲
Paonia
Eleven Mile ●
WEST ELK
COLLEGIATE PEAKS
Sweitzer Lake ●
Crawford ●
Arkansas Headwaters
Curecanti ■
Pueblo
BIG BLUE
Pueblo Reservoir ●
Ridgway ●
Lake Hasty ■
MT. SNEFFELS
LA GARITA
Miramonte ▲
LIZARD HEAD
WEMINUCHE
GREAT SAND DUNES
Lathrop ○
McPhee Reservoir ●
Mancos Lake ●
Monte Vista △
Alamosa △
SOUTH SAN JUAN
Trinidad ●
Navajo

● State Recreation Area
○ State Park
▲ State Wildlife Refuge
△ National Wildlife Refuge
■ National Recreation Area
COLORADO STATE FOREST
WILDERNESS AREA

10 0 10 20 30 40 50 Miles

RECREATION, WILDLIFE, AND WILDERNESS AREAS

51. RECREATION, WILDLIFE, AND WILDERNESS AREAS

Besides national forests, parks, monuments, and grasslands, the federal government has established a national recreation area and three national wildlife refuges in Colorado. The U.S. Fish and Wildlife Service, begun in 1871 as an independent agency, built the Leadville Fish Hatchery (1889) as the first federal hatchery in the Rockies. The Alamosa (1962)–Monte Vista (1953) Wildlife Refuge Complex is noted for its sandhill and whooping cranes. The service also tends the Browns Park (1963) and Arapahoe (1967) wildlife refuges. Colorado's national recreation area, Curecanti, is owned by the Bureau of Reclamation but managed by the National Park Service.

Once scheduled for development as a private resort, Trappers Lake in Rio Blanco County became a national prototype for a roadless wilderness area in the 1920s, thanks to the efforts of Arthur Carhart of the National Forest Service. After a forty-year crusade by Carhart and others, a Federal Wilderness Act, passed in 1964, authorized preserves within national forests where roads, vehicles, and permanent human fixtures are banned. Trappers Lake was included in one of the first wilderness areas, Flat Tops. Since then twenty-eight such areas have been established in Colorado. Another twenty-two areas and additions, totaling 850,000 acres, were designated in 1993. This doubled the space where, as the Wilderness Act put it, "the earth and its community of life are untrammeled by man; where man himself is a visitor who does not remain."

Federal recreation and wildlife areas attracted tourists as well as wildlife, inspiring the creation of the State of Colorado Parks and Recreation Department in 1957. Many state parks and recreation areas opened around flood-control and irrigation reservoirs, specializing in fun and games: kayaking and rafting on the Arkansas Headwaters, eagle watching at Barr Lake, great-blue-heron roosting at Chatfield Reservoir, trout and northern-pike fishing at Eleven Mile Reservoir, rock climbing in Eldorado Canyon, windsurfing at Harvey Gap, hay rides at Lory State Park on Horsetooth Reservoir, and spelunking at Rifle Gap. The State Division of Parks and Outdoor Recreation also administers the Colorado State Forest in Jackson County.

The Colorado Division of Wildlife traces its origins to the 1876 creation of a fish commission that opened the state's first fish hatchery in 1881. In 1893 the office was reorganized and placed under the state fish commissioner and game warden. Among its duties were to supervise hunters and fishermen and protect birds that controlled the insect pests that devastated Colorado crops. Hunting was organized and promoted as a major economic and recreational boon to many small communities. In a 1968 reorganization, the state of Colorado created a Natural Resources Department with five major divisions: Minerals, Lands, Water, Parks, and Wildlife.

The Parks Division supervises the thirty-eight state parks and recreation areas shown on the map, and more parks are being planned for the near future. The Wildlife Division handles hunting and fishing, various wildlife-management activities, and numerous small wildlife areas. Since 1978 the division has used a voluntary state income-tax checkoff to fund wildlife projects. In 1990 the division managed more than 500,000 acres of land, 252 wildlife areas, and 15 fish-hatching-and-rearing stations. To promote outdoor activities and publicize its work, the Colorado Wildlife Division issues a bimonthly magazine, *Colorado Outdoors.* Begun in 1938 as an in-house newsletter, named *Colorado Conservation Comments,* it was renamed *Colorado Outdoors* in 1956, and in 1992 it boasted 45,000 subscribers.

Not shown on this map are many municipal park systems that include sizable parcels outside city limits. Denver owns and operates approximately 13,500 acres of mountain parks, whose jewels are the Winter Park Ski Area and the Red Rocks Outdoor Amphitheater. Canon City, Colorado Springs, Pueblo, Trinidad, and some other cities likewise have parks outside their city limits. Boulder uses its extensive network of mountain parks and green space to insulate itself from sprawling Front Range development. Canon City's municipal parks include the scenic Skyline Drive and the Royal Gorge, over which a bridge, 1,053 feet above the Arkansas River, affords spectacular views.

Wildlife species, once in danger of going the way of the bison, grizzly bear, and the timber wolf, have been making a comeback. Mule deer, elk, coyotes, mountain lions, Canada geese, and red squirrels have returned with a vengeance, becoming a nuisance in some communities. Other creatures, such as jack rabbits, prairie dogs, rattlesnakes, and burrowing owls, are being displaced by the proliferating species called *homo sapiens.*

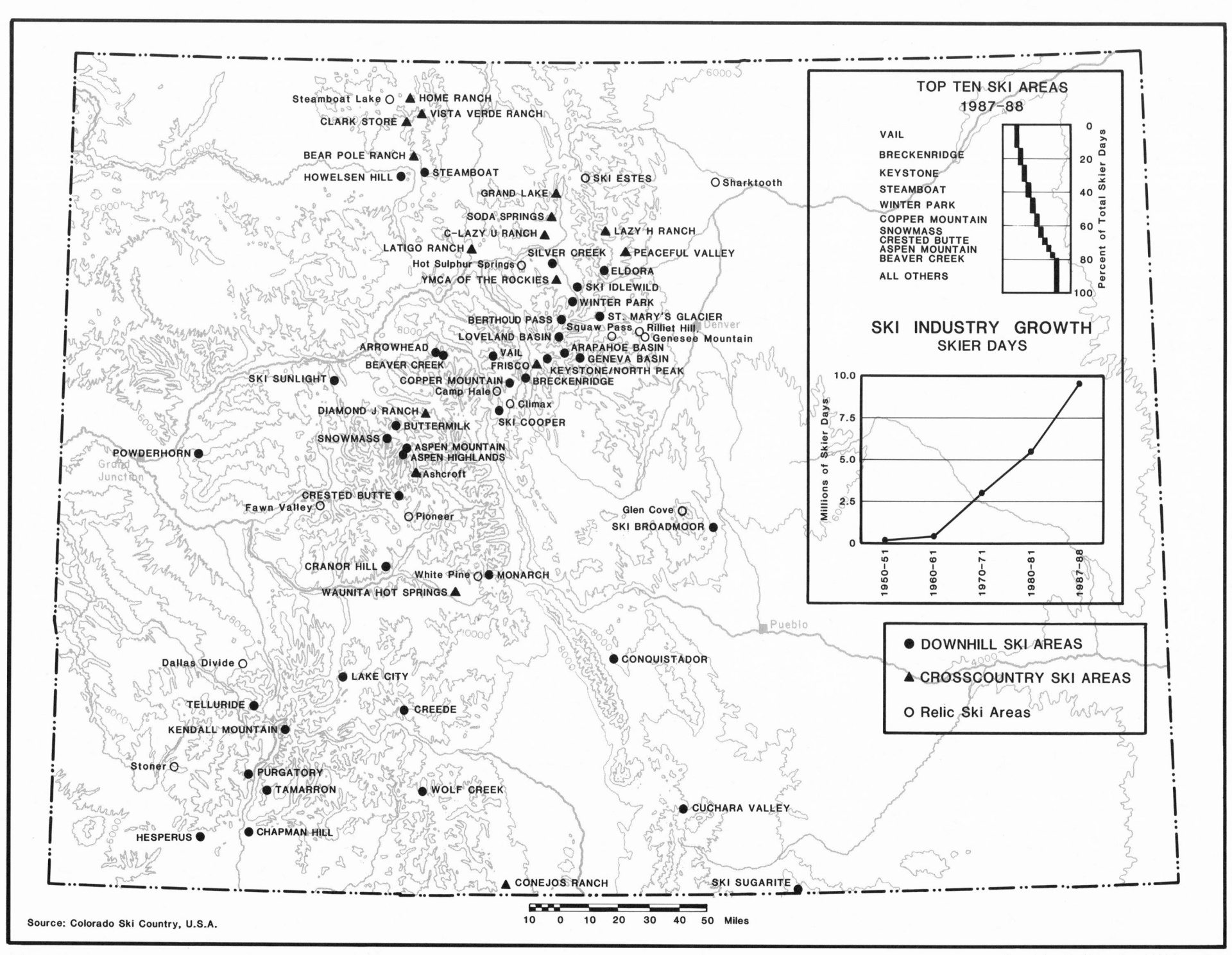

Steamboat Lake ○ ▲ HOME RANCH

▲ VISTA VERDE RANCH

CLARK STORE ○ ▲

BEAR POLE RANCH ▲

HOWELSEN HILL ● ● STEAMBOAT

○ SKI ESTES   ○ Sharktooth

GRAND LAKE ▲

SODA SPRINGS ▲

C-LAZY U RANCH ▲   ▲ LAZY H RANCH

LATIGO RANCH ▲

SILVER CREEK ▲   ▲ PEACEFUL VALLEY

Hot Sulphur Springs ○

YMCA OF THE ROCKIES ▲   ● ELDORA

● SKI IDLEWILD

● WINTER PARK

BERTHOUD PASS ▲   ● ST. MARY'S GLACIER

Squaw Pass ● ● Rilliet Hill   Denver

LOVELAND BASIN ●   ○ Genesee Mountain

ARROWHEAD ●   VAIL ●   ● ARAPAHOE BASIN

BEAVER CREEK ●   ▲ GENEVA BASIN

FRISCO ●   ▲ KEYSTONE/NORTH PEAK

SKI SUNLIGHT ●   COPPER MOUNTAIN ●   ● BRECKENRIDGE

Camp Hale ○

○ Climax

DIAMOND J RANCH ▲   SKI COOPER

● BUTTERMILK

SNOWMASS ●   ● ASPEN MOUNTAIN
                    ● ASPEN HIGHLANDS

POWDERHORN ●   ▲ Ashcroft

Grand Junction

CRESTED BUTTE ●

Fawn Valley ○   ○ Pioneer   Glen Cove ○

                    ● SKI BROADMOOR

CRANOR HILL ●

White Pine ○ ● MONARCH

WAUNITA HOT SPRINGS ▲

Pueblo

● CONQUISTADOR

Dallas Divide ○

● LAKE CITY

TELLURIDE ●

KENDALL MOUNTAIN ●   ● CREEDE

Stoner ○

● PURGATORY

● TAMARRON   ● WOLF CREEK

                    ● CUCHARA VALLEY

HESPERUS ●   ● CHAPMAN HILL

▲ CONEJOS RANCH   ● SKI SUGARITE

Source: Colorado Ski Country, U.S.A.

10 0 10 20 30 40 50 Miles

TOP TEN SKI AREAS
1987-88

VAIL
BRECKENRIDGE
KEYSTONE
STEAMBOAT
WINTER PARK
COPPER MOUNTAIN
SNOWMASS
CRESTED BUTTE
ASPEN MOUNTAIN
BEAVER CREEK

ALL OTHERS

Percent of Total Skier Days
0   20   40   60   80   100

SKI INDUSTRY GROWTH
SKIER DAYS

Millions of Skier Days
10.0
7.5
5.0
2.5
0

1950-51   1960-61   1970-71   1980-81   1987-88

● DOWNHILL SKI AREAS

▲ CROSSCOUNTRY SKI AREAS

○ Relic Ski Areas

SKI AREAS

Sliding over snow on long, narrow boards has been popular since the Middle Ages in Scandinavia. Immigrants from the Scandinavian countries of Norway and Sweden introduced skiing to Colorado's gold and silver camps, where at first it was known as "snow-shoeing." Winter travelers, mail carriers, and even circuit-riding ministers such as the "Snow-Shoe Itinerant," Father John Dyer, used skis.

Organized recreational skiing in Colorado may have begun in 1883 at Irwin in Gunnison County when workers at the Star Mine formed a racing club. The nearby towns of Crested Butte and Gunnison also joined in the sport, holding races on Tenderfoot Mountain overlooking Gunnison. Another Gunnison County ski area, Pioneer, boasted the first Colorado chair lift in 1938, but closed in 1951.

Carl Howelsen, a Norwegian immigrant, fathered recreational skiing in Colorado. A stonemason who gravitated to the mountains, he spearheaded Colorado's first winter-sports carnival and ski-jump competition in 1912 at Hot Sulphur Springs. The following year "the Flying Norseman" moved to Steamboat Springs and turned that town into a winter-sports center, where Howelsen Hill still attracts ski jumpers.

The Colorado Mountain Club, founded in Denver in 1912, organized ski parties to Rilliet Hill on Lookout Mountain. Ski enthusiasts also set up a course with a jump at Genesee Mountain Park, where the Colorado Mountain Club erected a stone ski hut. Other early ski areas now gone were Climax; Fawn Valley, near Paonia; Glen Cove, on Pike's Peak; Sharktooth, just west of Greeley; Ski Estes Park (Hidden Valley); Steamboat Lake; and White Pine, near Monarch Pass.

In the beginning skiers spent most of their day on long, difficult hikes up the slope. Then they descended ungroomed terrain with their ankles strapped onto long, heavy skis with bindings known as "bear traps." Development of cable bindings (1931), steel edges (1934), mechanical lifts, and groomed slopes improved the sport tremendously. Thor Groswold opened a factory in Denver to manufacture inexpensive, sturdy hickory skis that were sold at the May Company, a department store that installed a rope tow in 1937 on Berthoud Pass. Groswold, Clark Blickensderfer, and some sidekicks set up a homemade rope tow on Loveland Pass, where the Loveland Basin and Loveland Valley areas operate today.

Aspen Mountain opened as Colorado's first commercial ski area in 1937, using old mining-tram towers and cables to pull skiers uphill on a boat tow. Ashcroft, where locals gathered for winter sports in the 1930s, has emerged as a haven for cross-country skiing and dog sledding. Winter Park, a project of the Denver Parks and Recreation Department, opened in 1938 as the second commercial area. Winter Park has become one of the most-popular areas, noted for its family and handicapped ski programs. Its success led to nearby developments such as Ski Idlewild (1960) and Silver Creek (1983). Arapahoe Basin originated in 1941 when National Forest Ranger Wilfred ("Slim") Davis began a school there to teach fellow rangers how to ski and patrol ski areas, which are nearly all on land leased within national forests.

Camp Hale, on the north side of Tennessee Pass, opened in 1942 as the Army's Winter Ski Troops training base. On weekends some troopers from the Tenth Mountain Division skied nearby mountains. After World War II many Camp Hale veterans returned to Colorado to develop the ski industry. Camp Hale's training runs have been redeveloped as Ski Cooper.

Vail, opened in 1962 on a former sheep ranch, has become the largest ski area in North America. Vail spin-offs included lavish new resorts at Beaver Creek (1980) and Arrowhead (1989).

Aspen's spectacular transformation, from a fading silver camp to an internationally celebrated tourist mecca with five major ski areas (Aspen Highlands, Aspen Mountain, Buttermilk, Snowmass, and Ski Sunlight, near Glenwood Springs), encouraged other declining mining towns to exploit "white gold." Breckenridge (1961), Crested Butte (1963), Keystone (1970), and Telluride (1972) now attract hordes of skiers.

Other mining towns—Creede, Lake City, Silverton—have small-scale ski operations, while Durango boasts three area resorts—Chapman Hill, Hesperus, and Purgatory. The Broadmoor, grande dame of Colorado's resort hotels, built its own ski slope in 1961, as well as an ice-skating rink and school. As downhill ski-lift ticket prices climbed over forty dollars and the cost of skis, boots, and other attire soared, many turned to cross-country skiing. Cross-country touring can be done anywhere snow falls, but it became the specialty of some dude ranches such as Bear Pole, Conejos, Diamond J, Latigo, Vista Verde, Waunita Hot Springs, and the YMCA's Snow Mountain Ranch.

Approximately one hundred Colorado ski areas have come and gone over the years, ranging from small-town rope tows to slick, multimillion-dollar operations with high-speed quads and closed-gondola lifts. Some of the more memorable, better-documented downhill and cross-country commercial areas are mapped here. As the ski-industry charts indicate, this sport has snowballed into about 11 million skier days a year—a fourth of the U.S. total. What began as a quaint practice for a few Scandinavian miners has become big business in Colorado.

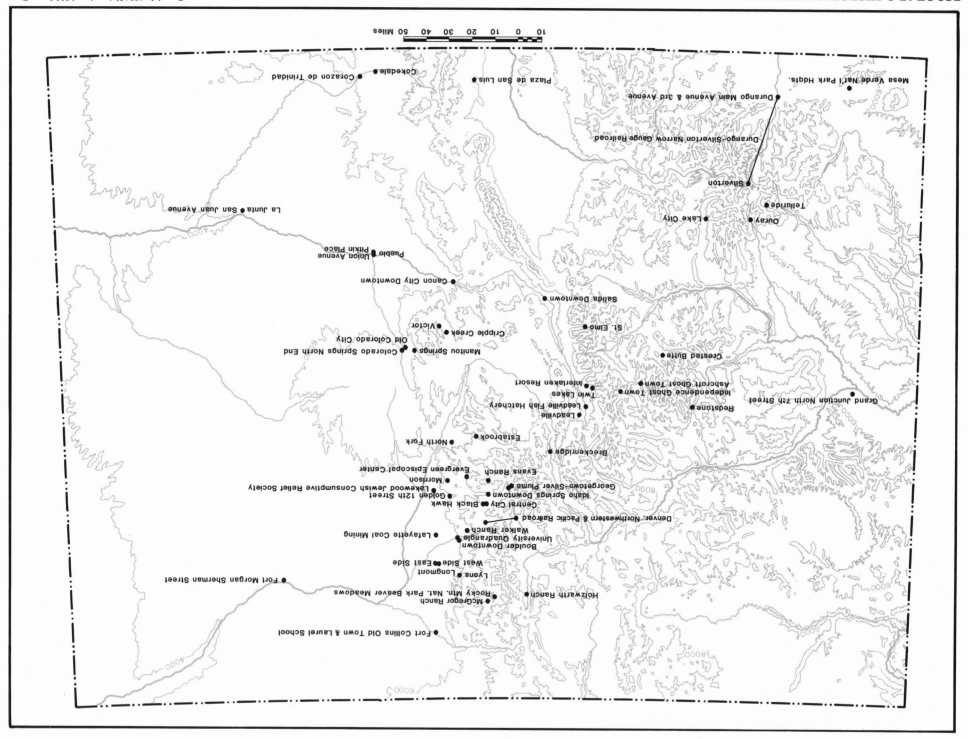

As a boom and bust state, Colorado built fast and recklessly, demolishing whole generations of buildings with each new wave of prosperity. Many nineteenth-century towns are gone, as are most of the landmarks built by the pioneers.

After losing so much architectural heritage, Coloradans slowly became interested in preservation. The first notable recycling took place in Central City, where the Opera House, a masonry landmark designed by Robert Roeschlaub, the state's first licensed architect, was restored in 1932 for a successful summer opera that continues to this day. This reborn building inspired other rehabilitations that led to the 1966 National Register designation of the Central City Historic District. In 1991 the Central City–Black Hawk–Nevadaville area was upgraded by the National Park Service to a national historic landmark district.

Another preservation pacesetter has been the tiny silver-mining community of Georgetown. During the 1970s this mountain village passed an ordinance that the Colorado Supreme Court rejected as too strict. Although Georgetown's redrafted ordinance is weaker, the town boasts of not losing a single structure—not even an outhouse—since its 1966 listing on the National Register as a historic district. Many decaying structures have been reconstructed, including the Lebanon Mine and the Georgetown Loop Railroad, the star attractions of the Colorado Historical Society's Georgetown–Silver Plume District. Georgetown also boasts the William A. Hamill House, a mining tycoon's home, yard, and six-hole outhouse restored and operated as a museum by the Georgetown Society.

Although Georgetown and Central City guarded their built environment, most communities did not. A turning point came in 1966 when the National Historic Preservation Act established state historic-preservation offices nationwide. This federally funded and supervised program, administered locally by the Colorado Historical Society, is charged with identifying, nominating, and monitoring landmarks for the National Register of Historic Places. Yet the only tools of the State Historic Preservation Officer (SHPO) in protecting landmarks are federal and Colorado state tax incentives, grants, reviews, and recommendations.

Communities wanting tougher preservation measures passed local ordinances to set up commissions to identify landmarks and prevent unsympathetic alterations and, in some cases, prohibit or delay demolitions. Since Savannah, Georgia, established the first Landmarks Preservation Commission in 1935, more than fifteen hundred similar bodies have been established across the country. In Colorado, local landmark agencies had been established in Aspen, Aurora, Boulder, Central City, Colorado Springs, Cripple Creek, Denver, Durango, Fort Collins, Georgetown, Golden, Idaho Springs, Lake City, Longmont, Manitou Springs, and Telluride.

Some mining towns have qualified as National Register historic districts, including the stabilized ghost town of Independence. Two company coal-mining towns, Cokedale and the planned workers' utopia of Redstone, are National Register historic districts. The humble frame cottages of the coal-mining era are best preserved in Lafayette. Landmark-district status has eluded Aspen, where a building boom fueled by wealthy newcomers has erased much of the old silver city, including the last miner's cabin. Aspen, Breckenridge, Crested Butte, and Telluride offer neo-Victorian architecture that imitates and sometimes spoofs historic styles.

Silverton exemplifies how poverty can enrich a community by encouraging the recycling of old structures. Cripple Creek and Victor, once a bustling metropolitan complex, produced millions in gold, but little money was sunk back into those communities. Even more than mineral wealth, health-care facilities and Colorado's sunny, dry climate attracted immigrants, a fact commemorated by the National Register designation of the Jewish Consumptive Relief Society campus in Lakewood.

Main Streets have generally decayed, their business stolen by suburban shopping centers. An exception is Durango's Main Avenue, which outsells new outlying shopping centers. Plaza de San Luis, Corazon de Trinidad, Union Avenue in Pueblo, Old Colorado City, Old Town Fort Collins, and the downtown districts of Salida, Morrison, Manitou Springs, Lyons, Leadville, Idaho Springs, Canon City, and Boulder are other fairly well-preserved commercial cores. Boulder's University of Colorado Quadrangle is the state's best example of consistent, planned campus architecture, with Tuscan-style structures of pink Lyons sandstone capped with red tile roofs.

Antique residential districts have been recognized on Golden's Twelfth Street, Grand Junction's North Seventh Street, Durango's Third Avenue, Colorado Springs's North End, Pueblo's Pitkin Place, La Junta's San Juan Avenue, Longmont's East and West Side, Fort Collins's Laurel School area, and Fort Morgan's Sherman Street. Colorado's livestock industry is commemorated by the Evans, Holzwarth, and McGregor ranches, which also function as open space. Estabrook, Evergreen's Episcopal Conference Center, North Fork, Twin Lakes, Interlaken, and Rocky Mountain National Park are examples of early resort areas. Railroad history has left Colorado with many landmark depots, as well as the Corona Pass roadbed of the Denver, Northwestern, and Pacific, and the still-rolling Durango-Silverton and Cumbres and Toltec narrow-gauge routes.

Besides the National Register historic districts shown here and on the Denver map (Map 54), more than nine hundred individual Colorado properties are listed on the National Register of Historic Places. These sites have been selected from among more than 28,000 historic and 48,000 prehistoric sites on file with the State Historic Preservation Office. Those designations and a 1990 statute providing state income-tax credits for restoring designated landmarks suggest that Coloradans have grown more concerned about their architectural heritage.

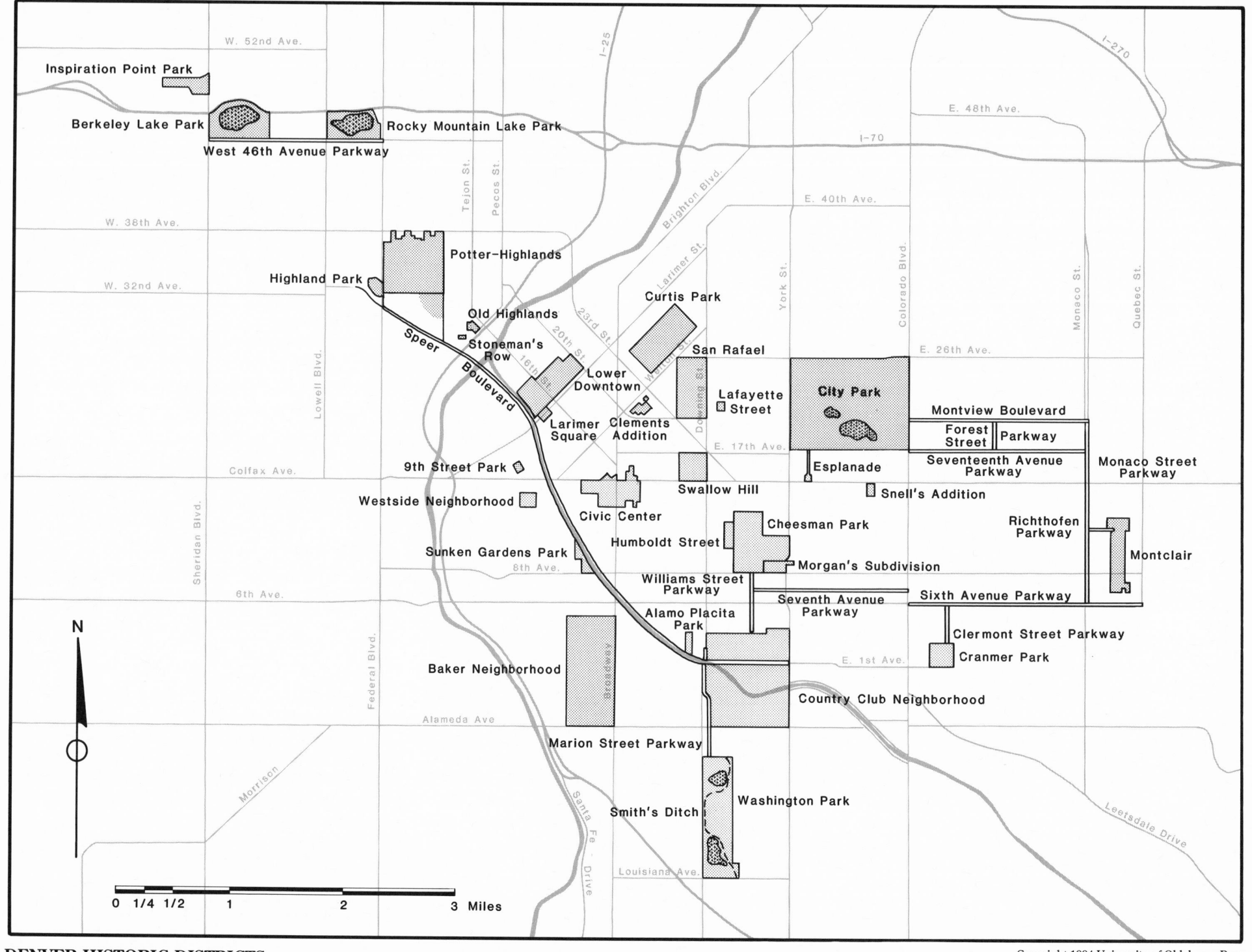

Inspiration Point Park

Berkeley Lake Park

Rocky Mountain Lake Park

West 46th Avenue Parkway

W. 52nd Ave.

W. 38th Ave.

W. 32nd Ave.

Teion St.

Pecos St.

Brighton Blvd.

Larimer St.

York St.

Colorado Blvd.

Monaco St.

Quebec St.

E. 48th Ave.

E. 40th Ave.

I-25

I-70

I-270

Potter-Highlands

Highland Park

Old Highlands

Stoneman's Row

Speer Boulevard

Lowell Blvd.

23rd St.

20th St.

16th St.

Downing St.

Curtis Park

San Rafael

Lafayette Street

City Park

E. 26th Ave.

Lower Downtown

Larimer Square

Clements Addition

Montview Boulevard

Forest Street Parkway

Seventeenth Avenue Parkway

Monaco Street Parkway

9th Street Park

Westside Neighborhood

Civic Center

Esplanade

Snell's Addition

Swallow Hill

E. 17th Ave.

Sheridan Blvd.

Colfax Ave.

Cheesman Park

Humboldt Street

Morgan's Subdivision

Richthofen Parkway

Montclair

Sunken Gardens Park

8th Ave.

Williams Street Parkway

Seventh Avenue Parkway

Sixth Avenue Parkway

Federal Blvd.

6th Ave.

Alamo Placita Park

Clermont Street Parkway

Cranmer Park

Baker Neighborhood

E. 1st Ave.

Country Club Neighborhood

Alameda Ave.

Marion Street Parkway

Morrison

Santa Fe Drive

Smith's Ditch

Washington Park

Louisiana Ave.

Leetsdale Drive

N

0 1/4 1/2   1   2   3 Miles

Copyright 1994 University of Oklahoma Press

A building boom that began after World War II and did not end until the 1980s erased much of Denver's nineteenth-century urban core. What remained of Auraria and Denver City, the two oldest neighborhoods, was largely leveled by the Denver Urban Renewal Authority during the 1960s.

The disappearance of downtown distressed some citizens. They persuaded the mayor and city council to create the Denver Landmark Preservation Commission in 1967. Modeled on commissions set up in Savannah, New York, Boston, Charleston, and other cities, the Denver Landmark Preservation Commission became a public forum for discussing proposed landmarks and landmark districts that might be recommended to the city council for official designation and protection. If the city council approves designation of a landmark or landmark district, any application for a building permit to alter a designated structure is flagged and sent to the landmark commission for design review. The commission has power to deny building or demolition permits within a district and to delay demolition of individual landmarks for a year. These actions buy time to find a new use for old buildings. Denver designations often overlap National Register designations, which are also mapped here.

Denver's first designated local historic district, Larimer Square, consists of antique buildings in the 1400 block of Larimer Street that were restored and recycled during the 1960s. Larimer Square supporters and other preservationists formed Historic Denver, Inc., in 1970 to rescue the Molly Brown House from demolition. They purchased the residence of the legendary poor Irish girl turned mining millionaire and converted it to a house museum. Historic Denver then turned its attention to Ninth Street and to Curtis Park, two early historic districts.

Despite scattered opposition from real-estate developers and property-rights advocates, Denver has designated more than 200 individual sites and some 22 local landmark districts, encompassing approximately 4,000 individual buildings. Several other neighborhoods are lobbying for additional historic-district designations to protect their historic residential ambiance. Opponents groan that little old ladies in tennis shoes and bow-tied dilettants are stopping progress, imposing the dead hand of the past on what has always been a knock-down, build-a-bigger-one town. Building saviors, on the other hand, dream of preserving many more of Denver's nineteenth-century neighborhoods.

Auraria, the original 1858 settlement leveled to construct the Auraria Higher Education Center, retains one block of historic homes and a corner store in Ninth Street Park. Nearby, the Westside neighborhood conserves another chunk of antique Auraria residences. Southside preservation efforts extended to the Country Club area, where local architects built expensive homes in predominately English, Italian, and Spanish revival styles.

Many vernacular versions of Italianate, Queen Anne, or eclectic design are preserved in the Baker Neighborhood. In east Denver, the Cheesman Park, Humboldt, Morgan, and Swallow Hill districts are studded with mansions erected by mining millionaires. Snell's Addition is a unique experiment in building street and alley homes, a prototype that did not catch on among Denverites, who were accustomed to detached homes with relatively spacious yards. The Montclair Historic District is an unusual neighborhood where nineteenth-century homes are infilled with more-modest twentieth-century bungalows and ranch-style houses. In northeast Denver, the Clements Addition, Curtis Park, Lafayette Street, and the San Rafael district preserve historic residential areas within the shadow of downtown high-rises.

The Civic Center Historic District protects the park-like heart of the city. It is ringed by monumental public buildings—the gold-domed State Capitol, the eagle-crowned City and County Building, and a trio of decidedly modern structures—the Denver Public Library, the Denver Art Museum, and the Colorado History Museum. The Lower Downtown Historic District next to Union Station offers sturdy, handsome commercial buildings and warehouses now recycled as art galleries, offices, lofts, shops, bars, brewpubs, and restaurants.

Northwest Denver, where many immigrants settled, remains primarily a residential area capped by church spires. Masonry structures grace Stoneman's Row, Old Highlands, and Highland Park. Potter-Highlands, the city's largest historic district, has a diverse stock of homes ranging from modest terraces to mansions. Vintage churches and taverns preserve the various ethnic flavors—German, Hispanic, Italian, Irish, Jewish, and Slavic.

Much of Denver's elegant park and parkway system, a legacy of the "City Beautiful" era, has been landmarked to discourage further street widenings and commercial intrusions. Restoration of tree lawns, antique light fixtures, street furniture, landscaping, and pedestrian amenities distinguish this verdant network. Speer Boulevard serves as the trunk of the parkway system with branches along Clermont, Forest, Marion, Monaco, Montview, Forty-sixth, Richthofen, Seventh, Sixth, and Williams parkways. Parkways lead to landmarked parks—Alamo Placita, Berkeley Lake, City, Cheesman, Cranmer, Highland, Inspiration Point, Rocky Mountain Lake, Sunken Gardens, and Washington.

Note the absence of landmark districts in southwest and southeast Denver, the last quadrants of the city to be developed. As landmarks usually are at least fifty years old, these bungalow, international-style, and ranch-house neighborhoods may contain future historic districts.

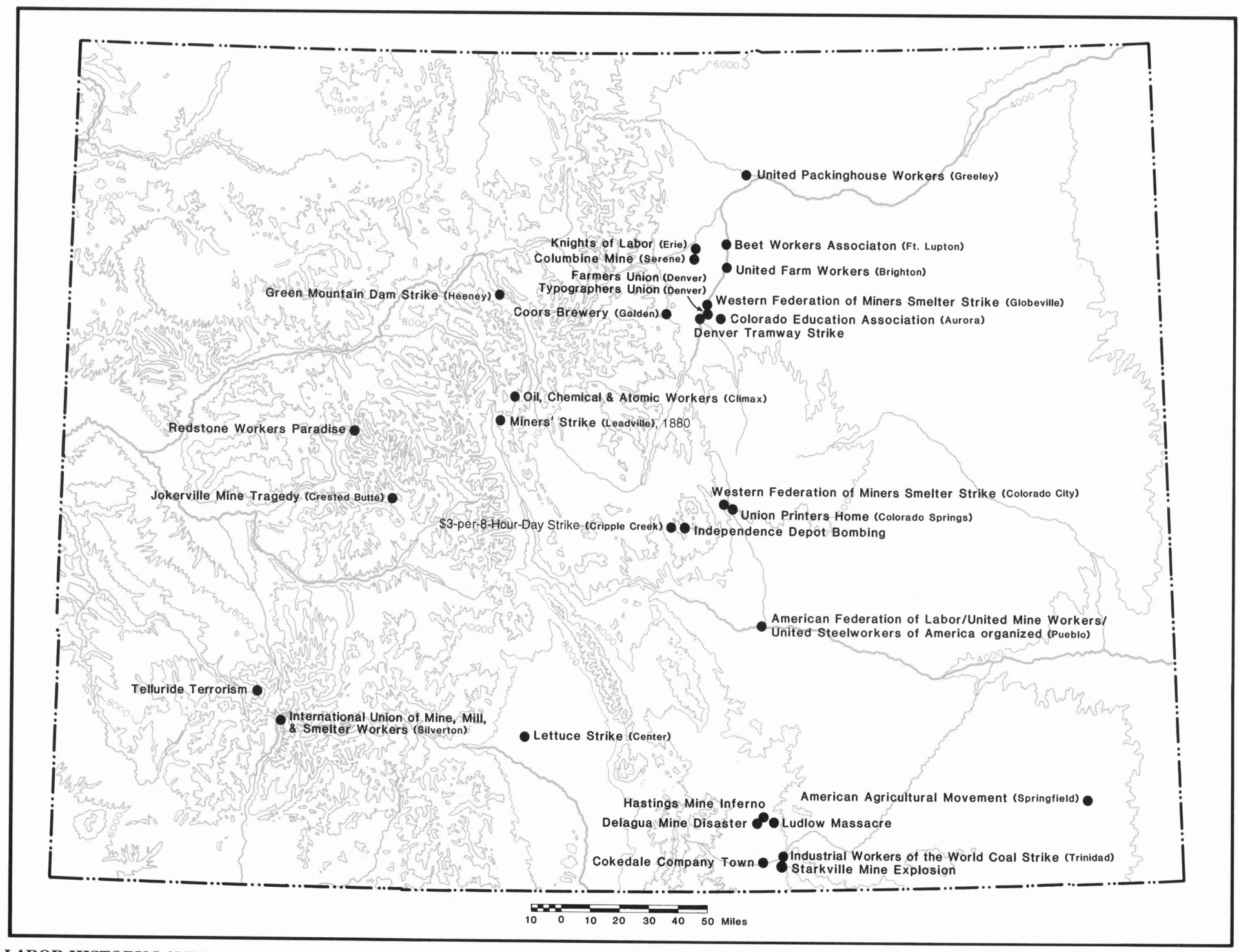

United Packinghouse Workers (Greeley)

Knights of Labor (Erie)
Columbine Mine (Serene)
Beet Workers Associaton (Ft. Lupton)
Farmers Union (Denver)
Typographers Union (Denver)
United Farm Workers (Brighton)
Green Mountain Dam Strike (Heeney)
Western Federation of Miners Smelter Strike (Globeville)
Coors Brewery (Golden)
Colorado Education Association (Aurora)
Denver Tramway Strike

Oil, Chemical & Atomic Workers (Climax)
Miners' Strike (Leadville), 1880

Redstone Workers Paradise

Jokerville Mine Tragedy (Crested Butte)
Western Federation of Miners Smelter Strike (Colorado City)
Union Printers Home (Colorado Springs)
$3-per-8-Hour-Day Strike (Cripple Creek)
Independence Depot Bombing

American Federation of Labor/United Mine Workers/
United Steelworkers of America organized (Pueblo)

Telluride Terrorism

International Union of Mine, Mill,
& Smelter Workers (Silverton)
Lettuce Strike (Center)

American Agricultural Movement (Springfield)

Hastings Mine Inferno
Delagua Mine Disaster
Ludlow Massacre

Cokedale Company Town
Industrial Workers of the World Coal Strike (Trinidad)
Starkville Mine Explosion

10 0 10 20 30 40 50 Miles

LABOR-HISTORY LANDMARKS

55. LABOR-HISTORY LANDMARKS

Deadly labor accidents and conflicts are a skeleton in Colorado's closet. Mining and smelting, the major occupations in the "good old days," were dangerous: at least one in twenty-five workers suffered death or injury each year. Survivors faced chronic health problems from exposure to smelter poisons and mine dust.

The deadliest single episode transpired at a coal mine in Hastings, twelve miles north of Trinidad. There, on April 27, 1917, an explosion blasted 121 men into eternity. Another blast at a Colorado Fuel and Iron Company coal mine in Starkville on October 9, 1910, had killed some 56 miners. A third Trinidad-area tragedy at Delagua ended 79 lives. At Crested Butte the 1884 Jokerville Mine explosion killed 59.

Despite wretched conditions, workers were slow and often unsuccessful at organizing unions. Colorado's labor history began happily enough with the 1860 formation of the Denver Local No. 49 of the International Typographical Union, which thirty-two years later opened its national retirement haven, the Union Printers Home, in Colorado Springs.

Miners first formally organized in Erie, near Boulder, where coal diggers started a local of the Knights of Labor in 1878. Leadville hard-rock miners organized another branch of this national union in 1880 and launched Colorado's first major strike that year. It was crushed in what became a familiar scenario: mineowners brought in strikebreakers and persuaded the governor to declare martial law and send in the state militia to protect mineowners, their mines, and "scab" labor.

To champion labor, the *Denver Labor Inquirer* began publication in 1882 and promoted the Denver Trades and Labor Assembly. This assembly successfully agitated for the creation of a Colorado Bureau of Labor Statistics and the proclamation of the Labor Day holiday in 1887. The *Inquirer,* the pioneer voice of the labor movement, was replaced subsequently by the *Colorado Labor Advocate.*

In 1894 the Denver-based Western Federation of Miners (WFM) won a Cripple Creek strike to maintain a minimum wage of three dollars a day and a maximum workday of eight hours. Under the leadership of William ("Big Bill") Haywood, the WFM hoped to make a minimum daily wage of three dollars for a maximum workday of eight hours a statewide standard for mine and smelter workers. The WFM began this crusade with a statewide 1903–1904 strike, a bloody confrontation that culminated in the bombing deaths of thirteen miners at the Independence Mine depot. Mine and smelter owners crushed the WFM with the help of private guards, private detectives, and state militia sent in by promanagement Gov. James M. Peabody.

Although some surviving unionists reorganized as the Industrial Workers of the World (IWW) and the International Union of Mine, Mill, and Smelter Workers (IUMMSW), hard-rock mining unions did not recover their pre-1903 strength. Antiunionists kidnaped and expelled union workers in Cripple Creek and Telluride during the 1903–1904 strike and an IUMMSW organizer in Silverton in 1938. The 1939 Green Mountain Dam strike was broken up by Summit County sheriffs and deputized vigilantes.

In an effort to keep workers satisfied and out of unions, mineowner John Osgood built a model company town at Redstone. Josephine Roche tried another unusual strategy at her Columbine Mine, where she settled what had been deadly confrontations by going into partnership with unionists and paying the highest wages in the industry.

The United Mine Workers Union (UMW) organized Colorado coal miners, whose working conditions were more wretched than the hard-rock miners. Coal companies often recruited immigrants, notably Greeks, Italians, and Mexicans, whom they expected to be docile. These miners and their families lived in company towns such as Cokedale, shopped at company stores, and initially accepted the long hours, poor pay, and dangerous working conditions. In 1913 and 1914 many went on strike in the southern Colorado coalfields at the urging of UMW organizers. At the tent town of Ludlow, strikers and their families were fired upon by the state militia and by gunmen hired by the mine owners. Among the nineteen who died that day were two women and nine children. This bloody Colorado Coalfield War ended only after Pres. Woodrow Wilson sent in federal troops.

Colorado farmers joined national organizations such as the Grange. Founded in 1867, this organization remains active, although it has evolved from an economic, educational, and political organization to more of a social one. During the dark days of the dust bowl and the Great Depression, many agrarians joined the Colorado Farmers Union, a part of the National Farmers Union. After the NFU moved its headquarters to Denver, it became Colorado's largest farm organization, with cooperative grain elevators, insurance programs, livestock facilities, and even a co-op oil company. Farm workers, embittered by their poverty and political ineffectiveness, have formed various unions over the years, including the Beet Workers Union, the American Agricultural Movement, and the United Farm Workers (UFW). The UFW, based in California, led strikes among carnation-greenhouse workers in Brighton (1968) and lettuce workers in Center (1970).

Such violent confrontations as the strikes of Denver Tramway workers (1920) and IWW Boulder County coal workers (1927) left unions battered. Since the 1970s unionized work forces at Pueblo's steel mill and Climax's molybdenum mine have been laid off, while the Coors Brewery, Continental Airlines, and the Monfort Packing Plant have broken unions. Since the 1950s union membership has fallen from around 25 percent to 13 percent of the nonagricultural work force in Colorado. The state's per capita union membership is about 30 percent lower than the national average.

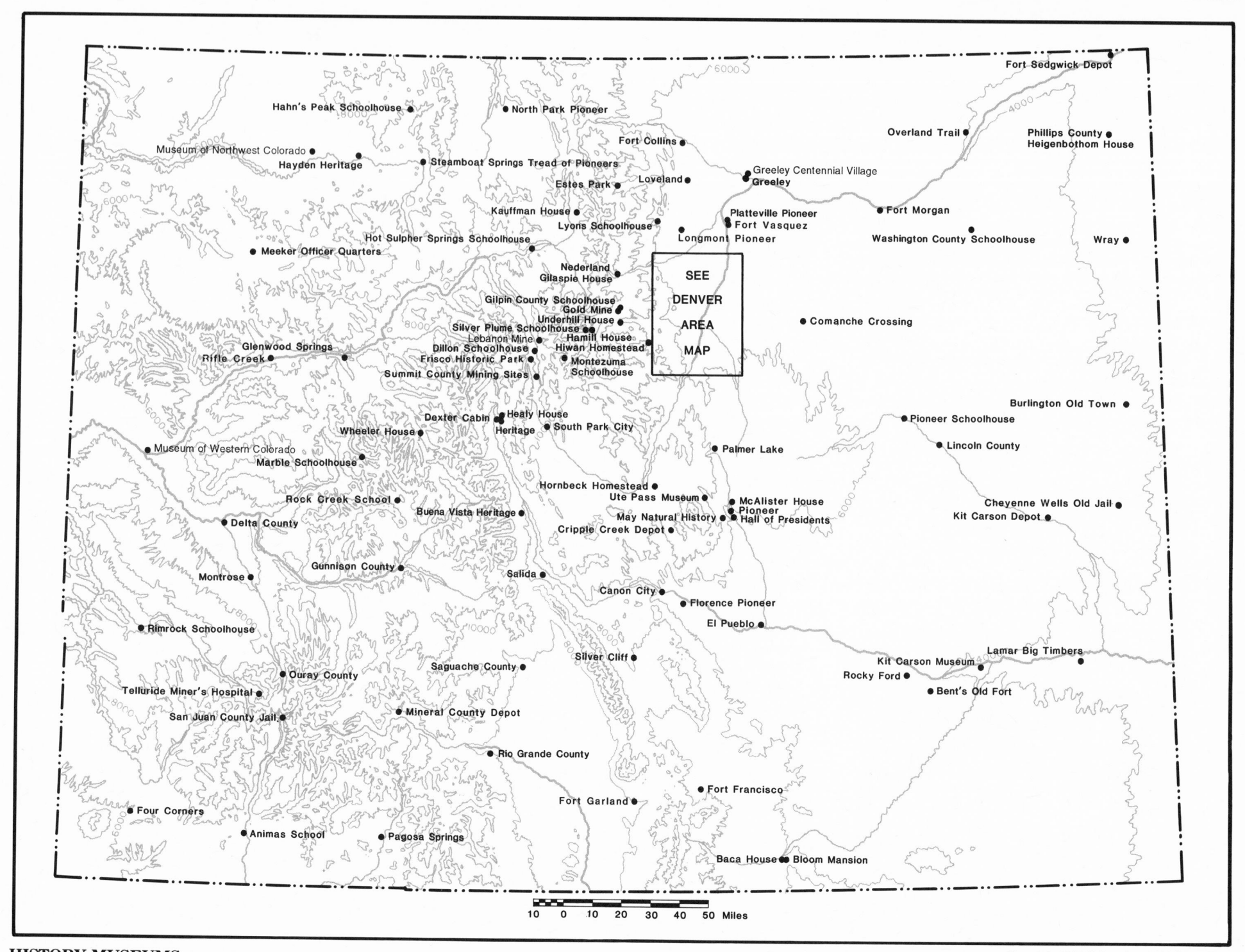

Fort Sedgwick Depot

Hahn's Peak Schoolhouse
North Park Pioneer
Overland Trail
Phillips County
Heigenbothom House

Museum of Northwest Colorado
Fort Collins
Hayden Heritage
Steamboat Springs Tread of Pioneers
Greeley Centennial Village
Greeley
Estes Park
Loveland
Fort Morgan
Kauffman House
Platteville Pioneer
Fort Vasquez
Lyons Schoolhouse
Washington County Schoolhouse
Wray
Hot Sulpher Springs Schoolhouse
Longmont Pioneer
Meeker Officer Quarters
Nederland
Gilaspie House
SEE
DENVER
AREA
MAP
Gilpin County Schoolhouse
Gold Mine
Comanche Crossing
Underhill House
Silver Plume Schoolhouse
Hamill House
Lebanon Mine
Hiwan Homestead
Glenwood Springs
Dillon Schoolhouse
Rifle Creek
Frisco Historic Park
Montezuma
Summit County Mining Sites
Schoolhouse
Burlington Old Town
Dexter Cabin
Healy House
Pioneer Schoolhouse
Wheeler House
Heritage
South Park City
Lincoln County
Museum of Western Colorado
Palmer Lake
Marble Schoolhouse
Hornbeck Homestead
Rock Creek School
Ute Pass Museum
McAlister House
Cheyenne Wells Old Jail
Buena Vista Heritage
Pioneer
May Natural History
Hall of Presidents
Kit Carson Depot
Delta County
Cripple Creek Depot
Montrose
Gunnison County
Salida
Canon City
Florence Pioneer
El Pueblo
Rimrock Schoolhouse
Lamar Big Timbers
Silver Cliff
Kit Carson Museum
Ouray County
Saguache County
Rocky Ford
Telluride Miner's Hospital
Bent's Old Fort
San Juan County Jail
Mineral County Depot
Rio Grande County
Fort Francisco
Four Corners
Fort Garland
Animas School
Pagosa Springs
Baca House
Bloom Mansion

10 0 10 20 30 40 50 Miles

A young state with many newcomers and tourists, Colorado has long used museums to promote a greater historical consciousness. Early settlers, proud of their achievements, formed the Colorado Pioneers Society in 1866 when Colorado Territory was only five years old. In 1879 some of those Pioneers helped form the Colorado Historical Society, which operates the state's largest and oldest history museum.

Besides its Denver headquarters and museum, the Historical Society has developed regional museums around the state. The Baca House and the Bloom Museum in Trinidad focus on southern Colorado. El Pueblo Museum commemorates an adobe trading post near the confluence of Fountain Creek and the Arkansas River where the city of Pueblo now stands. Fort Garland, which was once an 1850s adobe outpost commanded by Kit Carson, guards exhibits of nineteenth-century military history and the Hispanic traditions of the San Luis Valley. Fort Vasquez, a reconstructed 1830s adobe bastion on the South Platte River near Platteville, is used to interpret the fur trade. The reconstructed Georgetown Loop Railroad and Lebanon Mine are vivid living-history operations. The mining frontier and Victoriana are showcased in Leadville's Healy House and Dexter Cabin, while Colorado's oldest continuous residents are celebrated in the Ute Indian Museum at Montrose.

Uncle Sam also has established some splendid museums, including a $3 million reconstruction of Bent's Old Fort on the Arkansas River near La Junta. The Mesa Verde and Rocky Mountain national parks include historical exhibits in their visitor centers. The national monuments—Colorado, Curecanti, Dinosaur, Florissant Fossil Beds, and Great Sand Dunes—have visitor-center museums that combine history with natural history (see Map 50).

Many of the sixty-three counties have a county historical society and museum, with the glaring exception of Denver. One of the smallest and poorest, San Juan, has converted its three-story stone jail into a large museum and has built an archive next door. Summit County has showcased its mining history at a dozen interpretive sites, including an assay office, a placer-mining site, a lode mine, and dredge-boat ruins. Out on the eastern plains, Burlington has developed a historical village commemorating the often-overlooked, heroic efforts of the sodbusters. Other museum building collections may be seen at Fairplay's South Park City, Greeley's Centennial Village, and Strasburg's Comanche Crossing.

Despite limited hours, resources, and staff (usually volunteer) these county museums are gems, often occupying historic structures. Many of them sprang up around 1976, when Colorado celebrated its centennial as well as the national bicentennial. At that time communities began to assess and showcase their history. Residents began to look around for their pioneer railroad depots, schoolhouses, hotels, and other public buildings, only to discover that these historic resources often were gone or neglected. A rash of restorations started in the 1970s, encouraged by the national preservation movement. Consequently, many communities restored historic structures for museum use.

History museums vary widely in accessibility, quality, and presentation, with small towns often outdoing larger ones. Rangely, for example, recently converted its sturdy 1921 armory into the Museum of Northwest Colorado. Several other local museums aspire to regional coverage, including the Old Jail Museum in Cheyenne Wells and Grand Junction's Museum of Western Colorado.

In a footloose society searching for roots, museums provide a basic source of cultural transfer, introducing younger generations to the life-styles, goals, successes, and failures of earlier Coloradans.

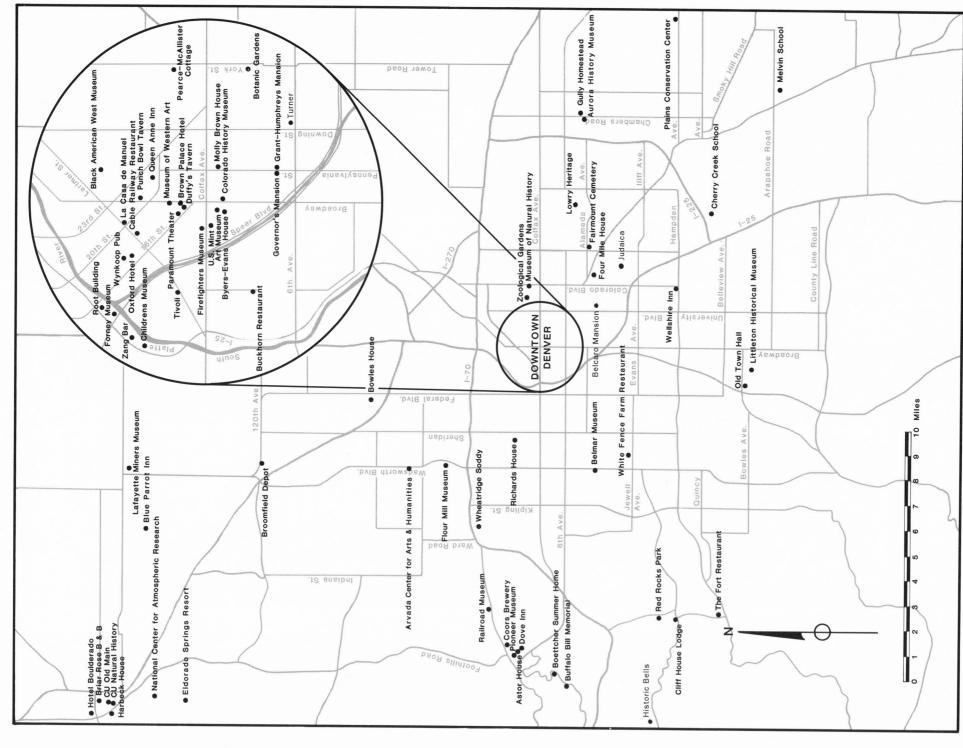

DENVER METRO MUSEUMS AND HISTORIC ACCOMMODATIONS

More than seventy-five museums and historic accommodations in the five-county metro area range from the Forney Transportation Museum, with its fleet of exotic vehicles, to an adobe replica of Bent's Fort in Morrison offering food and drink of the old West. New places open and old ones close every year, continually changing the list of attractions.

The Denver Museum of Natural History is the most popular museum in the state. Nearby, the Denver Zoological Gardens has become one of the nation's best zoos. Another top tourist target is the U.S. Mint in downtown Denver. From the mint, in Civic Center Park, it is an easy walk to the Byers-Evans House Museum, the Colorado History Museum, the Denver Art Museum, and the Museum of Western Art.

To cure museum fatigue, try some of the historic taverns and restaurants downtown, including the grand old Brown Palace Hotel, where nautical memorabilia adorn the Ship Tavern and a fortune in medieval armor decorates the Palace Arms Dining Room. Nearby are Duffy's Shamrock Tavern, the Denver City Cable Railway Building/Old Spaghetti Factory, La Casa de Manuel (with murals depicting Hispanic history), and the Punch Bowl, an old-time tavern with landscapes painted on the high-backed booths.

Urban-renewal projects erased much of old downtown Denver, with the notable exception of the Lower Downtown Historic District. LoDo is replete with restored resorts, including the city's oldest hotel, the Oxford, with its Art Deco Cruise Room. A block away, the J. S. Brown warehouse has been merrily recycled as Colorado's first brewpub, the Wynkoop Brewing Company. Only one 1920s movie palace, the Paramount, survives. Antique buildings have been restored as shops and cafes in Larimer Square and four blocks down Larimer at the Tivoli Brewery. Denver's century-old Buckhorn Exchange is jammed with hundreds of stuffed animals, antique weapons, traps, photos, and other western Americana, while menu items range from buffalo steaks to rattlesnake meat to Rocky Mountain oysters.

Free guided tours of the gold-domed State Capitol are available. The Capitol Hill neighborhood, once home for many mining millionaires, is studded with house museums: the Grant-Humphreys Mansion, the Governor's Mansion, the Molly Brown House, and the Pearce-McAllister Cottage, which features the Museum of Miniatures, Dolls, and Toys. Farther south, the Belcaro Mansion of Sen. L. H. Phipps is easily Denver's grandest house museum.

Cemeteries are often overlooked as preserves of architectural, historical, and horticultural interest. This is particularly true of Denver's Fairmount Cemetery, the largest cemetery park in the Rockies and the final home for many notables. It is also the state's largest arboretum. Local and exotic plants flourish in what was the old city cemetery, now the well-fertilized Denver Botanic Gardens, complete with a large domed conservatory for tropical plants.

Southeast Aurora offers unbroken prairie occupied only by prairie dogs, deer, antelope, and rattlesnakes at the Plains Conservation Center. Another natural wonder, worth a trip even when no performance is scheduled, is the Red Rocks Outdoor Amphitheater near Morrison, where huge red-sandstone outcroppings form a spectacular, acoustically superb setting in a large foothills park.

Other metro attractions include the Littleton Historical Museum and the Aurora History Museum, which has showcased its history in the old city hall. Lakewood's Belmar Museum is a collection of historic structures salvaged from the relentless developers in Colorado's third largest city. Other westside attractions include a free tour of Coors, the nation's third largest brewery, in downtown Golden, and a visit to Buffalo Bill's Grave and Museum atop Lookout Mountain.

Boulder's downtown historic district and Pearl Street Mall include such hospitable landmarks as the Boulderado Hotel. The University of Colorado Campus is a National Register historic-district showcase harboring the university's Old Main and natural history museums. Harbeck House, which houses the Boulder Historical Society, focuses on community history.

Specialized museums range from the splendid pioneer farmhouse museum at the Four Mile House, the area's oldest surviving structure, to the Turner Museum, housing some three thousand engravings, prints, and publications by and about the British artist J. M. W. Turner. Evergreen's Museum of Historic Bells boasts five thousand bells, everything from a tea bell to a gong from Hong Kong.

Ethnic history is the focus of the Black American West Museum, which concentrates on African American cowboys, miners, railroaders, and pioneers. The Mizel Museum of Judaica in the BMH Synagogue stresses Colorado's rich Jewish history. Immigrant coal miners are celebrated in Lafayette's Miners Museum.

At least twenty-five historic homes have been converted to bed-and-breakfast accommodations where you can get an insider's look at fascinating, cluttered, Victorian homes. Such hospitable landmarks, as well as some thirty museums in the metro area, will reward rubberneckers.

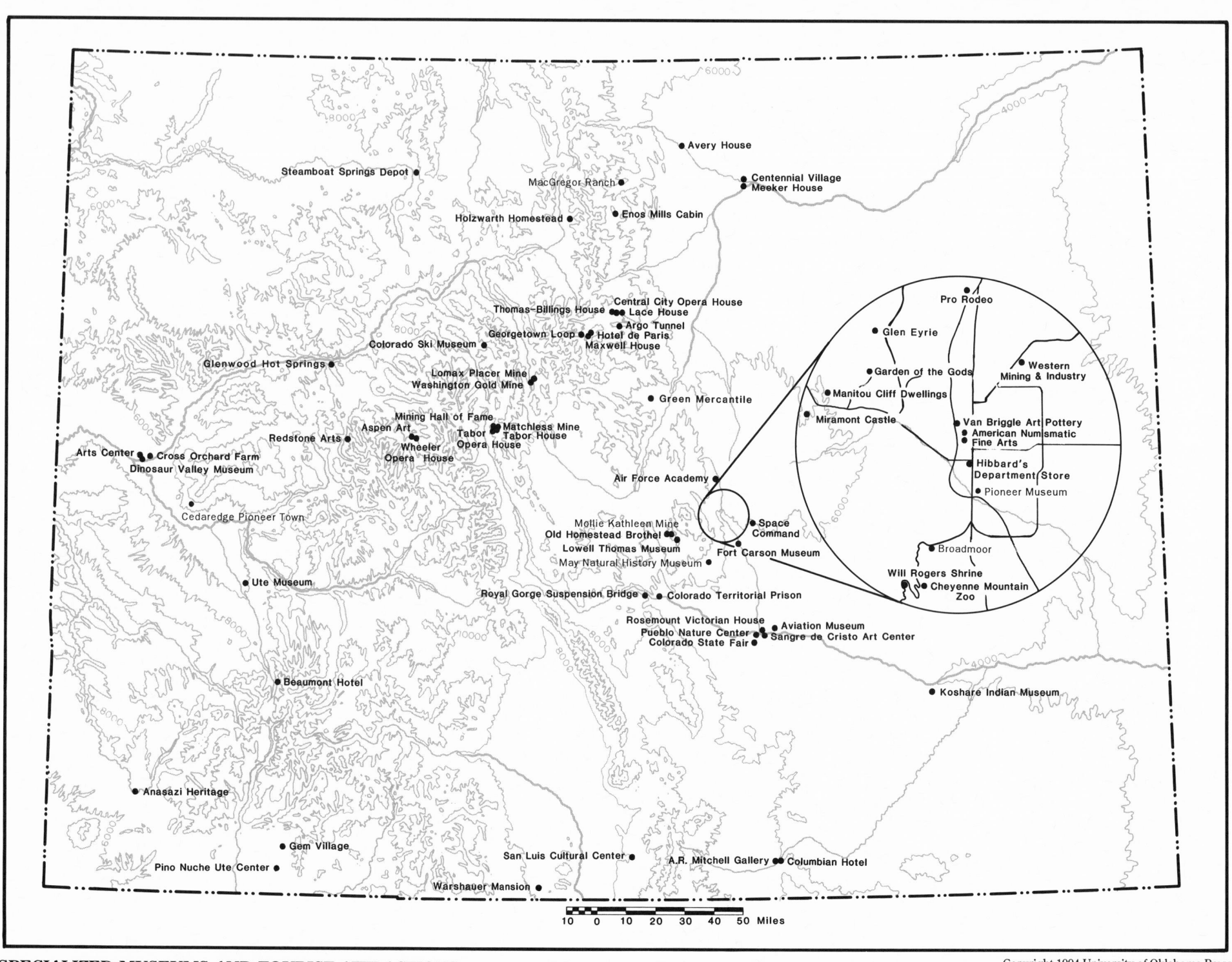

Avery House

Steamboat Springs Depot

MacGregor Ranch
Centennial Village
Meeker House

Holzwarth Homestead
Enos Mills Cabin

Central City Opera House
Thomas–Billings House
Lace House
Argo Tunnel
Georgetown Loop
Hotel de Paris
Colorado Ski Museum
Maxwell House

Glenwood Hot Springs
Lomax Placer Mine
Washington Gold Mine

Green Mercantile

Mining Hall of Fame
Aspen Art
Matchless Mine
Redstone Arts
Tabor
Tabor House
Wheeler
Opera House
Opera House

Arts Center
Cross Orchard Farm
Dinosaur Valley Museum

Air Force Academy

Cedaredge Pioneer Town

Mollie Kathleen Mine
Space
Old Homestead Brothel
Command
Lowell Thomas Museum
May Natural History Museum
Fort Carson Museum

Ute Museum

Royal Gorge Suspension Bridge
Colorado Territorial Prison

Rosemount Victorian House
Aviation Museum
Pueblo Nature Center
Sangre de Cristo Art Center
Colorado State Fair

Beaumont Hotel

Koshare Indian Museum

Anasazi Heritage

Gem Village

San Luis Cultural Center
A.R. Mitchell Gallery
Columbian Hotel
Pino Nuche Ute Center

Warshauer Mansion

Pro Rodeo

Glen Eyrie

Garden of the Gods
Western
Mining & Industry

Manitou Cliff Dwellings

Miramont Castle
Van Briggle Art Pottery
American Numismatic
Fine Arts

Hibbard's
Department Store
Pioneer Museum

Broadmoor

Will Rogers Shrine
Cheyenne Mountain
Zoo

10   0   10   20   30   40   50 Miles

SPECIALIZED MUSEUMS AND TOURIST ATTRACTIONS

58. SPECIALIZED MUSEUMS AND TOURIST ATTRACTIONS

Colorado has many specialized museums and tourist attractions in addition to the history museums previously listed on Maps 56 and 57. These museums and sites, mostly privately owned, usually have a very specific focus and often are geared toward family entertainment and education.

Colorado Springs, in particular, is loaded with such attractions. The Pioneer Museum in the old El Paso County Courthouse is a gold mine of information and exhibits, while Hibbard's Department Store is an operational antique. Colorado's grandest resort hotel, the Broadmoor, has a small Carriage Museum featuring an exquisite collection of horse-drawn and horseless carriages. The Broadmoor Figure Skating Museum and Hall of Fame is also on the hotel's spacious grounds. The Broadmoor Zoo, moved to Cheyenne Mountain after a monkey bit a hotel guest, still features primates in its largest exhibit. Farther up the mountain, the Will Rogers Shrine to the Sun commemorates the famed humorist who kept America laughing throughout the Great Depression and World War II. The May Natural History Museum displays some eight thousand insects. Various military installations in and around Colorado Springs also cater to sightseers, notably the Air Force Academy, Fort Carson, and the Space Command Center.

Of the various selected house museums shown here, one of the most spectacular is Glen Eyrie, the Tudor castle of D & RG railroad president and Colorado Springs founder William J. Palmer. Palmer built his English manor house in a wild canyon setting near the Garden of the Gods. The Van Briggle Art Pottery Company has been making its distinctive wares for almost a century, while the Colorado Fine Arts Center excels in southwestern art. The American Numismatic Museum showcases the nation's best exhibit of coins and paper money. Manitou Springs offers

fake cliff dwellings with items transplanted from Mesa Verde before it became a national park, saving tourists a long and difficult trip to see the real thing.

Cripple Creek offers the state's only brothel museum, the Old Homestead Parlor House, and the deepest and most-celebrated mine tour, the Mollie Kathleen. A few miles away the town of Victor commemorates its most famous resident in the Lowell Thomas Museum.

Pueblo's Rosemount Victorian House is one of the state's most elegant house museums, complete with a carriage-house restaurant. The many nearby Victorian homes and colorful ethnic neighborhoods, plus an old-fashioned downtown, make Pueblo one of the least expensive and more interesting urban experiences for sightseers. Pueblo's many other attractions range from the airport's Aviation Museum to the Sangre de Cristo Arts Center.

At the state penitentiary in Canon City, the old territorial prison is now a museum. Prisoners there carved their names into the stone blocks with which they built their own jail. Nearby, Canon City operates Royal Gorge, the world's highest suspension bridge, soaring a thousand feet above the Arkansas River canyon.

Southwestern Colorado showcases its Native American roots at the Anasazi Heritage Center and at nearby Crow Canyon, where the public can join archaeological digs. Ute and Hispanic cultures are spotlighted at the Pino Nuche Center on the Southern Ute Reservation, and at the San Luis Cultural Center, which is in an adobe village that is Colorado's oldest continually occupied town. Antonito, once the sheep-raising capital of Colorado, prizes the mansion of sheep king Fred Benjamin Warshauer. In Trinidad the A. R. Mitchell Gallery of Western Art is near the grand old Columbian Hotel in the Corazon de Trini-

dad Historic District. La Junta's Koshare Indian Museum celebrates Native American arts, crafts, and dances.

Leadville hosts the National Mining Hall of Fame as well as the home, opera house, and Matchless Mine of Horace Tabor, Colorado's most-celebrated mining tycoon. Aspen, another silver city, has become a cultural mecca, boasting a good art museum, the state's leading music festival, and a restored opera house. Central City, the first community to restore its mining-era opera house for modern extravaganzas, also features some of the best Victorian house tours. Since 1991 Central City has offered limited-stakes gambling, as have Black Hawk and Cripple Creek, often behind the restored facades of historic structures. Mining history is showcased in Breckenridge at the Lomax Placer, the French Gulch dredge-boat ruins, and the Washington Mine.

Grand Junction, the Western Slope's largest city, offers a fine arts center, a dinosaur museum, and a living-history museum at Cross Orchard Farm. Other agricultural museums are Centennial Village, in Greeley; Pioneer Town, in Cedaredge; MacGregor Ranch, in Estes Park; and Holzwarth Museum, in Rocky Mountain National Park. Visitors to Rocky Mountain National Park, the state's top tourist draw, may also visit the log cabin of Enos Mills, the founding father of the park.

Colorado has hundreds of hot springs, of which at least forty are open to the public. The largest outdoor hot-springs pool is at Glenwood Springs, and there are others at Alamosa, Eldorado Springs, Idaho Springs, Manitou Springs, Mount Princeton, Ouray, Pagosa Springs, Salida, Steamboat Springs, and Hot Sulphur Springs. Weary travelers may find rejuvenation and refreshment in these natural wonders before pushing on to the next museum or tourist stop.

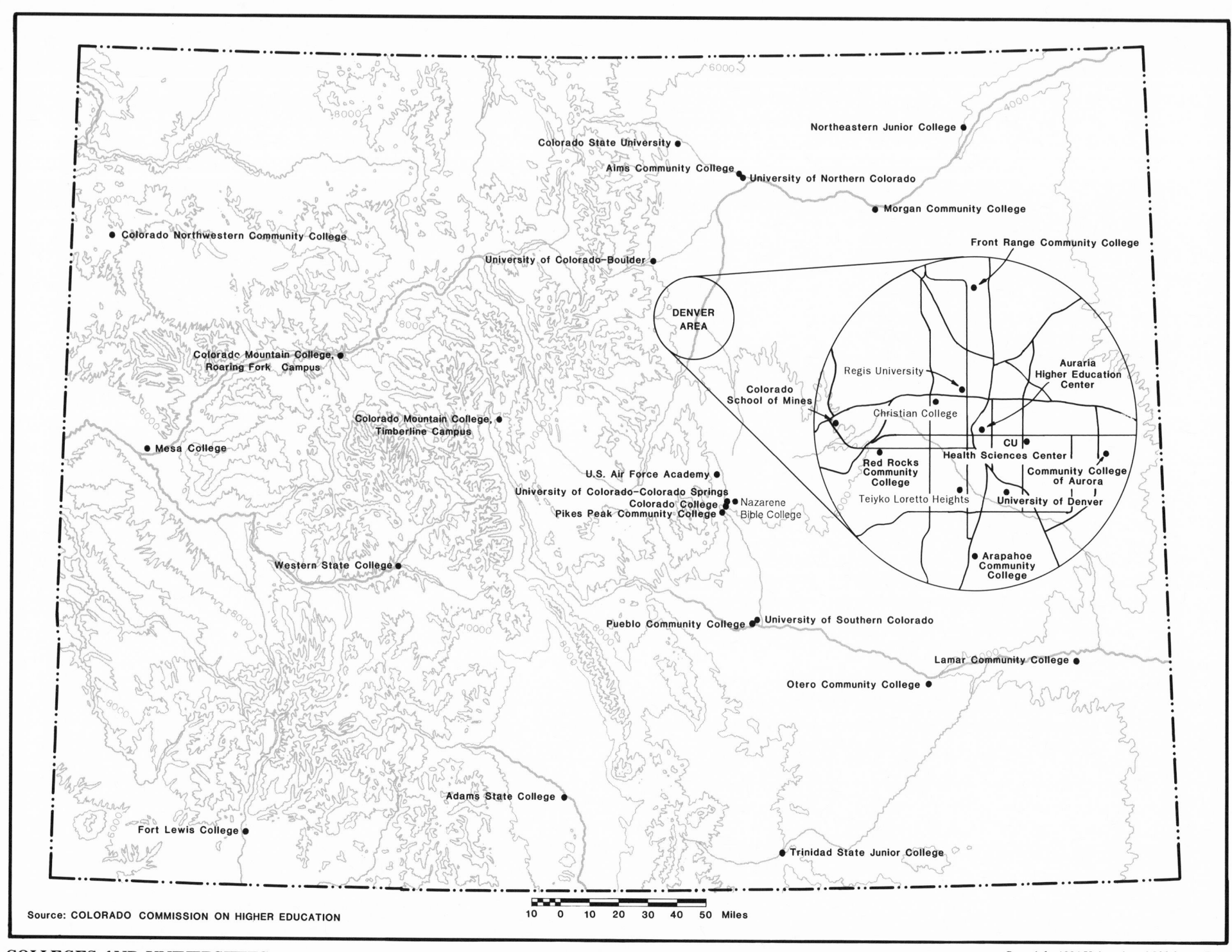

Northeastern Junior College

Colorado State University

Aims Community College • University of Northern Colorado

Morgan Community College

Colorado Northwestern Community College

Front Range Community College

University of Colorado–Boulder

DENVER AREA

Regis University

Colorado Mountain College, Roaring Fork Campus

Auraria Higher Education Center

Colorado School of Mines

Christian College

Colorado Mountain College, Timberline Campus

CU Health Sciences Center

Mesa College

Red Rocks Community College

Community College of Aurora

U.S. Air Force Academy

Teiyko Loretto Heights

University of Denver

University of Colorado–Colorado Springs
Colorado College
Pikes Peak Community College • Nazarene Bible College

Arapahoe Community College

Western State College

Pueblo Community College • University of Southern Colorado

Lamar Community College

Otero Community College

Adams State College

Fort Lewis College

Trinidad State Junior College

Source: COLORADO COMMISSION ON HIGHER EDUCATION

10 0 10 20 30 40 50 Miles

COLLEGES AND UNIVERSITIES

59. COLLEGES AND UNIVERSITIES

Colorado's state-supported higher-education system consists of five universities, five state colleges, and sixteen community or junior colleges. In addition, the state boasts four private colleges and two private universities.

The University of Colorado (1877), largest and oldest of the state schools, has more than forty thousand students and four campuses: Boulder, Colorado Springs, Denver, and the state's only medical school, the Health Sciences Center in Denver.

Colorado State University (1879), founded at Fort Collins as the state agricultural college, has become a full-blown university while retaining an emphasis on agricultural education and research. The University of Northern Colorado (1889), established at Greeley as the state teachers college, has undergone similar development. The Colorado School of Mines (1874), in Golden, claims to be the world's foremost college of mineral engineering, and it receives strong support in a state largely created by mineral wealth.

Colorado launched a system of state colleges to address educational needs in outlying areas. Adams State College (1925), in Alamosa; Fort Lewis College (1911), in Durango; Mesa College (1925), in Grand Junction; Trinidad State Junior College (1925), in Trinidad; and Western State College (1911), in Gunnison, offer various degree programs. Last to be established, Southern Colorado State (1933), in Pueblo, was promoted in 1975 when it became the University of Southern Colorado.

A system of two-year community, or junior, colleges, modeled on California's pioneer efforts to democratize higher education, was established in Colorado in 1967. These two-year colleges have sprung up in sixteen communities around the state. Among them are Aims, Colorado Northwestern, Colorado Mountain, Front Range, Lamar, Morgan, Northeastern Otero, Red Rocks, and Western State. Vocational-technical training for adults began with the Opportunity School established by Emily Griffith and the Denver Public Schools in 1916. Such training now is offered at regional "voc-tech" centers in Alamosa, Aurora, Boulder, Cortez, Delta, Fort Collins, and Trinidad.

The state's most-popular single campus is the Auraria Higher Education Center. Developed in the 1970s as an urban-renewal project in Denver's oldest neighborhood, this novel, low-budget campus has shared facilities (library, recreation center, student center, and so on) for the Community College of Denver, Metropolitan State College of Denver, and the University of Colorado at Denver. These three institutions have a joint enrollment of more than twenty-five thousand full-time-equivalent students.

The University of Denver (1864) is the state's oldest institution of higher learning and its largest private school, having merged with the Colorado Women's College during the 1980s. Founded by Territorial Governor John Evans as the Colorado Seminary, DU offers doctoral programs in a wide variety of fields, including international studies and theology. The Colorado College, founded in Colorado Springs in 1873, is the state's best-endowed private school with a fine reputation for undergraduate education. In 1877 the Catholic teaching order of Jesuits founded what has become Denver's Regis University, while the Sisters of Loretto established Loretto Heights in 1890 for Denver women. A century later it became Teikyo Loretto Heights, a Japanese-owned school for students from Japan. The Nazarene Bible College, in Colorado Springs, and Colorado Christian College, in Lakewood, are newer, smaller private colleges.

The United States Air Force Academy, with its dramatic chapel and huge campus, is a tourist target. Opened on the north side of Colorado Springs in the 1950s, it enrolls some four thousand male and female cadets aspiring to become Air Force officers.

During the nineteenth century chronic underfunding made Colorado's so-called universities and colleges little more than glorified high schools. Professionalism and academic distinction came slowly. The national attempt to make higher education available to the masses may be dated to the GI Bill passed after World War II to fund college and university training for veterans. Quonset huts and trailers sprang up on many campuses to handle the enrollment explosion. Not until the 1960s and 1970s did Colorado, with federal encouragement and financial aid, greatly expand its higher-education facilities.

Federal funding increased as a result of the 1964 Civil Rights Act and the Higher Education Act of 1965. State funding also soared, climbing from $28 million in 1962 to $332 million in 1982. Following a tremendous growth during the 1960s and 1970s in both the number and the enrollments of public colleges and universities, higher education has become more stable. Colorado still aspires to make higher education available to all its residents and prides itself on having one of the highest education levels in the country.

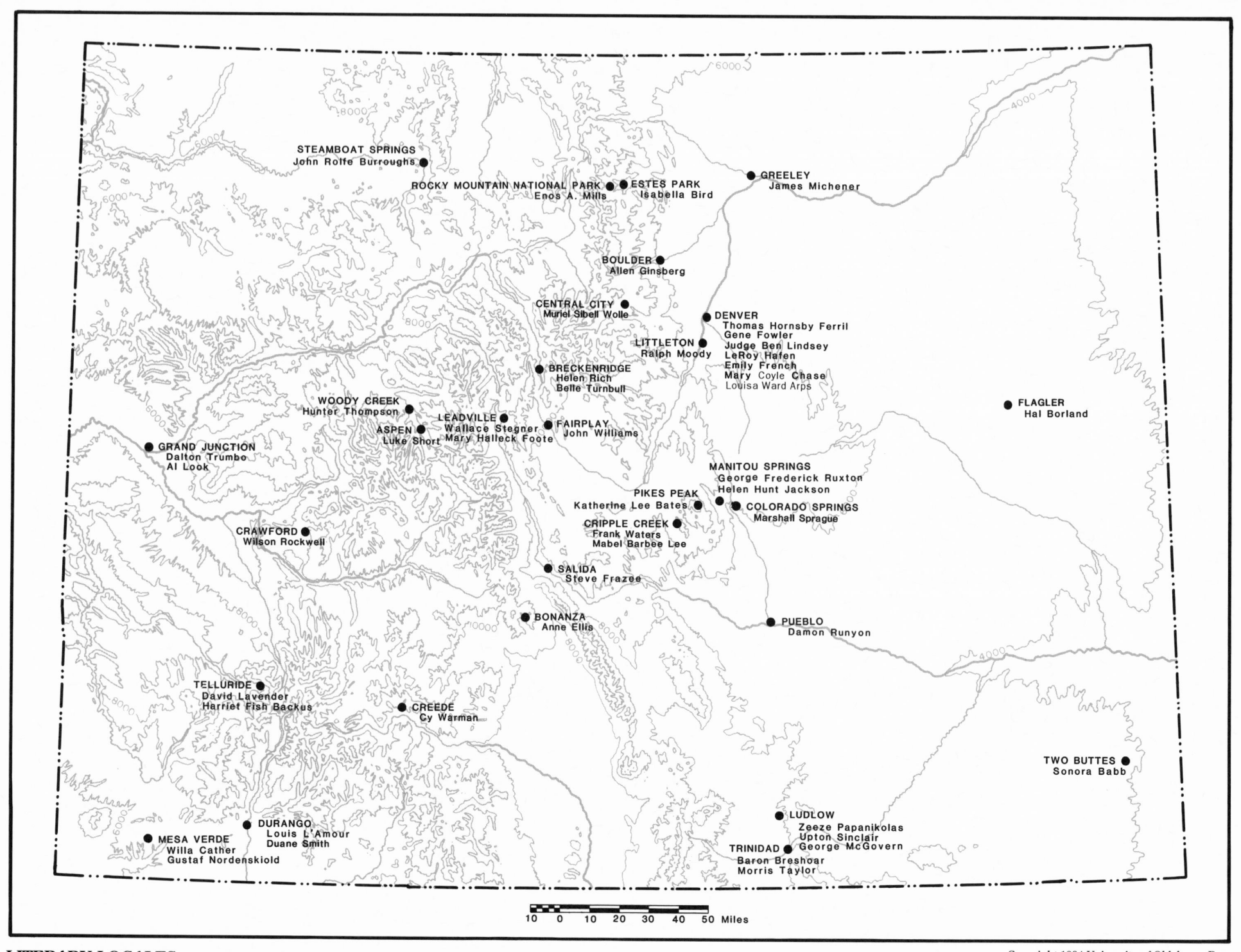

STEAMBOAT SPRINGS
John Rolfe Burroughs

GREELEY
James Michener

ROCKY MOUNTAIN NATIONAL PARK
Enos A. Mills

ESTES PARK
Isabella Bird

BOULDER
Allen Ginsberg

CENTRAL CITY
Muriel Sibell Wolle

DENVER
Thomas Hornsby Ferril
Gene Fowler
Judge Ben Lindsey
LeRoy Hafen
Emily French
Mary Coyle Chase
Louisa Ward Arps

LITTLETON
Ralph Moody

BRECKENRIDGE
Helen Rich
Belle Turnbull

FLAGLER
Hal Borland

WOODY CREEK
Hunter Thompson

LEADVILLE
Wallace Stegner
Mary Halleck Foote

FAIRPLAY
John Williams

ASPEN
Luke Short

GRAND JUNCTION
Dalton Trumbo
Al Look

MANITOU SPRINGS
George Frederick Ruxton
Helen Hunt Jackson

PIKES PEAK
Katherine Lee Bates

COLORADO SPRINGS
Marshall Sprague

CRAWFORD
Wilson Rockwell

CRIPPLE CREEK
Frank Waters
Mabel Barbee Lee

SALIDA
Steve Frazee

BONANZA
Anne Ellis

PUEBLO
Damon Runyon

TELLURIDE
David Lavender
Harriet Fish Backus

CREEDE
Cy Warman

TWO BUTTES
Sonora Babb

LUDLOW
Zeeze Papanikolas
Upton Sinclair
George McGovern

DURANGO
Louis L'Amour
Duane Smith

MESA VERDE
Willa Cather
Gustaf Nordenskiold

TRINIDAD
Baron Breshoar
Morris Taylor

10 0 10 20 30 40 50 Miles

LITERARY LOCALES

Certain Colorado communities have been enriched by exceptional literary efforts that bibliophiles may wish to investigate. This is only a start at a list.

Aspen. Fred Glidden, whose pen name was Luke Short, wrote fifteen western novels while living in a carpenter-Gothic cottage at 232 East Hallam Street.

Bonanza. Anne Ellis wrote an extraordinary biography, *The Life of an Ordinary Woman,* about lower-class life in this mining town.

Boulder. Allen Ginsberg, one of America's foremost living poets, and his beat sidekicks are celebrated in Boulder's Naropa Institute and Jack Kerouac School of Disembodied Poetics.

Breckenridge. Novelist Helen Rich and poet Belle Turnbull, who shared a cabin on French Street for over thirty years, captured Summit County's mining-country folkways and natural beauty in their high-country classics, recording with eloquent precision the lives of ordinary folk in a busted mining town.

Central City. Muriel Sibell Wolle, an art teacher at the University of Colorado, fell in love with Colorado mining camps and ghost towns during a 1920s tour of Gilpin County. Subsequently she produced the first of many ghost-town guides, *Stampede to Timberline,* which combines her lively text and realistic sketches of fading mining towns.

Colorado Springs. Marshall Sprague has captured much Colorado history in his best-selling books, including a witty look at his hometown, *Newport in the Rockies.*

Crawford. Rancher Wilson Rockwell explored the Western Slope in eight books portraying that region's evolution from Utes to uranium.

Creede. Cy Warman immortalized this silvery gulch with his poetry ("It's day all day in the daytime / And there is no night in Creede") and also wrote popular short stories about Rocky Mountain railroading.

Cripple Creek. Colorado's greatest gold camp inspired Frank Waters, one of the most-noted novelists of the Southwest, to capture the eccentric millionaire Winfield S. Stratton in *Midas of the Rockies.* Schoolteacher Mabel Barbee Lee produced *Cripple Creek Days* and *Back in Cripple Creek.*

Denver. Colorado poet laureate Thomas Hornsby Ferril celebrated his life-long hometown and favorite Colorado places in history-haunted verse. Journalist Gene Fowler portrayed Denver in two lively semiautobiographical books, *A Solo in Tom-Toms* and *Timber-Line,* and Judge Ben Lindsey, Denver's nationally noted reformer and muckraker, wrote the classic exposé of political corruption in Colorado, *The Beast.* Denver was also home for LeRoy Hafen, Colorado's most prolific historian and the founding editor of *Colorado Magazine.* In her diary Emily French, a laundress, provided an unusual perspective on women's work in Colorado. Denver's Mary Coyle Chase, captured a Pulitzer Prize for her play *Harvey,* which spoofed Denver's cowtown provincialism. Louisa Ward Arps contributed lively, accurate sketches of everything from Denver's boneyards to its waterways in works such as *Denver in Slices.*

Durango. Louis L'Amour, the most prolific and popular of western genre writers, covered much Colorado terrain in fiction, while Fort Lewis College professor Duane Smith has captured Colorado and Rocky Mountain history in more than twenty-four popular yet academically sound books.

Estes Park. Isabella Bird, an English world traveler, left a classic account of 1870s Colorado, *A Lady's Life in the Rocky Mountains.* She turned up her nose at most of Colorado, but fell in love with Estes Park, Longs Peak, and her "Mountain Jim."

Fairplay. John Williams, long-time University of Denver English professor, explored the South Park buffalo-hide trade in *Butcher's Crossing,* one of his highly acclaimed novels.

Flagler. Hal Borland, who grew up in Flagler and wound up at the *New York Times* as an editorial and environmental writer, wrote prose, poetry, and fiction, including three autobiographical classics of life on the Colorado High Plains, *Country Editor's Boy, The Seventh Winter,* and *High, Wide, and Lonesome.*

Grand Junction. Dalton Trumbo, a Montrose-born novelist and blacklisted Hollywood scriptwriter, wrote *Eclipse,* a novel about his life in "Shale City." Al Look, a longtime local journalist, explored Grand Junction and its Western Slope hinterland in a dozen fact-filled works.

Greeley. Best-selling novelist James Michener lived and taught in Greeley and recaptured the settlement of the South Platte Valley in his epic novel of Colorado, *Centennial.*

Leadville. Wallace Stegner, the novelist, poet, essayist, and conservationist, captured Leadville in his Pulitzer Prize winner, *The Angle of Repose,* which pays tribute to the earlier literary jewels of Mary Hallock Foote.

Littleton. Ralph Moody resurrected the days when he and ranching were young in his classic *Little Britches.*

Ludlow. Zeeze Papanikolas wrote a lyrical epic, *Buried Unsung,* of Greek strike leader Louis Tikas, who was captured and shot in the back by the Colorado National Guard. This is the most eloquent of many studies of the Ludlow Massacre, including Upton Sinclair's novel *The Coal War* and Sen. George McGovern's *The Great Coal Field War.*

Manitou Springs. George Frederick Ruxton and Helen Hunt Jackson captured the romance of this resort and the Native Americans and palefaces who patronized its mineral springs.

Mesa Verde. Pulitzer Prize–winning novelist Willa Cather explored Indians and Hispanics of the Southwest in various novels, including *The Professor's Wife,* set partly in Mesa Verde. Gustaf Nordenskiold conducted the first scientific dig of the famous cliff dwellings and left a report that has become a landmark of archaeological literature, *The Cliff Dwellings of Mesa Verde.*

Pikes Peak. Katherine Lee Bates drew inspiration for her song "America the Beautiful" from a trip to the top of America's most famous mountain.

Pueblo. Damon Runyon, who began his career with the *Pueblo Chieftain,* produced humorous stories written in a slangy idiom, known as Runyonese, about underworld characters, in such best-sellers as *Guys and Dolls, Blue Plate Special,* and *Money from Home.*

Rocky Mountain National Park. Enos A. Mills ("the Father of Rocky Mountain National Park") not only spearheaded efforts to create the park in 1915 but also wrote numerous books and articles about this high-country preserve.

Salida. Steve Frazee, who was born in Salida in 1909 and died there in 1992, wrote many short stories and novels set in the region, including *More Damn Tourists.* Frazee described himself in 1989 as "stooped, balding, squint-eyed and wrinkled," and he said, "A writer is sustained by stubborn determination and dogged effort, by honest anger, and by faith."

Steamboat Springs. John Rolfe Burroughs surveyed Steamboat and much of northwestern Colorado in generously illustrated books.

Telluride. David Lavender, who was born and raised in Telluride, has captured it and the Rocky Mountain West in books such as *One Man's West* and *The Rockies.* Harriet Fish Backus, wife of a mining engineer, produced a sensitive account of mining-town life in her autobiography, *Tomboy Bride.*

Trinidad. Baron Beshoar, a Trinidad native who became *Time Magazine's* Denver bureau chief, covered his hometown in *Hippocrates in a Red Vest* and the nearby labor wars in *Out of the Depths.* Trinidad history professor Morris Taylor explored his town and the surrounding Southwest in readable, well-researched publications.

REFERENCES

MAP 1. LOCATION

Beck, Warren A., and Ynez D. Haase. *Historical Atlas of the American West.* Norman: University of Oklahoma Press, 1989.

Colorado Atlas and Gazetteer: Topo Maps of the Entire State. Freeport, Me.: De Lorme Mapping, 1991.

Ellis, Erl H. *Colorado Mapology.* Frederick, Colo.: Jende-Hagen Books, 1983.

Griffiths, Thomas M., and Lynnell Rubright. *Colorado.* Boulder, Colo.: Westview Press, 1983.

Hafen, LeRoy, ed. *Colorado and Its People.* 4 vols. New York: Lewis Historical Publishing Co., 1948.

The WPA Guide to 1930s Colorado. New introduction by Thomas J. Noel. Topeka: University Press of Kansas, 1987.

MAP 2. MAJOR RIVERS

Davis, Clyde B. *The Arkansas.* New York: Farrar & Rinehart, 1940.

Fradkin, Philip L. *A River No More: The Colorado and the West.* New York: Knopf, 1981.

Horgan, Paul. *Great River: The Rio Grande in North American History.* New York: Rinehart & Co., 1954.

Mattes, Merril. *The Great Platte River Road.* Lincoln: Nebraska Historical Society, 1969.

Simmons, Virginia McConnell. *The Upper Arkansas: A Mountain River Valley.* Boulder: Pruett Publishing Co., 1990.

Waters, Frank. *The Colorado.* New York: Rinehart & Co., 1946.

MAP 3. LANDFORMS

Chronic, John, and Halka Chronic. *Prairie, Peak, and Plateau.* Denver, Colo.: Geological Society, 1972.

Chronic, Halka. *Roadside Geology of Colorado.* Missoula, Mont.: Mountain Press, 1980.

Helphand, Kenneth I. *Colorado: Visions of An American Landscape.* Niwot, Colo.: Roberts Rinehart Publishers and Colorado Chapter of the American Society of Landscape Architects, 1992.

Thornburg, W. D. *Regional Geomorphology of the United States.* New York: John Wiley & Sons, 1965.

MAP 4. THE 14,000-FOOT PEAKS

Borneman, Walter R., and Lyndon J. Lampert. *A Climbing Guide to Colorado's Fourteeners.* Boulder: Pruett Publishing Co., 1978.

Bueler, William M. *Roof of the Rockies: A History of Mountaineering in Colorado.* Boulder: Pruett Publishing Co., 1974.

Colorado Mountain Club. *Trail and Timberline.* A magazine published monthly since 1918.

Hart, John L. Jerome. *Fourteen Thousand Feet: A History of the Naming and Early Ascents of the High Colorado Peaks.* Denver: Colorado Mountain Club, 1931.

Ormes, Robert, with the Colorado Mountain Club. *Guide to the Colorado Mountains.* Denver: Sage Books, 1952.

MAP 5. CLIMATE

Colorado Planning Commission. *Climatological Data of Colorado.* Appendix 1 of *Water Resources of Colorado.* Denver: Colorado Planning Commission, 1939.

Trimble, Robert E. *Colorado Climatology.* Fort Collins: State Agricultural College of Colorado, 1918.

U.S. Weather Bureau. *Climatic Summary of the United States: Colorado:* Washington: Government Printing Office, 1941.

MAP 6. WET AND DRY YEARS

Trimble, Robert E. *Colorado Climatology.* Fort Collins: State Agricultural College of Colorado, 1918.

U.S. Weather Bureau. *Climatic Summary of the United States: Colorado.* Published annually. Washington: Government Printing Office.

MAP 7. NATURAL VEGETATION

Ewan, Joseph. "The Growth of Our Knowledge of Colorado Plant Life." In *Colorado and Its People,* ed. LeRoy R. Hafen, 2:17–26. New York: Lewis Historical Publishing Co., 1949.

Kuchler, A. W. *Vegetation Mapping.* Netherlands: Kluwer Academic, Junk Publishers, 1988.

Mutel, Cornelia F., and John C. Emeric. *From Grassland to Glacier: The Natural History of Colorado.* Boulder: Johnson Books, 1984.

Peattie, Donald Culross. *A Natural History of Western Trees.* Illustrated by Paul Landacre. New York: Bonanza Books, 1950.

Ryberg, Per Axel. *Flora of Colorado.* Fort Collins: State Agricultural College, 1906.

Weber, William A. *Rocky Mountain Flora.* Boulder: Colorado Associated University Press, 1972.

MAP 8. SPANISH AND FRENCH EXPLORERS

Chavez, Fray Angelico. *The Dominguez-Escalante Journal.* Provo, Utah: Brigham Young University, 1976.

Espinosa, J. Manuel. "Journey of the Vargas Expedition into Colorado, 1694." *Colorado Magazine* 16, 3 (May 1939).

Folmer, Henri. "The Mallet Expedition of 1739 through Nebraska, Kansas, and Colorado to Santa Fe." *Colorado Magazine* 16, 5 (Sept. 1939).

Thomas, Alfred B. *After Coronado: Spanish Exploration Northeast of New Mexico, 1696–1727.* Norman: University of Oklahoma Press, 1935.

MAP 9. U.S. EXPLORERS

Carter, Carrol Joe. *Pike In Colorado.* Fort Collins: Old Army Press, 1978.

Fremont, John Charles. *The Expeditions of John Charles Fremont.* Edited by Donald Jackson and Mary Lee Spence. Urbana: University of Illinois Press, 1970.

Goetzmann, William H. *Exploration and Empire.* New York: Alfred A. Knopf, 1966.

Hollon, W. Eugene. *The Lost Pathfinder: Zebulon Montgomery Pike.* Norman: University of Oklahoma Press, 1949.

Long, Stephen. *From Pittsburgh to the Rocky Mountains: Major Stephen Long's Expedition, 1819–1820.* Edited by Maxine Benson. Golden: Fulcrum, 1988.

Mumey, Nollie. *John Williams Gunnison.* Denver: Artcraft Press, 1955.

MAP 10. MEXICAN LAND GRANTS

Hafen, LeRoy. "Mexican Land Grants and Adobe Towns." Chap. 8 in *Colorado and Its People,* edited by LeRoy Hafen, 1:99–121. New York: Lewis Historical Publishing Co., 1948.

Van Ness, John R., and Christine Van Ness. *Spanish and Mexican Land Grants in New Mexico and Colorado.* Manhattan, Kans.: Sunflower University Press, 1980.

MAP 11. TERRITORIAL DISPUTES

Ellis, Erl H. *International Boundary Lines across Colorado and Wyoming.* Boulder: Johnson Publishing Co., 1966.

Hafen, Leroy, ed. *Colorado and Its People,* 1:9–122. New York: Lewis Historical Publishing Co., 1948.

Marshall, Thomas M. *The History of the Western Boundary of the Louisiana Purchase, 1819–1841.* Berkeley: University of California Press, 1914.

Richie, Eleanor L. "Background of the International Boundary Line of 1819 along the Arkansas River in Colorado. *Colorado Magazine* 10 (July 1933).

MAP 12. BOUNDARY AND INTERIOR SURVEYS

Bartlett, Richard A. *Great Surveys of the American West.* Norman: University of Oklahoma Press, 1962.

Ellis, Erl H. *Colorado Mapology.* Frederick, Colo.: Jende-Hagen Books, 1983.

Goetzman, William H. *Exploration and Empire.* New York: Knopf, 1966.

Hayden, F. V. *Geological and Geographical Atlas of Colorado and Portions of Adjacent Territory.* Washington: U.S. Geological and Geographical Surveys, 1877.

Stegner, Wallace. *Beyond the Hundredth Meridian: John Wesley Powell and the Second Opening of the West.* Boston: Houghton Mifflin, 1954.

MAP 13. THE PUBLIC DOMAIN

Colorado Bureau of Mines. *Colorado Mining Laws.* Golden: 1899–.

Mall, Loren L. *Public Land and Mining Law.* Seattle, Wash.: Butterworth, 1981.

Robbins, Ray. *Our Landed Heritage: The Public Domain, 1776–1936.* Lincoln: University of Nebraska Press, 1962.

MAP 14. COLORADO AS PART OF KANSAS, NEBRASKA, NEW MEXICO, AND UTAH

Allen, James B. *The Evolution of the County Boundaries of Utah.* Salt Lake City: Utah Historical Quarterly, 1955.

Ellis, Erl H. *Colorado Mapology.* Frederick, Colo.: Jende-Hagen Books, 1983.

Gill, Helen G. "The Establishment of Counties in Kansas." *Transactions of the Kansas Historical Society* 8 (1903–1904): 449–72.

MAP 15. THE SEVENTEEN ORIGINAL COUNTIES

Ellis, Erl. *Colorado Mapology.* Frederick, Colo.: Jende-Hagen Books, 1983.

Hall, Frank. *History of the State of Colorado.* 4 vols. Chicago: Blakely Printing Co., 1889.

MAP 16. COUNTY EVOLUTION

Colorado Planning Division. *Colorado Year Book, 1962–1964.* Denver: State Planning Division, 1964.

Ellis, Erl. *Colorado Mapology* Frederick, Colo.: Jende-Hagen Books, 1983.

MAP 17. COUNTY SEATS, PAST AND PRESENT

Ellis, Erl H. *Colorado Mapology.* Frederick, Colo.: Jende-Hagen Books, 1983.

MAP 18. CONGRESSIONAL DISTRICTS

Colorado Yearbook. Denver: State Planning Commission, 1918–64.

Congressional Directory. Washington: Government Printing Office.

MAP 19. MAJOR WATER DIVERSIONS AND RESERVOIRS

League of Women Voters of Colorado. *Colorado's Water Resources.* Denver, 1958.

Sherow, James E. "The Chimerical Vision: Michael Creed Hinderlider and Professive Engineering in Colorado." *Essays and Monographs in Colorado History* 9 (1989): 37–59.

Steinel, Alvin T. *History of Agriculture in Colorado.* Fort Collins: State Agricultural College, 1926.

Tyler, Daniel. *The Last Water Hole in the West.* Niwot: University Press of Colorado, 1992.

U.S. Geological Survey. *Water Resources Data For Colorado.* 3 vols. Washington: Government Printing Office, 1980.

MAP 20. LIVESTOCK

Goff, Richard. *Century in the Saddle.* Denver: Colorado Cattleman's Centennial Association, 1967.

Gressley, Gene M. *Bankers and Cattlemen.* New York: Knopf, 1966.

Peake, Ora B. *The Colorado Range Cattle Industry.* Glendale, Calif.: A. H. Clark Co., 1937.

Simms, Willard E. *Ten Days Every January: A History of the National Western Stock Show.* Denver: Western Stock Show Association, 1980.

MAP 21. AGRICULTURAL CROPS

Colorado Agricultural Statistics. Denver: Colorado Department of Agriculture, 1948–.

Colorado Year Book. Denver: State Planning Office, 1918–64.

Pabor, William E. *Colorado as an Agricultural State: Its Farms, Fields, and Garden Lands.* New York: Orange Judd Co., 1883.

Steinel, Alvin T. *History of Agriculture in Colorado.* Fort Collins: Colorado Agricultural College, 1926.

MAP 22. MAJOR AGRICULTURAL INDUSTRIES

Dunbar, Robert G. "History of Agriculture." In *Colorado and Its People,* ed. L. R. Hafen, 2:121–57. New York: Lewis Historical Publishing Co., 1949.

Nelson, Elroy. "Manufacturing History of Colorado." In the same volume, 2:571–607.

MAP 23. AGRICULTURAL GHOST TOWNS

Bauer, William H., James L. Ozment, and John H. Willard. *Colorado Post Offices, 1859–1989.* Golden: Colorado Railroad Museum, 1990.

Eberhart, Perry. *Ghosts of the Colorado Plains.* Athens, Ohio: Swallow Press/Ohio University Press, 1986.

Noel, Thomas J. "Chavez Town: Lost City on the Huerfano." *Greenhorn Valley News,* June 22, 1978.

Schaffer, Ray. *A Guide to Places on the Colorado Prairie, 1540–1975.* Boulder: Pruett Publishing Co., 1978.

Federal Writers Project for Colorado. "The Thousand Town File." 5 vols. Typescript in the Works Progress Administration, Writers Project Mss. collection, ca. 1940, Colorado Historical Society Library, Denver.

MAP 24. PASSABLE PASSES

Brown, Ralph L. "The Mountain Passes of Colorado." *University of Colorado Studies* 18, 1 (Aug. 1930): 29–42.

Edmondson, Clyde and Chloe Edmondson. *Mountain Passes.* Longmont: Clyde and Chloe Edmondson, 1963.

Koch, Don. *The Colorado Pass Book.* Boulder: Pruett Publishing Co., 1980.

Martin, Bob. *Hiking the Highest Passes.* Boulder: Pruett Publishing Co., 1984.

Ruhoff, Ron. *Colorado's Continental Divide: A Hiking and Backpacking Guide.* Evergreen: Cordillera Press, 1989.

MAP 25. FUR TRADERS

Beckwourth, James P. *The Life and Adventures of James P. Beckwourth. . . .* New York: Harper & Bros., 1856.

Hafen, LeRoy. "Mountain Men and Fur Trade Days." In *Colorado and Its People,* ed. LeRoy Hafen, 1:63–81. New York: Lewis Historical Publishing Co., 1949.

Hafen, LeRoy, ed. *The Mountain Men and the Fur Trade of the Far West: Biographical Sketches of the Participants by Scholars of the Subject. . . .* 7 vols. Glendale, Calif.: A. H. Clark Co., 1965–69.

MAP 26. GOLD RUSH ROUTES

Blue, Daniel. "Statement of Daniel Blue." *Colorado Magazine* 8 (Nov. 1931): 232–33.

Hafen, LeRoy R., ed. *Colorado Gold Rush: Contemporary Letters and Reports, 1858–1859.* Glendale, Calif.: A. H. Clark Co., 1941.

Long, Margaret. *The Smoky Hill Trail: Following the Old Historic Trails on the Modern Highways.* Denver: W. H. Kistler, 1943.

Mattes, Merrill J. *Platte River Road Narratives: A Bibliography. . . .* Urbana: University of Illinois Press, 1988.

MAP 27. MAJOR STAGECOACH LINES

Butterfield, Ella A. "Butterfield's Overland Dispatch." *The Trail,* Dec. 1925, 3–9.

Long, Margaret. *The Smoky Hill Trail: Following the Old Historic Trails on the Modern Highways.* Denver: W. H. Kistler, 1943.

Scott, Glenn R. *Historic Trail Map of the Greater Denver Area, Colorado.* Map I-856-G. Washington: U.S. Geological Survey, 1976.

Taylor, Morris. "The Barlow and Sanderson Stage Lines in Colorado, 1872–1884." *Colorado Magazine,* Spring 1973, 142–62.

MAP 28. PIONEER RAILROADS

Beebe, Lucius, and Charles Clegg. *Narrow Gauge in The Rockies.* Berkeley: Howell-North, 1958.

Colorado Railroad Museum. *A Detailed Map: Railroads in the State of Colorado.* Golden: Colorado Railroad Museum, 1969.

Hauck, Cornelius W. *Narrow Gauge to Central City and Silver Plume.* Colorado Rail Annual #10. Golden: Colorado Railroad Museum, 1972.

Le Massena, Robert A. *Colorado's Mountain Railroads.* Denver: Sundance Publications, 1984.

Noel, Thomas, J. "All Hail the Denver Pacific: Denver's First Railroad." *Colorado Magazine* 50, 2 (Spring 1973).

Poor, M. D. *The Denver, South Park, and Pacific.* Denver: Rocky Mountain Railroad Club, 1949, 1976.

Wilkins, Tivis E. *Colorado Railroads: Chronological Development.* Boulder: Pruett Publishing Co., 1974.

Wilson, O. Meredith. *The Denver and Rio Grande Project, 1870–1901.* Salt Lake City: Howe Brothers, 1982.

MAP 29. MAJOR RAILROADS CONSTRUCTED, 1880–1913

Athearn, Robert G. *Rebel of the Rockies: The Denver and Rio Grande Railroad.* New Haven: 1962. Reprint. Lincoln: University of Nebraska Press, 1977.

Athearn, Robert G. *Union Pacific County.* 1971. Reprint. Lincoln: University of Nebraska Press, 1976.

Beebe, Lucius, and Charles Clegg. *Rio Grande: Main-line of the Rockies.* Berkeley, Calif.: Howell-North, 1962.

Bollinger, Edward T. *Rails That Climb: The Story of the Moffat Road.* 1950. Reprint. Golden: Colorado Railroad Museum, 1979.

Bryant, Keith L. *History of the Atchison, Topeka, and Santa Fe Railroad Company.* New York: Macmillan Publishing Co., 1974.

McFarland, Edward M. *The Midland Route.* Boulder: Pruett Publishing Co., 1980.

Overton, Richard C. *Burlington Route: A History of the Burlington Lines.* New York: Alfred A. Knopf, 1965.

MAP 30. SURVIVING PASSENGER RAILROADS

Abbott, Morris W. *The Pike's Peak Cog Road.* San Marino, Calif.: Golden West Books, 1972.

Colorado Historical Society. *The Georgetown Loop: A Capsule History and Guide.* Denver: Colorado Historical Society, 1986.

Ormes, Robert M. *Tracking Ghost Railroads in Colorado.* Colorado Springs: Century One Press, 1975.

Osterwald, Doris B. *Cinders and Smoke: A Mile by Mile Guide for the Durango to Silverton Narrow Gauge Trip.* Lakewood: Western Guideways, 1965.

Osterwald, Doris B. *High Line to Leadville: A Mile by Mile Guide for the Leadville, Colorado and Southern Railroad.* Lakewood: Western Guideways, 1991.

Osterwald, Doris B. *Ticket to Toltec: Mile by Mile Guide for the Cumbres and Toltec Scenic Railroad.* Lakewood: Western Guideways, 1976.

Patterson, Steve, and Kenton Forest. *Winter Park Ski Train.* Denver: Tramway Press, 1984.

MAP 31. PAVED ROADS, 1940 AND 1980

McGinn, Elinor M. "Trying to Profit: Inmate Labor at Canon City, 1872–1927." *Colorado Heritage,* no. 2, 1987, 14–24.

Morrison, Jack. "Early Colorado Auto Trails," *Denver Westerners Roundup* 47 (Jan.–Feb. 1991): 3–18.

Noel, Thomas J. "Paving the Way to Colorado." *Journal of the West* 26 (July 1987): 42–49.

Wiley, Marion C. *The High Road.* Denver: Colorado Department of Highways, 1976.

MAP 32. COMMERCIAL AVIATION

Colorado Department of Local Affairs, Division on Local Government. *Colorado Airport Directory.* Denver, 1986.

Colorado State Yearbooks. Denver: Colorado State Planning Office, 1918–64.

Federal Aviation Administration, Air Commerce Traffic Pattern and Air Traffic Activities.

Miller, Jeff. *Stapleton International Airport: The First Fifty Years.* Boulder: Pruett Publishing Co., 1983.

Scamehorn, H. Lee. "The First Fifty Years of Flight in Colorado." *University of Colorado Studies in History* (Boulder), no. 2, 1961, 102–21.

MAP 33. METALLIC MINERAL DEPOSITS

Henderson, C. W. *Mining in Colorado.* Washington: Government Printing Office, 1926.

Pearl, Richard M. *Colorado Rocks, Minerals, Fossils.* Denver: Sage Books, 1964.

Smith, Duane A. *Colorado Mining: A Photographic History.* Albuquerque: University of New Mexico Press, 1977.

Vanderwilt, John W. *Mineral Resources of Colorado.* Denver: Colorado Mineral Resources Board, 1947.

MAP 34. GOLD RUSH, 1858–1870s

Fossett, Frank. *Colorado: Its Gold and Silver Mines.* 1879. New York: Arno, 1973 Reprint.

Henderson, Charles W. *Mining in Colorado.* Washington: Government Printing Office, 1926.

Smith, Duane A. *Colorado Mining: A Photographic History.* Albuquerque: University of New Mexico Press, 1977.

MAP 35. SILVER BOOM, 1870s–1893

Blair, Edward. *Leadville: Colorado's Magic City.* Boulder: Pruett Publishing Co., 1980.

Leyendecker, Liston E. *Georgetown: Colorado's Silver Queen.* Fort Collins: Centennial Pubs., 1977.

Vandenbusche, Duane. *The Gunnison Country.* Gunnison: B and B Printers, 1980.

MAP 36. THE SAN JUANS

Backus, Harriet Fish. *Tomboy Bride.* Boulder: Pruett Publishing Co., 1969.

Brown, Robert L. *An Empire of Silver.* Denver: Sundance, 1984.

Griffiths, Thomas M. *San Juan Country.* Boulder: Pruett Publishing Co., 1984.

Nossaman, Allen. *Many More Mountains.* 2 vols. Denver: Sundance Books, 1989 and 1993.

Rickard, Thomas A. *Across the San Juan Mountains.* New York: Engineering and Mining Journal, 1903.

Smith, Duane A. *Song of the Hammer and Drill: The Colorado San Juans, 1860–1914.* Golden: Colorado School of Mines Press, 1982.

MAP 37. CRIPPLE CREEK GOLD

Feitz, Leland. *Ghost Towns of the Cripple Creek District.* Colorado Springs: Little London Press, 1974.

Levine, Brian. *A Guide to the Cripple Creek—Victor Mining District.* Colorado Springs: Century One Press, 1987.

Sprague, Marshall. *Money Mountain.* Boston: Little, Brown & Co., 1953.

Taylor, Robert G. *Cripple Creek Mining District.* Palmer Lake, Colo.: Filter Press, 1973.

Waters, Frank. *Midas of the Rockies: The Story of Stratton and Cripple Creek.* Denver: Sage Books, 1937.

MAP 38. LOST MINES AND BURIED TREASURES

Bancroft, Caroline. *Colorado's Lost Gold Mines and Buried Treasure.* Boulder: Johnson Publishing Co., 1961.

Cornelius, Temple H. *Sheepherder's Gold.* Denver: Sage Books, 1964.

Eberhart, Perry. *Treasure Tales of the Rockies.* Denver: Sage Books, 1961.

Marshall, John B., and Temple H. Cornelius. *Golden Treasures of the San Juan.* Denver: Sage Books, 1961.

MAP 39. OIL AND GAS

Gulliford, Andrew. *Boomtown Blues: Colorado Oil Shale, 1885–1985.* Niwot: University Press of Colorado, 1989.

Jensen, Fred S., Henry H. R. Sharkey, and Daniel S. Turner. *The Oil and Gas Fields of Colorado.* Denver: Rocky Mountain Association of Geologists, 1954.

Rountree, Russ. *Western Oil Reporter's Rocky Mountain Oil History.* Denver: Hart Publications, 1984.

Scanlon, A. H., comp. *Oil and Gas Fields of Colorado: Statistical Data through 1981.* Denver: Colorado Department of Natural Resources, Geological Survey, 1982.

MAP 40. COAL

Colorado Bureau of Mines. *Report of the Inspector of Coal Mines.* Denver: Colorado Bureau of Natural Resources, 1897–.

Vanderwilt, John W., et al. *Mineral Resources of Colorado.* Denver: Colorado Mineral Resources Board, 1947.

Whiteside, James. *Regulating Danger: The Struggle for Mine Safety in the Rocky Mountain Coal Industry.* Lincoln: University of Nebraska Press, 1990.

MAP 41. MAJOR EXTRACTIVE INDUSTRIES

Fell, James E., Jr. *Ores to Metals: The Rocky Mountain Smelting Industry.* Lincoln: University of Nebraska Press, 1979.

1988 Directory of Colorado Manufacturers. Boulder: University of Colorado Business Research Division, College of Business and Administration, 1988.

Vanderwilt, John W. *Mineral Resources of Colorado.* Denver: State Mineral Resources Board, 1947.

MAP 42. SELECTED MANUFACTURERS

Directory of Colorado Manufacturers. Boulder: University of Colorado Business Research Division, College of Business, 1992.

MAP 43. PREHISTORIC COLORADANS, 10,000–0 B.C.

Cassells, E. Steve. *The Archaeology of Colorado.* Boulder: Johnson Books, 1983.

Wormington, H. Marie. *Ancient Man in North America.* Denver: Denver Museum of Natural History, 1957.

MAP 44. ANASAZI, FREMONT, AND PLAINS CULTURES, 1–1300 A.D.

Nordenskiold, Gustaf. *The Cliff Dwellers of the Mesa Verde.* 1893. Reprint. La Glorietta, N. Mex.: Rio Grande Press, 1979.

Underhill, Ruth. *The First Penthouse Dwellers of America.* 1938. Reprint. Santa Fe, N. Mex.: William Gannon, 1976.

Watson, Don. *Indians of the Mesa Verde.* Mesa Verde National Park: Mesa Verde Museum Association, 1953.

Wormington, Marie. *A Reappraisal of the Fremont Culture. . . .* Denver: Denver Museum of Natural History, 1955.

MAP 45. NATIVE AMERICAN TRIBES

Conn, Richard. *Colorado's Native Heritage: A Handbook for Students and Teachers.* Denver: Denver Art Museum, 1981.

Hughes, J. Donald. *American Indians in Colorado.* Boulder: Pruett Publishing Co., 1977.

MAP 46. MILITARY SITES

Beckner, Raymond M. *Old Forts of Southern Colorado.* Canon City: O'Brien Printing & Stationery, 1975.

Brandes, T. Donald. *Military Posts of Colorado.* Fort Collins: Old Army Press, 1973.

Nankivell, John H. *History of the Military Organizations of the State of Colorado, 1860–1935.* Denver: W. H. Kistler, 1935.

MAP 47. COUNTY POPULATION TRENDS

Colorado State Yearbook. Denver: State Planning Commission, 1920–64.

U. S. Census Bureau. *Census of Populations.* Washington: Government Printing Office, 1860–1990.

MAP 48. URBAN POPULATION GROWTH

Leonard, Stephen J. and T. J. Noel. *Denver: Mining Camp to Metropolis.* Niwot: University Press of Colorado, 1990.

Smith, Duane A. *Rocky Mountain Mining Camps: The Urban Frontier.* Bloomington: University of Indiana Press, 1967.

U. S. Census Bureau. *Census of Population.* Washington: Government Printing Office, 1860–1990.

MAP 49. DENVER AND SUBURBS

Abbott, Carl. "Boom State and Boom City: Stages in Denver's Growth." *The Colorado Magazine* 50 (Summer 1973):205–30.

Leonard, Stephen J., and Thomas J. Noel. *Denver: Mining Camp to Metropolis*. Niwot: University Press of Colorado, 1990.

Mehls, Steven F., Carol J. Drake, and James E. Fell, Jr. *Aurora: Gateway to the Rockies*. Evergreen: Cordillera Press, 1985.

MAP 50. NATIONAL FORESTS, GRASSLANDS, MONUMENTS, AND PARKS

Buckholtz, Curt. *Rocky Mountain National Park: A History*. Boulder: University Press of Colorado, 1983.

Carhart, Arthur H. *The National Forests*. New York: Alfred A. Knopf, 1959.

McCarthy, G. Michael. *Hour of Trial: The Conservation Conflict in Colorado and the West, 1891–1907*. Norman: University of Oklahoma Press, 1977.

Shoemaker, Len. "National Forests." *Colorado Magazine* 21 (July 1944):182–84.

Smith, Duane A. *Mesa Verde National Park*. Topeka: University Press of Kansas, 1988.

MAP 51. RECREATION, WILDLIFE, AND WILDERNESS AREAS

Baldwin, Donald Nicholas. *The Quiet Revolution: The Grass Roots of Today's Wilderness Preservation Movement*. Boulder: Pruett Publishing Co., 1972.

Colorado Division of Wildlife. *Colorado Outdoors,* 1951–.

Colorado Mountain Club. *Trail and Timberline*. Denver: Colorado Mountain Club, 1918–.

Fielder, John. *Colorado: Our Wilderness Future: Proposed Additions to the Wilderness System*. Englewood: Westcliffe Publishers, Inc., 1990.

Kleinsorge, Martin G. *Exploring Colorado State Parks*. Niwot: University Press of Colorado, 1992.

MAP 52. SKI AREAS

Fay, Abbott, *Ski Tracks in the Rockies*. Evergreen: Cordillera Press, 1984.

MAP 53. COLORADO HISTORIC DISTRICTS

Colorado Historical Society. *National Register Listings for Colorado*. Denver: Colorado Historical Society, Office of Archaeology and Historical Preservation, 1966–.

MAP 54. DENVER HISTORIC DISTRICTS

Denver Planning Office. *Historic Building Inventory*. Rev. ed. Denver: Denver Planning Office, 1974, 1981.

Morris, Langdon. *Denver Landmarks*. Denver: Charles W. Cleworth, 1979.

MAP 55. LABOR-HISTORY LANDMARKS

Colorado Bureau of Labor Statistics. Biennial reports, 1884–1932.

Knight, Harold. *Working in Colorado: A Brief History of the Colorado Labor Movement*. Boulder: University of Colorado Center for Labor Education and Research, 1971.

Whiteside, James. *Regulating Danger: The Struggle for Mine Safety in the Rocky Mountain Coal Industry*. Lincoln: University of Nebraska Press, 1990.

MAP 56. HISTORY MUSEUMS

American Museum Association. *Directory*. Annual. New York.

Caughey, Bruce, and Dean Winstanley. *The Colorado Guide*. Golden: Fulcrum, 1989, 1991.

Joy, Carol M., and Terry Ann Mood. *Colorado Local History: A Directory*. Denver: Colorado Historical Society, 1985.

MAP 57. DENVER METRO MUSEUMS AND HISTORIC ACCOMMODATIONS

Numerous guidebooks are available, but the phone book classified section will give you the most complete and current list of museums and historic accommodations.

MAP 58. SPECIALIZED MUSEUMS AND TOURIST ATTRACTIONS

Cahill, Rick. *Colorado Hot Springs Guide*. Boulder: Pruett Publishing Co., 1983.

Caughey, Bruce, and Dean Winstanley. *The Colorado Guide*. Golden: 1992.

MAP 59. COLLEGES AND UNIVERSITIES

Le Rossignol, James E. *History of Higher Education in Colorado*. Washington: Government Printing Office, 1903.

McGiffert, Michael. *The Higher Learning in Colorado: An Historical Study, 1860–1949*. Denver: Sage, 1964.

INDEX